FALLING IN LOVE WITH DARKNESS

OSHO

Extemporaneous talks given by Osho in Udaipur, India

falling in **love** with **darkness**

overcoming the fear of darkness and discovering its qualities of rest, relaxation, and profound peace

OSHO

Originally published in Hindi as *Jeevan Sangeet*. The material in this book is a series of talks by Osho given to a live audience. The complete OSHO text archive can be found via the online OSHO Library at www.osho.com/Library

OSHO MEDIA INTERNATIONAL
New York—Zurich—Mumbai
an imprint of
OSHO INTERNATIONAL
www.osho.com/oshointernational

Library of Congress Catalog-In-Publication Data is available

Printed in India by Manipal Technologies Limited, Karnataka

ISBN: 978-1-938755-71-2
This title is also available in eBook format ISBN: 978-0-88050-093-7

contents

preface

There is a beautiful story about one of the most significant women who has ever lived – Rabiya al-Adabiya. One evening, as the sun was just setting…she was very old, perhaps ninety years. And she was searching outside on the street for something she had lost.

A young man saw her, and just out of compassion for the old woman – he was a stranger to the village, he had no idea who she was – he just asked, "What are you searching for? Can I be of any help? You are very old, the sun has set, and it is becoming darker; it will be impossible for you to find it. Just tell me. I am not engaged in any other work, I can help you."

Rabiya laughed. She said to him, "Thank you for your kindness, stranger."

He said, "Why do you call me stranger?"

She said, "Because nobody of this village would have come to help me; they think I am mad. And perhaps they are right. But I have lost my needle."

The young man said, "Such a small thing like a needle, with your so-ancient eyes, in the darkening evening, how can you hope? Just tell me exactly where it has fallen. Perhaps – because the road is big – if you show me the exact spot, I may still be able to find it."

Rabiya said, "It would have been better if you had not asked that question, because I have not lost it on the road. I have lost it inside my house, but there is too much darkness. I am a poor woman, I don't even have a lamp. Thinking that inside there is so much darkness, finding the needle would be impossible, I was searching outside because there was a little sunlight at the time that I started the search."

The young man said, "Then perhaps your village people are right. You have lost your needle inside the house and you are searching for it outside! But your madness has a method in it, you have a certain rationality. The reason is, because inside the house there is so much darkness, finding it would be impossible. And outside there is a little light yet, perhaps there is some possibility. But if you have not lost it there, the light will not help."

Rabiya said, "But this is what everybody in the world is doing, and nobody calls them mad. They have all lost their treasures within themselves and they are all searching for them outside, because outside there is more light. Because all the senses open outside, it is easier to search there."

The question is not: Where is it easier to search? The question is: Where have you lost it? You know perfectly well you have not lost it outside yourself. You cannot remember any incidents when you lost your treasures: your consciousness, your being, your love, your blissfulness, your silence, your innocence. Nothing is outside. And if you have not lost it outside... There are not many sides in the world. There are only two. It is just a simple arithmetic: if you have not lost it outside, you must have lost it inside.

Inside there is darkness – about that I agree. But that darkness is not a hindrance – that is my experience. That darkness is immensely helpful because it is peaceful, it is silence. That darkness is luminous; it is a different kind of light. That's why in the beginning you feel it as darkness, but as you go deeper, slowly, slowly it starts becoming a different kind of light that you have not known before.

You have known lights which need fuel – even sunlight needs fuel. The sun is being exhausted of its fuel every day and scientists say that this sun can last another few million years, at the most. And then suddenly one day it will have lost its light and there will be darkness all over. Every day there are stars which become dark – bigger stars than your sun. Because they have lived far longer than your sun, they have exhausted their fuel. Outside, all light is dependent on fuel; inside is a totally different quality of light – it does not need any fuel. That's why it is eternal; it cannot be exhausted.

What appears as darkness in the beginning, slowly, slowly becomes luminous. And the day it becomes totally luminous – that's what is called enlightenment, you have come to the true light. Up to now you have seen only shadows of light in the outside world; you have not seen the authentic light which knows no beginning, no end.

Just gather courage, you have nothing to lose. What can you lose? What have you to lose? So why be afraid? Just go inside, fearlessly – it is your own territory, it is your own being. And once you have found just a ray of light, that is the beginning of the greatest experience of life. Nothing is comparable to it in bliss, in benediction.

Osho
The Rebel

CHAPTER 1

darkness is peace, relaxation

MY BELOVED ONES.

Darkness has its own bliss, so why do we desire light? Why do we hanker so much for light? We never think that the desire for light is a symbol of the fear rooted within us; it is a symbol of fear. We want light so that we can become free of that fear. The mind is scared in the dark. The longing for light is not a great quality; it is just evidence of the fear lingering in the consciousness: the frightened man wants light. And a man who is fearless no longer thinks of even darkness as darkness. The anxiety around darkness and the struggle with it are because of fear. Once man is without fear, the desire for light will also disappear.

There have been very few people on the earth who have dared to say that God is darkness. Most people have considered God to be light. "God is light" – most people have said that God is light. But these may be the same people who believe in God out of fear. Those who have interpreted God as light must be frightened people. They can accept God only as light. A man of fear cannot accept darkness.

But there have been a few people who have said that God is

the ultimate darkness. My own understanding is that God is the ultimate darkness. Why? Light has an end; darkness is endless. No matter how far you stretch your imagination about light, you will find a limit. No matter how many different ways you think about it, or how far you extend your thinking, you will come across the borders of light.

Just think of darkness: are there any borders to it? It is hard to even imagine a limit to darkness. There is no end to it; darkness is endless.

Also, because light is an excitement, it is a tension. Darkness is peace, relaxation. But because we are all frightened people, we call life light, and death darkness. The truth is that life is stress and death is relaxation. The day is unrest, the night is rest. If someone names the chaotic activities of millions of lives "light," they will be right. But then the ultimate freedom will certainly be called darkness.

Maybe you have never considered that when rays of light touch your eyes, it creates stress, disturbance. If you want to sleep at night and the light is on, you cannot sleep. It is difficult to rest in light. Darkness is the ultimate peace; it leads you into profound peace.

But when we face even a little darkness, we feel restless and uneasy. Just a little darkness and immediately we are in difficulty and start wondering what is going to happen. Remember, anyone who is restless, frightened, and scared by darkness will be equally afraid of entering *samadhi*, a peaceful state of being. Anyone who is so afraid of darkness, remember, will be equally afraid of entering *samadhi*, the state of divine ecstasy. For *samadhi* is an even greater silence than darkness.

We are afraid of death for the same reason. What is the fear of death? What harm has death ever caused anyone? One has never heard of death harming anyone. It is quite possible that life has caused great damage in some cases, but death causing any damage? It has never been heard of.

Who has ever been hurt by death? Life gives you many problems. What is life – a series of problems! When has death tormented anyone? When has it disturbed anyone? When has it caused suffering to anyone? But we are afraid of death. And we cling to life.

Death is unknown, and what is there to be afraid of in the unknown? You can be afraid of something which is known. But what is there to be afraid of in what we don't know, when we don't even know whether it is good or bad? Actually, our fear is not the fear of death; it is the fear of being lost in the dark. Life seems to be illuminated: everything is visible, familiar – familiar people, a familiar home, a familiar house, and village. Death appears to be a pitch-black phenomenon where, once you are lost in it, nothing will be seen and there will be no contact with any friend, any family, or loved ones, or with all that we have built around us. All that will be lost. And who knows what kind of darkness we will be entering? The mind is afraid to go into darkness.

Remember, the fear of darkness is based on the fear of being alone: the fear of being alone comes together with the fear of darkness. You know that you are never totally alone in light, you can see others. Whereas in darkness, no matter how many people are sitting there, you will be alone. The other is not visible. You are not sure whether the other is there or not. Man is alone in darkness. And someone who intends to be alone must enter darkness.

Yoga, *meditation*, and *samadhi* are just other words for the ability to enter profound darkness.

So it is good that there is little light here. It is not right that someone has just now brought a few candles to our meeting here. If there were more wedding ceremonies happening in this village, so that he would not have been able to find any candles, it would have been even better!

Darkness is unknown. We are alone in it. We feel lost and all that was known and familiar seems to have vanished. And remember, only people who can start the journey on the path of truth – who have the ability to let go of the familiar, who are ready to drop the known, who can enter the unknown where there is no path or track – only they can enter truth.

I am saying these few things as an introduction because without falling in love with darkness, you will be deprived of loving the great truths of life. Next time you find yourself in darkness, take a direct look into it and you will discover that it is not so frightening after all. When darkness surrounds you, become absorbed in it, become one with it. And you will find that darkness offers you something that light can never give you.

All the important mysteries of life are hidden in darkness.

Trees are visible on the surface, but their invisible roots are spread deep down in the darkness. The trunk of the tree, its leaves and fruits, can be seen, but the roots are not observed because they work in darkness. If you pull the roots of a tree out into the light, the tree will simply die. So the eternal play of life happens in darkness.

Life is born in the darkness of a mother's womb. We come from darkness through the doors of birth, and disappear into darkness through the doors of death.

Someone has sung a song about life... What is life? Imagine a building surrounded by an ocean of utter darkness. There is a small candle alight inside the building. A bird flying from that vast dark sky enters the candlelit building, flutters its wings for a while, and then flies away through the other window. In the same way, we come from one darkness, flutter our wings around the flame of life, and disappear into another darkness.

It is darkness that is going to be our companion at the end. If you are very afraid of darkness, you will face great difficulty in your grave. If you are so afraid of darkness, you will face great difficulty entering death. No, one has to learn to love death too.

It is very easy to love light. Who does not love light? So, it is not a great thing to love light. Love darkness. Love even darkness! And remember, someone who loves light will start hating darkness. But someone who loves darkness will naturally still love light. Please understand this too.

How can someone who has embraced loving darkness deny loving light? A love of darkness includes the love of light, but a love of light cannot embrace the love of darkness.

For example, to start loving beauty is very easy. Who does not love beauty? But if I start to love ugliness, then I will naturally love beauty too. Someone who is able to love ugliness will naturally embrace the love of beauty too. But vice versa is not true. The lover of beauty is not able to love ugliness also. Flower lovers love flowers, but they deny loving thorns. Their love for flowers becomes a hindrance in loving thorns; but if someone starts loving thorns, there is no hindrance to loving flowers.

These few words I wanted to share with you to start.

Now, I am reminded of a short story, and with that I will begin the talks of the coming three days…

It must have been a night like tonight, a full-moon night, and a crazy man was passing along a lonely path. He stopped by a tree and there was a huge well just by the side of the tree. When he peered into the well and saw the moon reflected there, he thought that the poor moon had fallen into the well: "What shall I do? How can I save the moon? No one is here to help! If the moon is not rescued, it might even die."

And there was another problem… It was the month of Ramadan, and if the moon stayed in the well, what would happen to the people who were fasting for Ramadan, if there was no full-moon night to end the fast? They would die. Anyone fasting for Ramadan keeps on thinking for twenty-four hours about when it is going to be finished; everyone who fasts thinks the same way. All those who perform religious rituals think desperately about when the bell will ring and finish it – the state religious followers are in is no better than that of school children!

He went on thinking: "It is the month of Ramadan and the moon is stuck in the well. What will happen? I have nothing to do with such things as Ramadan, but… And there is no one else around." Somehow he found a piece of rope, made a loop of it and threw it into the well to pull out the moon. Since the moon was not there, it could not be caught in the rope, but a rock got stuck in the loop! He began to pull on the rope with great force, but as it was trapped by the rock, the rope didn't come up. He muttered to himself, "The moon is very heavy and I'm alone here. How am I going to pull it up? No one knows for how long the moon has been drowning in the well, whether it is alive or dead, and it has become so heavy.

"And what kind of people are there out in the world, people who have not even heard the news yet! So many people read and sing poems about the moon, and now when the moon is in trouble, no poet is here to rescue it. And there are people who just keep on singing their songs of poetry, but never show up when there is a need." In fact, those who never show up at a time of need are the ones who learn to write poetry!

He kept on pulling and pulling. Finally the rope broke; he was pulling with such great force and the rock was heavy. When the rope broke, he fell on the ground, with his eyes closed and his skull injured.

When he finally opened his eyes, he saw that the moon was moving in the sky! "Oh! Finally I managed to rescue the poor moon! It doesn't matter that I was hurt a little, but at least the moon is rescued," he said to himself.

We laugh at that madman. Where exactly did he miss the point?

People come to me and ask, "How to be free?" I just tell them this story. They ask, "How to find ultimate freedom?" I share this story with them.

They laugh at the story and then ask, "Tell me the path to freedom." And I see that they did not understand the story. When someone is trapped, he can be freed. If someone is fettered, he can be released. But if someone has never been trapped, and just by looking at a reflection he believes that he is trapped, then there is a problem.

The whole of mankind is caught in the same trouble as that crazy man whose moon was stuck in the well. The whole world is in the same trouble.

There are two kinds of people in the world, and that madman had both types of personality in him. There are two types of crazy people in the world; the first consists of those who believe that the moon is trapped. The second type tries to release the trapped moon. The first are the worldly people and the second are the ascetics, the monks. There are two types of crazy people. The ascetics say, "We will liberate the soul at any cost!" and the householders say, "Now we are caught, what to do? How can we get out of it? We are trapped!" Those who are caught touch the feet of those who are trying to liberate themselves. There are two types of crazy people: one who says that the moon is trapped, and the other who tries to free it. And the one who feels trapped falls at the feet of the one who is trying to liberate.

The truth is totally different. And once you grasp the truth, the whole of life undergoes a transformation. A different quality of life arises.

The truth is that man has never been trapped. The being is constantly free; it has never been in bondage. But the reflection is caught: we are always on the outside, but our image is caught. And we know nothing of the fact that we are more than the mere image; we know only that we are our image. That has created the difficulty: we think the image of ourselves is our being.

Someone is a leader, someone is a poor man, someone is a rich man, someone is a master, someone is a disciple, someone is a husband, someone else is a wife, and so on. All these are reflections that appear to us in the eyes of others. But I am what I am; I am not the way I appear in your eyes. What you see with your eyes is my shadow and somehow I have become stuck in that very shadow.

Suppose you met me today on the path and greeted me. And I became happy: "I am such a good person that people greet me with respect." Now it is so ridiculous: how will someone become good through being greeted by a few people? It does not really matter whether four people are greeting him or fifty or a thousand people. What is the connection between being good and someone showing you respect? In this world, even the evil people can have thousands of people who adore them, so don't be under this illusion that if a few people admire you or bow down to you, you have become a good man. Otherwise you will be caught in your own great image; and when these same few people stop paying you respect and turn their backs on you, you will be in trouble. Now the image has become stuck and it will demand respect! We become identified with the image, and now it will demand "Respect me." And when it is refused, that will be the start of a great problem.

You must have seen political leaders when they had a post as a minister of some department and then later lose the post. Have you seen the condition they end up in? They look like clothes after they have been worn, having lost all their pressing and starch. As if those clothes have been slept in for several days. That is exactly the condition of a political leader who is forced to step down – absolutely good for nothing! What happens to the person in such cases?

He was caught in his image. He was identified with the image. Now he says, "I am the image which was there before. I am that.

I refuse to become someone else." If he can get a greater image, then he will accept it. If a low-ranking minister is promoted to the status of a higher minister, or a clerk is promoted to the post of chief clerk, then it is a different matter. If the image is improved, it is fine. If the image is degraded, then the trouble begins. Man is identified with his image.

When someone respects us or someone insults us, do we realize that we have never actually seen our own face? We are absolutely unaware of the original face which we can call our own face. We don't know it; we have only seen our image.

Have you seen the arrogance of a father when he stands in front of his son? When a father says to his son "What do you know about life? I have been through life, I have the experience of many years. When you grow older and have some life experience, you will know," who is this father talking to? Is *he* talking to his son? No. Is he speaking on his own? No, an image is speaking. The image is speaking, and it is interacting with how his son's eyes see him. The father has grabbed his son by the neck and the son is afraid: an image is reflected in his father's eyes. The one who is afraid can be made even more afraid, and yet the same father wags his tail when he is in front of his boss, saying "Yes sir" to whatever his boss orders.

I have heard...

A mystic once became the servant of a king for a few days. Just like that. Can a mystic ever become the servant of someone? Someone who does not want mastery over anyone can never be enslaved. Then why did he do it? He wanted to experience how the king's servants spend their lives.

He was acting as the servant of the king. The very first day, a particular vegetable dish was cooked. The king really liked it and the cook was ordered to prepare the same food every day. The dish was also offered to the mystic and the king asked, "What is your opinion? How was the food?"

He replied, "Master, there is no better vegetable than this one in the whole world. It is nectar." The cook kept on preparing the same vegetable for the next seven days – on the order of the king himself.

Now, if someone has to eat the same vegetable for seven days, what will happen? The king became very angry. Even in heaven one could become bored after seven days, and ask to visit hell for a short period. According to Hindu scriptures, the gods descend at times to the earth. Why do they come here? – they must be so sick and tired of heaven that they are asking "Let us visit the earth."

The king got utterly sick and tired of the same vegetable being served day after day. After a week, he threw the dishes away and shouted at the cook, "What kind of nonsense is this? The same food is served day after day!"

The cook replied, "Master, I was just following your command!"

Then the mystic commented, "This vegetable is poison! If you eat it every day, you will simply die."

The king replied, "This is too much! Seven days ago you said this same vegetable is nectar."

The mystic replied, "Master, I am your servant, not the servant of the vegetable. I am your servant: I look into your eyes and catch the image that is formed there, and then I speak according to that. The other day you said that it was delicious, so I added, 'It is nectar. There is no other vegetable higher than this one.' I am your servant, not the servant of the vegetable. I am only your servant: today you said that you do not like it, so I added, 'It is poison, anyone eating it will die.' If you change your opinion tomorrow and you say it is nectar and you really like it, then I will say that you cannot find better nectar than this.

"I am your servant; I am not the servant of the vegetable. I am living according the images formed in your eyes."

We all live in the same way. Neither we are aware of what is within us nor has it ever been trapped anywhere. Nor can it ever be trapped; there is no way for it to fall into any bondage. And the interesting thing is that all kinds of effort are being made to free it. It has never been in bondage; there is something else that has fallen into bondage. And we do not even give that a thought. We pay no attention to that which is in bondage.

What is the disturbance which is occupying human beings? What is their suffering? What is the agony? It is the image. When that is shaky, the mind becomes shaky. When it is broken, the mind is suffering. When that image is applauded, the mind feels encouraged.

I have heard...

One day, early in the morning, a fox went hunting, searching for something to eat and drink. It was a sunny day and because of the early morning sun, a long shadow of the fox appeared. On seeing it, the fox said, "A small meal will not satisfy me today!" He thought himself as big as a camel: "What a big shadow! A small meal will not work for me; I am not a small animal. I need to hunt a lot today."

The fox started strutting around, searching for prey. By then, the sun was moving toward the middle of the sky. But by midday the fox had not been able to find any prey. It looked back at its shadow and saw the shadow had shrunk. The fox said, "Not eating anything has put me in such a bad way. What a great body I came out with this morning and look at it now! Even a small meal will satisfy me now. But I am feeling so sad." The fox's mind was suffering.

We all start our lives in this way; great shadows are projected. The sun shines in the beginning of life, and each child embarks on life's journey filled with such great aspirations to conquer the world. Each and every man is Alexander the Great in his childhood. The shadow shrinks in old age. He starts thinking everything is pointless; there is no meaning in anything. But man lives on shadows: our image is formed in the eyes of people around us. And even those who desire to be liberated live through the same shadows.

There are sannyasins who wear ochre clothes. Now, what does sannyas, the search for truth, have to do with ochre clothes? But the robes create an image in other people's eyes, and that image is greatly respected. At the very sight of the ochre robes, the other person is ready to bow down. Such an image is formed in the other person's eyes; the ochre robe is used to create that image. Otherwise, what is the need for ochre clothes?

Can the ochre color, which you can buy for a few rupees, help you to be a sannyasin? Otherwise you could buy all the ochre color, store it in your house and paint everything that color – paint the whole house and all your clothes. Paint your body ochre too. You will just look like a lion in the circus. You will never become a sannyasin, a seeker of the truth, by doing so. And in the name of sannyasins, mostly circus lions are gathered!

What is mind? Have you ever seen someone going to the temple early in the morning and loudly chanting prayers? Just think about this phenomenon. If he is chanting on a lonely road where there is no one to notice him, his singing will turn into mere humming. The moment he sees a few people coming toward him on the road, suddenly the volume of his chanting increases. Very strange! Are you concerned with God or with those few people passing by? I have seen people worshipping in the temple and turning to look back again and again to see whether any spectators have arrived or not. If no one has arrived, the religious ceremony is finished quickly; but if anyone comes, the whole ritual is prolonged. And if someone who is useful in some way to the worshipper is present, performing the rituals lasts even longer. What is happening? – this person lives through images.

For instance, someone visits a temple every day, early in the morning, with the desire that people should consider him a religious person. What is the point in public opinion? But we base our life on public opinion, the image formed in people's eyes. This is the image of the moon in the well which has become trapped. And it is a great problem. How to take it out, how to release it? For that reason, so many paths to liberation are invented. There are people who offer freedom by repeating "Rama, Rama," someone else says there is no way to liberation other than repeating "Om, om" and someone else suggests repeating "Allah, Allah." There are people who have even created a mixed path – they chant "Allah, Ishvara," and say, "They are both names of God, chanting them together will be good. Maybe just one is not strong enough, so I have put both together. Perhaps the combined power can work. Who knows which one is the real one?" So just join both together. Pray to all the enlightened ones; bow down to all the saints; fall at the feet of all holy ones. If one saint does not save you, then catch hold of all the saints and try to find a way to save yourself. You must save yourself because life is full of suffering and agony.

It is true. There is pain, suffering, and agony in life. And man has so much anxiety. Why is there all this anxiety? Why are there so many difficulties? Don't look at the reason that causes the problem...

A man came to me and told me, "I am very disturbed; show me how to find peace." He fell at my feet.

I said, "Keep your hands away from my feet – what relation can your peace have to my legs and feet? Never heard of it! No matter how much you dissect my legs, you will not find your peace in my legs. What wrong have my legs done to you? How are my feet to blame for your condition? If you have become disturbed, did my legs cause that?"

The man was startled. He said, "So this is what you say! I went to Rishikesh, there was no peace; I visited Aurobindo's ashram and there was no peace; I have returned from Arunachala and from the ashram of Ramana, but could not find any peace. I could not find it anywhere. Everywhere they are playing games of pretension in the name of spirituality. Someone mentioned your name, so I came to you."

I said, "Get up and leave immediately, otherwise afterward you will go and gossip that you came to me but could not find any peace even here. And the important thing is, when you first became disturbed, which ashram did you visit, which master did you consult in order to become restless? Who trained you in how to become disturbed? Did you come to me? Who did you go to ask, 'Master, I want to become disturbed, please show me the way?' You managed to become disturbed on your own, you were enough unto yourself! And now you want to become peaceful, you have come here to blame others. If you do not become peaceful, I will be responsible. As if I have made you disturbed! Did you come to ask me then?"

He said, "No, I didn't come to ask you."

"Then who did you go to ask?" I asked.

"I didn't go to anyone," he replied.

And I told him, "In that case, try to understand that you have become disturbed on your own. Try to find out how you became disturbed and what caused it. When you find out what is creating disturbance, stop doing it and you will be peaceful."

There is no method to become peaceful. But there are ways to become disturbed. And someone who drops out of the ways of being disturbed becomes peaceful. There is no way to become free, but there are ways to be in bondage. There are methods to become enslaved. And someone who does not fall into bondage is free.

Suppose I am making a fist, holding it tight, and I ask you how to open it. What will you say? "Just open it. What are you asking for? Just don't tighten it and it will be released. You do not need to do anything to release the fist, just don't hold it tight. When you tighten your hand, only then do you make a fist. Stop tightening it and it will open." To be open is the nature of the hand, to tighten it is an effort. It is natural for it to be open.

Man's self-nature is naturally free, calm, and blissful. If you are miserable, you must be using some device. If you are in bondage, you have created those handcuffs. You are suffering – you are very skillful in creating suffering. It is by your own craftsmanship that you create suffering. And you are no ordinary craftsman, because you are able to build a house of suffering on the soul, which is beyond suffering. And you are no ordinary blacksmith; you are able to put chains on that soul which has never been chained and cannot be. What a funny thing! You first put on those chains yourself and then you carry them around, asking "How can I be free from these chains? I need a way out. How can I become peaceful, blissful, and end the suffering?"

In this introductory talk, I want to say to you that image equals suffering, image is agony, and image is bondage. We live through images. How can one who is living on images live with himself? And how can one whose eyes are focused on images turn in on himself?

I have heard…

There is a small child in a house and he is running and crying, running and crying. His mother asks him, "What is the matter?

He says, "I want to catch my shadow." He runs… He is in great difficulty: the reflection is very clever, you can chase it, but it leaves you behind. The child is crying, weeping. He runs, and once again the shadow overtakes. He wants to touch the shadow of his head – how to catch hold of it? How to grab the head of your shadow?

A mystic had come begging at the door and he started laughing. Even the mother was upset. The mystic started to laugh and said, "Not like this, not like this. That is not the way. This boy will be in difficulty; he has already started acting in the ways of the world."

The boy's mother asked, "What ways of the world? He is just playing."

The mystic said, "Even in his play, this child is caught in the ways of the world."

The mystic went inside. He held the crying child's hand and placed it on his head. The moment the hand reached the boy's head, simultaneously it also touched the head of the shadow. The boy said, "Got it! Strange, you helped me to catch it so easily. By putting my hand on my head, the shadow was caught because the hand reached the head of the shadow."

The shadow becomes the same as we are. If you try to do something to the shadow, you cannot change it; but if *you* change, the shadow changes. We are all engaged in trying to do something with the shadow, from birth until death. And not just one life, infinite lifetimes. We are people who run after shadows – run behind the shadows. And by running after shadows we can never get hold of the shadows. Rather, our minds end up in misery. No shadow is ever caught, and the mind is defeated. The shadow slips out of our hands again and again and we feel that we are inferior, we are not powerful. We are defeated. And the shadow appears to be trapped in so many prisons, so we start doing things to try and free it. We start chanting mantras, reading the Gita, reading Ramayana, reading the Koran and so on. Who knows how many devices we use? We do everything! And nothing will happen because we never do what actually needs to be done.

The right action is to perceive and realize who has been entangled. Me? Have I ever been trapped? Who has become disturbed? Me? Have I ever been disturbed? You may say that you have been disturbed thousands of times, every day, even right now while sitting here.

I want to say to you that if you search, you will be amazed to discover that you have never been disturbed. That which is your innermost core, that depth which is your being, that innermost being, your innermost existence, that which is you, has never been disturbed. The reflection is caught. The self-nature has never been disturbed, has never been in suffering, but the reflection is hurt, disturbed, and is suffering.

I have heard...

There was a small stream, not flowing much. It must have been an Indian river – nothing flows in India! Not even the rivers flow; everything just remains stagnant. Everything stands still and that is why everything has become rotten. If something is stagnant, it will rot. It must have been an Indian river, absolutely stagnant. If rubbish is thrown into it, it just goes on lying there. If you return after many lives, you will still find it lying there! It will still be found there, rotten. Everything has become so dirty.

A dog came to the river to drink. The river was still, unmoving, and when the dog looked down, he saw his reflection. When he saw another dog in the water, he became afraid and stepped backward. But his thirst was strong and he had to drink. The thirst was compelling him to go back to the water, so he went again to the river, but seeing a dog appear when he looked in, he became frightened and stepped back again. The water was so close and he was so thirsty inside. The water was just there, outside, and his thirst was inside. The thirst was there, the water was available, and there was no real hindrance. The dog went to the water again and went away again, afraid of the dog he saw there. But how long could he continue taking that step backward?

A man was passing nearby, and seeing this, he laughed loudly. Not at the dog. Only fools would laugh at the dog. He laughed at himself. He laughed at himself: "I too have returned many times in the same way, after becoming shaky around my own reflection."

He went close to the dog and pushed him in. The dog put up a great resistance: if you push anyone, he is going to resist. Even if you are pushing him into a pool of nectar, he is going to resist. Everyone resists being pushed. Man freezes when he is pushed and does not want to move at all.

That man pushed the dog and it fell into the water. There was no more reflection, the reflection was shattered. The dog drank and the mystic laughed.

If the dog could have asked, he would have asked, "Why are you laughing?" It could not ask, but we can easily ask. Ask the man, "Why did you laugh?"

The man would say, "I am laughing because my state has been exactly the same. This has been my condition too: my own reflection has turned into so many difficulties, obstacles; it turns into so many walls. My shadow has been turning into a hindrance.

Our image is not formed on any river nor is it formed on a mirror. There is no difficulty with a mirror or a river; the image that we are entangled in is projected in the eyes of the people around us; *that* is our standpoint. When it is said that a man is entangled, identified in the world, it is not his self-nature that is entangled, rather it is just his image.

When you are suffering, when great suffering is there, close the door, sit in solitude for a moment, and ask yourself, "Am I suffering?"

And I say to you that if you ask with honesty and total authenticity whether you are suffering, you will instantaneously discover: an answer will come from within you that the suffering can surround you, but you are not suffering.

Suppose your leg is broken, the leg is in pain, it is hurting. Then ask yourself, "Is the pain happening to me, am I suffering?" And surely it will become absolutely clear that the leg is hurting, the information that there is pain is received by you, but where are you? You are the witness standing aloof, far away, you are just watching.

I have a friend, an old man. He fell down the stairs and broke his leg. The doctors told him to rest in bed, and told him he should not move around at all for three months. He is an active man and cannot stand being static; even if movement is unnecessary, he cannot stay without moving.

And how many people are there whose movement truly has any meaning? How often are they moving consciously? If someone keeps an account of his movement from morning till evening, he will find out that ninety eight percent of his movements are unnecessary. He is just restless. There are many things that one does not want to see, and which may become visible just by being unoccupied.

He was told to rest in bed. I went to see him and he started crying, and he said, "I am in great difficulty. It would be better if I had just died. How am I going to survive these two or three months lying in bed? It is such suffering."

I said to him, "Close your eyes and search – are you and the suffering one or separate?

He replied, "What will happen by doing that?"

I said, "First try it, and then we will talk afterward. Close your eyes; I am sitting here. And don't open your eyes until it becomes clear to you. Try to find out whether you and the suffering are one or two. If you and the suffering are one, you can never know that you are suffering. How can suffering know that there is suffering? Can suffering know that it is suffering?"

It is as if a thorn can become aware that it is pricking. A thorn pricks the other; the other feels the prick. There have to be two. The pain, the suffering is one, and the one who is feeling pain and suffering is the other. He is separate. If he becomes one, there will be no experience of suffering.

Do you feel anger arising? If you and the anger are one, will there be any experiencing? Then you will become anger itself. Then the anger will never end; it cannot be erased. Because when you yourself have become anger, how can it end? And if the anger disappeared, you too would be finished.

No, you are always separate. Anger comes and goes; suffering comes and passes, turmoil comes and then goes away. Smoke surrounds from everywhere and disappears. But the one who stands in the center always remains. The name of that constant remembrance is meditation; that search which is beyond bondage, which is beyond suffering, which is beyond pain, which is beyond disturbance, which is always beyond everything, is called meditation. That which is always beyond everything. No matter how hard you try, it can never be touched by anything. It is beyond every happening, beyond every becoming. Whatever is taking place, it remains beyond that.

It happened...

I was on a trip with three friends and we were travelling by car. They were taking me to a village, but the car overturned on a bridge. It fell almost eight feet, the car turning completely upside down. The whole car was crushed. It was a small car with only two doors and one of the doors was blocked by a rock. There was another door, but my friend, his wife, and his driver all were in such panic that they were crying and screaming, but not climbing out of the car! They were screaming, "Oh, we died, we died!"

I told them, "If you were dead, who would have screamed? Please get out. If you were dead, the entire problem would be finished. Who would be there to scream? You are screaming, so it is obvious that you are not dead!"

But they were not listening at all. His wife went on screaming, "Oh, we have died!"

I shook her and said, "Have you gone crazy? If you were dead, there would be silence. Who would scream?"

She said, "You are right, but I *have* died!"

Now this is a very interesting point. Who has died? Who has died – if you are experiencing it, then you have not died. The one who is experiencing is a separate entity. That which is happening is one thing, and the person who is experiencing it is something different. And the person who is seeing it is present.

Then we all climbed out. They were busy calculating what parts of the car had been broken, what had been destroyed and so on. I asked the friend, "Is your car insured?"

"Yes, it is," he replied.

"Then," I said, "stop worrying, the matter is finished. Do you have any life insurance?"

He replied, "Yes, for that we are also insured."

I said, "That is even better. Even if you had died, there would be no problem. Now the question is whether you are going to learn something from this incident or not."

He replied, "What is there to learn from it? The first lesson is, as far as possible, do not ride in a car! The second lesson is, on arriving home, immediately fire the driver. And the third lesson is, never drive a car over the speed limit. These are the things to be learned."

I replied, "What a great opportunity, and you learned so much junk! It is as if you went to university and learned only how to count to ten; that knowledge was all you returned home with. You were satisfied that you had learned how to count to ten and you went back home. You had such a great opportunity and you ended up only learning how to count till ten."

He asked, "What else is worth learning in this?"

I told him that the moment was a great opportunity. When the car turned over, in that moment he should have observed: "Who is dying? Who is falling? Who is going through an accident?"

It was a great opportunity because in such a moment of danger, the whole consciousness awakens. In danger, the whole consciousness becomes aware.

If a man attacks you, threatening you with a knife at your chest, within a second all thoughts will stop: whether you were going to a movie or not; or what to do and what not to do; or what news was in the newspaper that day; or who had become the president, and so on. All this chattering would come to an immediate end. Within a fraction of a second, everything would stop. In that moment there is an opening, an opportunity to see what is taking place. In that moment, you will also be able to see that what is happening is outside of you. And that there is someone who is standing outside of all the happening, just witnessing.

Meditation means: discovering the one who is beyond all happening and has never been a part of anything. There is no other meaning to meditation. We are going to experiment only with this during these three days.

And how are we going to discover that which is beyond everything, even though it is at the center of everything? How can we find that which seems to be born and seems to die; and still it has never been born nor has it ever died? How can we discover that which is in the body, which appears to be the body and yet is not the body? How shall we discover that which thinks, but has never been involved in any thinking? That which seems to be worried, seems to get angry, and yet has never been touched by any anger, no worry has ever reached it. How are we going to search for that?

We cannot discover it as long as we perceive the moon in the well. The moon is somewhere outside and it has never fallen into the well. Have you ever seen it moving toward the well? But it *appears* to fall into the well! It looks bigger there. Sometimes it is seen more clearly in the well than in the sky. It depends on the cleanliness of the water in the well; the moon has nothing to do with it. If the well is absolutely clean, then it is seen very clearly.

That is why we don't want to look into the eyes of our enemy; there is a dirty well in the eyes of the enemy, and so the reflection is not good in those eyes. We prefer to look into the eyes of a friend. A husband looks into the eyes of his wife, and in India, the wife is preconditioned that her husband is a god. Now her eyes are totally clear, the husband reflects in her eyes as a god, and he feels great joy to see himself there as a god. When the wife writes letters to him she signs the letter "your servant" and the husband is very happy that he is the master.

Now the interesting thing is, in whose eyes are you seeing yourself? These are the eyes of your own wife.

It happened...

One day, a man declared in the marketplace, "No one is more beautiful in the world than my wife."

The villagers asked him, "Who told you that?"

He said, "Who else would tell me that? My wife has told me herself."

People said, "You are really crazy! You are manipulated by your own wife."

And he replied, "Everyone is manipulated by his wife, and all the wives are convinced by their husbands. Everyone is manipulated by the people around them. So if I am convinced by my wife, what is wrong in it?"

There are many kinds of wells. If a well is dirty, you cannot see the moon clearly. If the well is clean, you can see the moon clearly. But the moon has never gone into any well. Remember this. And if you start believing that the moon has fallen into the well, your whole life will be in difficulty. The first difficulty you will face is that you will never be able to grasp the moon that has entered the well. When it slips again and again from your hands, your life will become miserable. You will start thinking how to free the moon: "I want to get out of the well. I want liberation! I want to become an ascetic!" Then another kind of complication starts. How are you going to get out of the well something that has never entered?

The moon is always standing outside. The soul is always standing outside; it has never entered any well. But the illusion of it entering the well is created. And the more it seems to enter these wells, the greater we appear to be. That is why if one person bows down to us, we are pleased, and if ten people show their respect, the joy increases. If ten million were doing it, then even more joy, and if ten billion were doing that – or the whole world was doing it – how can you describe the ecstasy from that! I can see my image in so many wells and it seems as if I have expanded so much. I have become so vast. I occupy so much space. And in all this, just one place is missed – where I actually exist. I start appearing at places where actually I am not present.

Meditation means to come out of those wells where you have never been. Now, that is a very paradoxical thing. How to get out of those wells that you have never been in? The meaning of coming out of the well is to discover that perhaps you have always been outside. Let us begin that discovery from today. Now we will sit here for fifteen minutes and try to discover this.

Even this one light here will be turned off; there will be utter darkness and you will remain absolutely alone. In that aloneness, sit peacefully by relaxing the whole body completely, in every way. Close your eyes. Slow down your breathing. And start your inner search with the question "Am I outside, am I beyond all experience?"

You don't have to believe in it and start repeating in your mind "I am beyond, I am outside, I am untouched." Nothing will happen by doing that because when you repeat "I am beyond," it simply means that you have a feeling that you are inside, and you are trying to convince yourself that you are beyond. This happens often. You do not have to repeat, you have to search. Am I really inside, am I a part of any experience?

If an ant bites your leg, in that moment you have to observe: "Is the ant biting me or is it biting my legs? I am witnessing." When your leg becomes heavy, losing sensation, and you feel pins and needles pricking in your leg, observe: "The foot, the needles, the heaviness – is it me or am I just aware of them? Am I just noticing, witnessing them? You will hear sounds, there will be noises, someone will pass by on the road, someone will shout, someone will sound a car horn – then witness: "This sound that I am hearing, is this very sound me? Or am I just the listener standing absolutely aloof?" There is darkness surrounding you:

"I am experiencing this darkness, I am experiencing the silence of this darkness."

Remember; do not just *think* that you are beyond disturbance. In fact, when you reach the inner depths, you are even beyond peace. Where disturbance has never reached, even peace cannot reach. That place is beyond both. There is neither darkness nor light.

Go on digging deeper and deeper, move to the very innermost core of your being and search: "Am I beyond, am I outside?" Keep on asking this, go on knowing, and go on searching. And as you continue this search, your mind will start disappearing into silence. Such a thick silence will surround you as you may never have experienced. There will be such a great explosion within you as you may never have known. For the first time, you will experience: "I am always outside of the well, and have never been inside."

During these three days of the meditation camp, you have to search for this as intensely and as deeply as possible. I will talk about different keys each day, but all the keys will be pointing only to this. I will give you a push from different angles, but all those pushes will take you into the same space.

Let us prepare for tonight's meditation.

Please have enough space around you when you are sitting; don't touch anyone while sitting. Have enough space around you so that no one can be touched. And don't make any noise at all; move away quietly and sit anywhere. If you can listen to my voice, that is enough. And please do not talk to anyone because no one can be your companion or friend in this. Silence, no chattering.

Completely relax your body. No talking is allowed anymore: now, no chattering at all! Stop all talking.

Sit absolutely still, close your eyes. I will give some suggestions and then you slowly move into the search for that which is already within you.

First, relax your body completely, feeling your body to be completely frozen: as though there is no body, as if the body is dead. Relax completely, relax. Relax your body, relax your body utterly.

You have closed your eyes, have relaxed your body, have relaxed your body. Relax your body, relax your body absolutely…

Now relax your breath completely. You don't have to slow it down, just let go, relax it. It is coming and going on its own, do not bother whether it comes or not and whether it is more, or is less. Relax your breath completely. The breath will slow down, it will move as slowly as if it has stopped. Relax your exhalation, letting go of the breath.

The body is relaxed, the breathing is relaxed. Now, within your very self – that which is standing far away from everything – you will be listening to all the sounds here. You are listening. You are beyond, you are separate, and you are the other: "I am the witness, whatever is taking place around me, whether it is happening outside or inside, within my body, whatever is happening, everything is outside of me.

"There might be lightning, there might be a shower of rain, or there may be sounds. The body will stay frozen – the body may even fall down. Everything is outside of me. Everything is outside of me. I am separate. I am beyond. I am standing aloof. I am witnessing, all this is happening. I am nothing more than just a witness. I am a witness, I am just a witness.

"I am a witness, I am a witness. I am watching. Everything is, everything is outside of me. And everything is happening, all is happening far away from me; I am standing far aloof, far beyond, I am standing above, I am standing totally separated. I am just watching, I am just experiencing, I am just a witness.

"I am a witness, I am just experiencing, I am just aware... I am just aware of that which is happening. I am just a witness..."

And this experience will move deeper and deeper, will take you into such a deep peace as you have never known. It will take you into such profound silence, which is totally unknown to you. It will drown us in such great bliss as is totally unknown to us.

"I am a witness... I am a witness... I am just a witness..."

CHAPTER 2

don’t seek, stop

A MAN IN BONDAGE can be liberated; a man in prison can be freed. A man who is sleeping can be awakened. But someone who is awake and under the illusion that he is fast asleep is very difficult to awaken. And someone who is free and thinks that he is constrained is very difficult to untie. When someone who has no chains around him, but who is dreaming with closed eyes that he is chained, asks how to break those chains, how he can become free, how he can be released, then there is great difficulty.

In this context, I talked to you about the first key last night. Man's being is not in bondage, but we believe it to be bound. You don't need to free your being, you just need to know that your self-nature is already free.

Today, in my talk on the second key, this will be the direction I will be pointing to, but from a different angle. The moon is one, but you can point to it with different fingers. In the same way, the truth is one, but you can come to it through different doors. In the second key we are going to ponder over the question: What are we searching for?

Everyone is searching for something: someone is searching for money, someone else is searching for fame. And those who avoid wealth and fame end up searching for religion, ultimate freedom, God. They are compelled to search for something; they cannot escape the searching itself.

Generally we think that someone who is searching for riches is irreligious and someone searching for spiritual matters is religious. I want to say to you that whoever is searching is irreligious and whoever is not searching is religious.

What you are searching for is irrelevant. As long as you are searching, you will go away from yourself. So anyone who is searching will only move farther away from himself. Only someone who stops searching can come upon himself. *Search* means – the very word *search* implies – going far away.

What does it mean to search? To search implies that we want to reach where we are not. We want to find what we don't possess and we want to search for what we haven't yet found. What I am, my very being, is already there, always available. It is my very being – how can I search for that? And the more I get involved in searching, the more I will move away from what I am.

We have lost ourselves through being obsessed with searching. Then whether someone is running after money or fame or enlightenment does not matter. It makes no difference. These are just different names of the same disease; the disease of searching. Our basic disease is not about what we are searching for, rather it is the very searching itself. We have the disease of searching. We cannot be without searching – we have a compulsion to search. And search implies that the eyes will be focused far away: seek and you will lose yourself!

Naturally, that which is far away can be searched for. The stranger can be searched for; the distant one can be searched for. But if there is not even a needle's distance between me and the object – in fact we are one – and it is not possible to go away from it, even if I would want to; wherever I go, it will remain with me, how can I search for that?

Searching is the greatest illusion. And the seeker goes astray; this illusion of searching has a strong foundation stone: when we get bored with one search, we get attached to another search as a substitute, but the searching continues.

Anyone who is continuously running after money gets bored. Once he has gathered a lot of money, he starts saying, "Running after money has no attraction for me anymore, now I will search for religion!" That is why it often happens that someone who has gathered tremendous riches sets out on the search for religion.

Do you know why only rich people start searching for the truth? All twenty-four *tirthankaras* of Jainism were the sons of kings. Buddha was the son of a king. Rama and Krishna were sons of kings. In India, all the *tirthankaras*, the enlightened masters, all the buddhas and all the reincarnations of God were sons of kings. Why do children of wealthy people go in search of spirituality?

They are finished with gathering riches. It doesn't interest them anymore. Whatever is achieved loses its charm. Now you have to search for what has not been achieved. Hence, the man who is tired of riches turns toward religion. The man who is bored with worldly affairs starts searching for ultimate freedom.

The subject of the search changes, but searching itself continues. And the searching mind remains exactly the same; it does not matter what you are searching for.

A shopkeeper goes on worrying about money all day long. Similarly, a seeker of God wakes up in the morning, visits the temple, and spends the day concerned with finding God, just as the shopkeeper is concerned with money. A worldly man goes on running after things and goes on hoarding things. If you observe an ascetic, then you will see that he is also continuously running after something. They are turned in opposite directions, but there is no difference in their chase – both are running. The chase continues. A worldly man dies unfulfilled because he could not get everything he desired for. And an ascetic dies unfulfilled because he could not meet God. The marathon is on for both of them.

I would like you to understand that the real thing is to become free from running, to put an end to chasing. The very running implies that my eyes are focused on something else. And as long as my eyes are focused on something else, how can they turn toward myself? Then it makes no difference whether they are focused on God or on a great position in Delhi. My eyes are looking somewhere else, not where I exist.

This is the symptom of a mind that runs after something. You can change the object; you can change the goal you are running after, select another goal, but the same activity continues. The runner remains the same old runner.

For an ox who works in an oil-press, going around and around with the pulley, it does not matter what kind of oil is being produced. The ox is forced to walk, totally unconcerned with the oil; whatever kind of oil is produced, the ox goes on walking. A running mind goes on running. What it is running after does not make any difference to it.

But we differentiate. We say that a certain man is worldly and dying for money, but another man is very spiritual because he is searching for God. They are exactly the same type of person, there is no difference whatever between them. Both are running. Both are crazy to achieve something. Both have desiring minds. Both are suffering for something outside of themselves; both are desperate to reach somewhere outside of themselves. Both are thirsty. Both say that they will be happy if they achieve their goal, otherwise there will be no joy. There is something they must find before they can have any joy, otherwise they will be miserable. That something can be called by any name, *A*, *B*, *C*. Changing the name makes no difference.

This running mind... This running mind, this searching mind, is the greatest hindrance in the search for truth.

Then what is the way out? You will ask, "If we don't search, what will happen? Then we will remain just as we are!" No, in reality if you go on searching, you will remain exactly as you are. But if you drop searching even for a moment, you will be transformed into that which you have always been. But it is very difficult to drop searching, even for a moment.

The end of searching means that for a moment the mind is not searching for anything at all. You have said, "No, I don't want to find anything. Nowhere to go, no becoming, no goal, I am enough unto myself. Just what I am is enough in itself. For a moment, I have come to a stop. All the running stops. All the wind stops – neither a leaf moves nor any ripple on the water. I am not going anywhere or asking anyone anything. No worshipping or praying with folded hands. I don't bother about my safe deposit or about any scriptures. I have come to a sudden stop. I have become quiet, silent, and no longer search." In this moment of silence, that which is always present and needs no search comes into being. That which we have been forgetting because of our constant running reveals itself.

There was a great mystic in China named Lao Tzu. He has said, "As long as I was searching I could not find, but when I dropped the search itself, it was revealed that the seeker was the searched."

When someone starts searching for himself, then no matter how far he wanders or what great distance he travels, where can he find himself?

I have heard...

A man came home drunk one night. Somehow, following the mechanical habit of his legs, he managed to arrive home.

Our legs don't need to learn the direction of our homes each day. You manage to reach home without much conscious thinking; you don't have to think now take a left turn or now take a right turn and here comes your home. It is all mechanical habit. You go on being occupied with other thoughts and your legs move, they lead you home, they climb the stairs and you find yourself inside the home. You change your clothes, start eating your meal, and you never even consciously think that you have arrived home.

The man was drunk, but still he managed to arrive home. But being drunk, when he arrived, a doubt arose in his mind, "Have I reached my own home, or is it someone else's?" He asked the neighbors, "Brothers, I am little drunk, can you please show me my home?"

He was sitting on the steps of his house. The neighbors started making fun of him. He kept asking, "It's not the right time to joke around, please show me my home. My mother must be waiting for me!"

The people were shaking him and saying, "You are sitting outside your house and trying to fool us!"

The drunk said, "Please don't talk nonsense. Where is my home, please take me to my home!"

By then, his mother had woken up. It was midnight. She came outside, put her hands on her son's head, and said, "My son this is your home. What has happened to you?"

He fell at her feet and said, "O lady! Please take me to my home, my mother must be waiting for me!"

There was a clever man in the neighborhood. There is no lack of clever people anywhere – every neighborhood is filled with them. And clever people cause great trouble. A fool knows that he is a fool, but clever people lack this awareness. A clever man arrived and said, "Wait a minute! I am going to fetch a bullock cart and I will drive you home."

The neighbors said, "What nonsense! This man is already sitting on his doorstep. If you bring your bullock cart and drive him somewhere, then no matter where in this world you drive him, he will be far away from his home."

But the clever man didn't listen. He brought his bullock cart. "If you want to go anywhere then you need a bullock cart," he argued. Now, someone sitting at his own home does not need a bullock cart to reach home. But the argument seems right that to travel anywhere you need a vehicle.

The people started forcing that drunken man into the bullock cart. His mother kept on screaming, "What kind of craziness are you doing? When someone is at home, no matter how far you drive him in the bullock cart, he will end up going farther away from home!"

But who listens?

Our condition is exactly like this. What we are searching for exists exactly where we are. What we are calling for is the person who is calling.

It is a very strange situation. And because of this strange situation, great difficulty arises. The more we pray, the more we search, the more the difficulty increases. And it never occurs to us to at least take a look inside and ask who it is who is searching.

That's why I say to you that a religious man or a seeker is not someone who asks, "What shall I search for?" Rather, a true seeker asks, "Who is it who is searching?" The question is not what to search for. An irreligious man asks, "What should I search for?" A religious man asks, "Who is it who is searching? Let me first discover that. Then I will search for something else. First let me find myself, and then I will start on the search for the truth. Let me first know myself, and then I can experience God, the world, and worldly things such as money. Someone who does not know himself, what else can he know?"

A true seeker does not ask where God is. And a man who asks where God is has nothing to do with religiousness. A religious man does not ask where ultimate liberation is. And someone who does ask has nothing to do with religiousness. The religious man asks, "Who is it who has the desire to be liberated? Who is this person who wants to be liberated? Who is it who has this thirst to realize godliness? Who is longing to find truth? Who does this longing to find bliss belong to? Who is this person who is crying, longing, and praying for bliss? Who am I? Who is this very seeker, let me just know it! Let me just recognize it."

But in the name of religion, only meaningless things have been taught and explained. The very direction of religious search has been wrong. Religiousness has nothing to do with the search and the object of search; it is only concerned with the seeker himself. Who is this seeker? And if you want to find the seeker, where do you need to go? Where do you have to go – to the Himalayas or to holy places such as Kashi? Where do you have to go to search for yourself?

It happened…

A great crowed was gathered in a village. A mystic came out of his hut and asked the people, "What a great crowd, where are all these people going?"

The people replied, "Don't you know that a man has returned from Mecca? All these people are going to visit him."

The mystic said, "Aha! I thought since it is such a great crowd that Mecca had come to visit a man, and that is why people are flocking toward him. What is so great if a man has visited Mecca? When Mecca comes to visit a man, there is some significance in the happening." And he went back into his hut.

A religious man is not one who goes in search of godliness: a religious man is one who arrives at the center of his being; because the moment someone reaches the center of his being, the whole of God drops into him. You cannot search for God, only God can search for you.

How can we search for God? We are not even able to find ourselves. We are not even able to know ourselves and yet we long to know God.

In fact, it is man's ego which claims that he will find God. This is the greatest ego; the ego of a money-minded person is not so big. It is difficult to find greater egoists than ascetics. What is their ego all about? The illusion to find God! And the truth is that no one can ever find God. One just has to find oneself and then godliness is realized. No one can come close to existence directly; one just comes close to his own being and he immediately finds intimacy with the whole of existence.

Hence, I want to talk about the second key: don't search, be still. Don't run, stop. Withdraw your eyes from others, but don't focus on some substitute. Withdraw your eyes from looking outward, so that your eyes turn in. And remember that you cannot focus your eyes on yourself. You cannot focus your eyes on yourself, you cannot concentrate on yourself. Concentration is always focused on others; there have to be at least two entities for the process of concentration – the one who is concentrating and the object of concentration.

So when I say to withdraw your attention from everywhere, I don't mean that you should concentrate on yourself. When your attention is withdrawn from everywhere, it simply turns toward the center of your being. You don't have to concentrate on the center of your being; no one can concentrate there. Hence, the whole process of meditation is negative, *neti-neti*, neither this nor that. Not this, not this, and not even this. You are going to withdraw your attention from this, this, and even this. From everything. And let it remain unoccupied. Leave it empty. The moment the attention is utterly unoccupied, immediately it turns inward.

To understand the second key, you must understand the illusion of worldly people and the illusion of the religious ascetics.

People like Alexander and Genghis Khan are trying to conquer the world, declaring they will succeed in conquering the whole world. In their case, the "I" is saying, "I will conquer the whole world!" The ego says, "I will have the whole world in my fist!" And on the other hand there is another kind of man who declares, "I am going to search for God!" The ego says, "I will have God in my fist! I will find God at any cost." What is the difference between these two?

Yes, there is some difference. The pursuit of the worldly man is small, the world is small. Whereas God or existence implies the whole, the total, that which is absolute. The ascetic says, "I will take the whole in my fist." Neither of them is religious.

A true seeker says, "I will find out who my fist belongs to. I am not out to capture someone in my fist; rather I want to find out who this fist belongs to. Who closes this fist and who opens it? I don't care about what is in the fist, I care about who is behind it. Who is behind my fist, who closes and opens this fist? I am not concerned about what I see with my eyes – whether I see a beautiful girl or a beautiful flower or a beautiful building or God. The real issue is not what I see. It is not a question of object. The question is who is seeing through the eyes." You must have a clear distinction between these two, between the observer and the observed.

The object of observation can change. Someone gets tired of being focused on money and starts focusing his eyes on God. People who are obsessed with the marketplace turn around and start seeing visions of heaven. There are people who suddenly have visions of Lord Krishna playing on his flute while they are engaged in counting money! But all these experiences are separate from us; they are the observed, but we are totally unaware of the observer: "Who am I?" Whether you have a vision of Krishna playing on his flute or you are watching a play, in both cases you are watching something outside of you. You are unaware of the watcher.

A truly religious man tries to discover the observer, the witness. He is concerned with the seer not the seen. He is not concerned with the observed; he asks about the observer, "Who is he?" And in this search for the observer, running after something will not work. In this dimension, searching has no place. Stopping will work. Doing nothing will work. Sitting silently will work.

But we are experts in running after things and searching. That is why, if someone advises you that you should drop the search that you are on and pursue something else, it is easy to feel it must be right: "Now I will end this search and start pursuing something else."

The man who is obsessed with money easily gets engaged in the search for God. So don't be too surprised when you see a wealthy man becoming an ascetic. There is no difference. The same money-seeking mind says, "I want to search, I will search for something. If I am not going to search for money then let me search for religion." That money-seeking mind asks, "Why do I search for wealth? So that I can get prestige from it." That same mind says, "Alright! If I am not searching for money I will search for religion, since religion draws even more respectability." How many people respect a wealthy man? And if the wealthy man becomes a saint, the same fools who never respected him before, or even when they showed respect, it was false… They used to show respect when they met him on the way and talked about him behind his back. Now the same idiots start touching his feet.

Running after money is motivated by a desire for respectability and the search for religion can also be caused by the same reason. But the mind needs to search; the mind demands a search. It cannot survive without searching. Why? Because without a search, the mind will die. The moment searching ends, the mind dies. Searching finished, the mind is finished. No searching, no mind. As long as searching continues, the mind continues. If you understand it rightly, the mind is the very instrument of searching. The mind survives as long as searching persists. When searching ends, the mind ends.

Generally we say that the mind is searching. It is a wrong statement. But our language has many wrong expressions. Last night there was thunder and lightning and someone said in Hindi that electricity is lightning. Now ponder on this expression a little. It sounds as if the electricity produced from thunder and lightning are two different phenomena. In fact, that which is lightning is called electricity. It is a wrong expression to say that electricity is lightning. *Lightning* and *electricity* mean the same. When you say that electricity is lightning, it seems that they are two separate things, that electricity is one thing and lightning is something different. Can you separate lightning from the electricity produced during thunder? If you remove the lightning, then the electricity is not there. If there is no electricity produced, there will be no lightning. *Electricity* and *lightning* are just two names of the same phenomenon. But we say electricity is lightning! It is a wrong expression.

In the same way, we say that the mind is searching. This too is a wrong expression. The very process of searching is called *mind.*

It is meaningless and pointless to say that the mind is searching. The mind means search. As long as you are searching, there will be mind. Then the object of search does not matter, and the mind will continue. When you stop searching, the mind disappears. And when the mind disappears, there is the realization of that which is.

You do not have to search for that which is. That which is, is. Just stop searching.

There is a garden where many flowers are blooming; you pass over the garden in a jet plane, with tremendous speed. Even if you circle the garden thousands of times, still you will not be able to see the flowers in the garden. The flowers are there, but how can you notice them when you are in such speed, in such a hurry? You have to stop, and only then will you be able to see that which is. And if you continue running, you will miss that which is.

The faster you run, the faster you will miss that which is. The faster a mind runs, the farther it moves away from the truth. The more a mind becomes unmoving and tranquil, the closer it comes to the truth. The truth is that which a still mind implies: no-mind. Mind dies – the moment it stops, it departs.

We must understand this rightly, because we use common expressions like this in our daily life: we say that a certain person has a very peaceful mind. It is a totally wrong saying. There can be nothing like a peaceful mind; the *mind* is another word for disturbance. The mind is always disturbed. When disturbance is gone, the mind disappears.

Try to understand it in another way. There is a storm over a river and the waves are going wild. There is a tempest and everything is disturbed. We say that the waves are very disturbed. Then all the waves become calm, and will we say: "Now all the waves have become tranquil"? It means the waves have disappeared, doesn't it? Now there are no more waves.

There is nothing like a motionless wave. The very word *wave* means a disturbance. As long as there is a wave, there will be a disturbance. There is nothing like a still wave. A still wave implies the death of the wave. There is no wave anymore. This is the very meaning of a still wave.

The mind is always disturbed. And why is it disturbed? The

one who seeks is bound to be disturbed. Searching implies tension. I am here, and the thing I want to find is *there*; it is at a distance. The thing I want to achieve is there, and the achiever is right here. There is a tension between the two. Until I achieve it, I cannot be at rest. And the moment I arrive there, my search will move forward because the seeking mind will say, "Further! More and more and more..." and only then can it survive. Only as long as the mind maintains a search for more and continues searching further can it stay alive. Hence, the mind takes you further and further away, day after day. Your mind takes you into the future and you are in the present.

A search takes you into the future and existence is in the present. A search says, "Tomorrow." A search says, "Tomorrow you will achieve. Tomorrow you will have wealth, tomorrow you will attain status, and tomorrow you will realize God – tomorrow!"

A search says, "tomorrow" and that which is, is today. It is now and here.

I have heard...

A few saints were traveling together. There was a Sufi mystic, a yogi, and a devotee among the travelers. They had an overnight stay in a village. There, they begged and then one of them went to the market to buy some food. At the market he bought some sweet halvah. Since he had very little money, he could buy only a small amount of food. But there were more hungry people than there was food, so each one of them started to claim his right to eat the halvah. The devotee said, "Since I am a great devotee of God, and I often have a vision of Lord Krishna playing on his flute, the halvah should be given to me."

The yogi said, "What nonsense! I have spent most of my life practicing the headstand. No one has ever practiced the inverted Yoga positions more than me. I possess all the extrasensory powers of Yoga. So I will take the halvah."

The dispute continued, but nothing was decided. There was only a little halvah and they could not reach any agreement about who should eat it. It was sunset and finally the Sufi mystic suggested, "Let us all go to sleep. Whoever has the sweetest dream can eat the halvah in the morning. We will share our dreams in the morning."

They all went to sleep. When they woke up in the morning, they started describing their dreams. Certainly, they all had great dreams! Now, no one can have control over their dreams, but even so they created such dreams…

The devotee said, "God himself came into my dream and said, 'You are my greatest devotee. There is no devotee greater than you.' So I have the right to eat the halvah."

The yogi said, "I went into *samadhi*, reached ultimate freedom, and experienced divine bliss. So I have the right to eat the halvah." They went on arguing and claiming.

Finally they asked the Sufi mystic, "What is your idea?"

"I am in great difficulty. I dreamed that God was commanding me, 'Get up, and eat the halvah!' No one can refuse God's command. How could I do so?" replied the Sufi mystic.

The Sufi mystic who has told of this incident in his biography has written that those who get up and eat the halvah are the real ones. Those who say, "Tomorrow," those who postpone even for a moment, miss it. And searching always postpones. Searching is a postponement. Searching can never happen now and here. A search has to go on and on – then we will arrive somewhere tomorrow and some fulfillment will be waiting for us there. But when we arrive, the searching mind will still focus beyond that point and it will say "Farther away, farther away."

Have you seen how the horizon appears to us? When you go out of your house, you see the horizon touching the earth all around. It appears to be just a little distance away from you. As though, if you went a little beyond where we are sitting here, beyond the hills, the sky must be merging with the earth. But when you go there, it will keep on moving farther away. The horizon never touches the earth anywhere. The farther you move, the farther away it will appear. You can take a journey around the whole earth; it will always appear as if the earth and sky are just merging into each other in front of you, calling you onward. And the farther you move, the farther away it will appear.

In the same way, the horizon of desire never ends anywhere. The sky of desire never touches the earth of your being anywhere. You follow it, and its horizon moves farther away from you. You go on running, rushing, searching, and finally reach only the end of your life. One life, two lives, infinite lifetimes… And the madness of searching never ends.

Yes, only one thing happens and that is that you get bored with one search and replace it with another search. But searching continues. A truly religious man is one who is finished with searching – not with any particular search, but with search itself. He is bored with searching and he declares, "Now no more searching. Now I will sit silently and find out what happens in the absence of searching."

Sitting silently and witnessing without searching is called meditation. A non-seeking mind, a mind that has stopped seeking, enters meditation. It attains meditation. The very state of a non-seeking state of mind is meditation.

We have not known the state of non-seeking even for a moment. We are always seeking something or other. This seeking is a symptom of our inner restlessness. If you leave someone unoccupied in an empty room – nothing is in there – and you keep on observing him through a hole, you will see that he will try to search for something in the room. He will not sit idle. There is nothing there, but if he finds a piece of old newspaper, he will start reading it. Once, twice, ten times. He will read the same newspaper repeatedly. He will open and close the window. He will do something or other. If he lies down, he will toss and turn; if he gets up, he will constantly move his hands and legs.

One day, a man was sitting in front of Buddha and was moving his toe. Buddha stopped speaking and said, "My friend, why is this toe moving?" The moment Buddha said that, the man stopped moving his toe.

The man answered, "Please continue with your talk. Why are you bothering about things like a toe? What have you got to do with my toe?"

Buddha said, "You are not concerned with your toe, but I am. Why is this toe moving?"

"It was moving automatically, I was not aware of it," the man replied.

Buddha said, "It is your toe and you are not aware of it? Then there is a great difficulty! Are you a conscious man or are you unconscious? Why was the toe moving?"

The man retorted, "Why are you bothering about such trivia? Why are you concerned about my toe?"

It is not a question of the toe. It shows that your mind is agitated inside and is moving.

You must have observed someone sitting on a chair unoccupied and moving his legs unknowingly. If you ask him why he is moving his legs… "If you are going somewhere and moving your legs, it is understandable. You are not going anywhere and just moving your legs while sitting! What has happened to you?"

The mind is restless inside. The mind says, "Do something. If you are not engaged in anything, then do something useless."

Someone is smoking a cigarette. Now, there is no point in smoking a cigarette. He is taking smoke in and out. If someone asks him, "Why are you taking smoke in and out?"… Such things go on and we have got used to seeing them.

If someone takes water in his mouth and gargles with it, we will call him crazy. But if it becomes a fashion and is accepted by the culture as a device for entertainment, then you will see that in each and every house people will be sitting and gargling water in their mouths. And if it goes on for thousands of years, the priests will start preaching that gargling water is a bad habit. And people will say, "Sir, we are not able to drop it. We are addicted to it. When we don't gargle, we feel something is missing. We feel obsessed with it and have to do it four or six times a day."

Perhaps you don't know – no one chews gum in India. But people are doing it all over America. They put chewing gum in their mouths and go on chewing. They are unable to drop chewing gum. But here, we don't have the idea of sitting silently and chewing gum. Why? It is just a matter of fashion there; it is in fashion, so it is happening.

People are smoking cigarettes; they are just taking smoke in and out. What are they doing? It is not a question of whether someone should smoke or not. It just shows that a restless man wants to do something or other. If he sits unoccupied, what to do? He is just taking smoke in and out! This becomes something that he does: cigarette smoking is an occupation. It is just a device for an unoccupied man to stay busy.

Slowly, slowly all over the world, even women have started smoking. Do you know that in the countries where women have started smoking, women talk and gossip less because they have found a new occupation?

In countries like India where women do not smoke, they gossip more. What you exhaust by smoking, women have to exhaust by gossiping. It is the same thing, there is no difference. And in my understanding, it is better to smoke than to fill up somebody's brain. While you are smoking you are caught up in yourself, and whatever you are doing you are doing it to yourself – at least you are not causing any damage to someone else's head.

Around the world, women chatter more than men because they have no simpler way to keep their lips busy. But in countries where women have started smoking, they have become more silent. Now they sit in a corner and go on smoking, they do not gossip much.

Our minds seek pointless occupation. People wake up in the morning and start reading the newspaper. The moment they wake up, they ask where the newspaper is. Do you think that they are desperate to know about the world? Don't assume so. They don't even bother to know about themselves, how can they be concerned about others? But they need some engagement, some involvement. It will keep them occupied for a while. Then they will turn on the radio and stay busy with that. They need something to be occupied with. Man is restless inside; he needs to be occupied with some search. If there is no search it is a problem.

We have escaped from ourselves. People are trying to escape from themselves and we go on giving new names to this escape.

It will not work – you must stop. There is no need to escape from yourself. Just stop. Take a break sometimes and go in. Stop going anywhere, stop doing anything, stop seeking anything, stop being occupied – freeze your legs and hands, no cigarette smoking, no newspaper, and no chanting mantras. Whether you are taking smoke in and out or chanting "Rama, Rama," both activities are the same. Chanting a mantra and using prayer beads are just the same urge to remain occupied.

In a better world, children will have a more evolved intelligence and they will be puzzled to know that in the old days some crazy people used to sit for half an hour or forty five minutes and chant mantras on prayer beads. But we are unable to see that; we think it is all right. The person who has become religious goes on praying with beads. What has using prayer beads to do with being religious? It is the same thing – just the method is different; there is no difference between a smoker and a devotee using prayer beads. One is taking smoke in and out and the other is fingering prayer beads, but both are occupied with some activity. They cannot remain in a non-doing state.

Doing nothing is meditation. To stay absolutely unoccupied is meditation. This is the second key I am giving you: for a while, remain without doing anything. Absolutely nothing.

People come to me and ask, "Okay, then what should we do in that period of non-doing? Should we chant 'Om' or 'Rama, Rama'? What should we meditate upon, which mantra should we chant, should we repeat some mantra from Jainism? What should we do?"

I say to them that this is exactly what I tried to explain to them: do nothing. Then they say, "We must do something! Could you please give us something to do?" If I give them something, they relax because they have found another substitute to be occupied with. They need something to do. They are ready to do anything. But you must give them something to keep them busy; they will keep on doing just that and stay occupied with it. Then the same old pattern of doing will continue.

I say to you: for a while, no action. For a period of time, no doing! If even for a second you are able to remain in a state of non-doing, in that very moment the door to existence will open.

We will experiment with this during the evening meditation. When you sit for the evening meditation, just remember that we are meditating – that is, doing nothing. It is just the limitation of our language that we say, "We are doing meditation." Now, the very meaning of *meditation* is doing nothing. This is the difficulty of the language. Languages are created by the unenlightened ones; the enlightened ones have not been able to create any language. When the enlightened beings try to create a language, the fools try to stop them. If the enlightened beings were to create a language, it would be totally different. All our languages have been created by unenlightened people.

I will end my talk with a short story. And then we will enter this non-doing.

Please think during your waking hours about what this non-doing is; sharpen your understanding of it a little. Whatever I have shared with you, you must also take some time to consider it. You are not going to understand just by listening to what I say. It does not work that way. But when I share it, then you also have to contribute something to it. You have to continuously meditate on it – only then will something happen.

I have heard...

There was a monastery in Japan and the emperor came to visit. It was a big monastery with hundreds of rooms for the monks. The head of the monastery showed each and every room to the emperor: he showed him the bathrooms, toilets, gym, and the study room.

The emperor asked, "You have shown every corner of this place, except the great building over there. What do you do there?"

But whenever the emperor asked about what they did in that building, the master remained silent, just as if he was deaf and had not heard anything. Yet he was listening to everything else.

The emperor became angry because he was not showing him what he had come to see, he was not showing him that building. And the master went on showing him the uninteresting places such as the barn where they sheltered their cattle! Finally, the emperor said, "Have you gone crazy? I don't care about where you shelter your cattle. I have come here to see that building and what you do there."

The moment he asked, "What do you do there?" the master became absolutely silent. The emperor angrily returned to the gate and said, "I am leaving with sadness, either you are mad or I am crazy. Why don't you tell me what you do there in that big building?"

The master said, "You are asking a wrong question. And if I answer you, it is bound to be a wrong answer. There cannot be a right answer to a wrong question."

"What am I asking? I am just curious to know what you do in that building," answered the emperor.

The master replied, "That is exactly why I stay silent. You understand only the language of doing, so I explained to you where the monks take their bath, where they study, where they exercise and so on. That building is our meditation hall – we do nothing there. When you ask what we do there, I keep quiet because you will not understand our language. You know only the language of doing. Hence, I am showing you where we shelter our cattle. And what we do over there? When someone wants to do absolutely nothing, then he goes there. That is our meditation hall. We do nothing there, your honor! When we feel like being absolutely unoccupied, then we go there. We don't do anything there; we just rest in our being. Doing nothing. Just being. We stay there, doing nothing."

Think over this during the day, then the evening meeting will be significant for you. Just listening to me is not enough! If you meditate on it, it becomes clearer. You also need to contribute a little, you also need to participate in it.

I have heard...

A king had invited his friend to be his guest on a hunt. The king's friend was a wise man, so just to tease him the king gave him the worst horse, which was so slow that it was impossible to hunt anything with it.

They went out for the hunt, and everybody arrived in the jungle, but the friend could not even leave the borders of the village. The horse was so slow that he could have gone faster if he had gone without the horse. Often it happens that the vehicle becomes a hindrance. But fortunately it rained – and it rained heavily. The wise man, just at the edge of the village, took off all his clothes, put them under him on the saddle, and went back to the palace. When he arrived at the palace, he put on his clothes again.

The king and everyone who had been hunting in the jungle came rushing back. They were absolutely soaked in the rain. They saw that the wise man was still wearing dry clothes, was not wet at all! They asked, "What happened?"

"The horse is extraordinary. It brought me back home so skillfully that my clothes did not get wet at all," replied the friend.

The next day they went hunting again. The king said, "I want to take that horse today."

The friend replied, "As you wish." The king gave the fast horse to his friend and rode the slow horse. It rained again. And the wise man took off his clothes, put them underneath him again, and returned with great speed. He was even drier than the previous day because the horse was faster.

The king was soaking wet, even more so than the previous day because the horse was extremely slow. The rain poured on him. On returning home, the king said to his friend, "You lied to me. This horse made me even wetter than the other day."

The wise man replied, "Your honor, the horse alone is not enough. You have to contribute something; you also have to do something. What will the horse do alone? Did you do something or just depend on the horse?"

"I was just sitting on the horse and everything went wrong," was the king's reply.

The friend said, "I contributed something, then the horse cooperated. Today also, I added something, so the horse collaborated."

The king asked, "What did you do?"

The friend said, "Please don't ask me about that. Don't ask that at all. That is a secret. But one thing is certain; you always have to contribute something. If you don't contribute at all, even the fastest horse is useless. And if you contribute a little, even the slowest horse will be cooperative and friendly to you."

This story was about a horse. Just like with the horse in that story, after listening to my talks, you have to do something with what you have heard. If you do something, something is possible; otherwise, you will just hear it and then it will disappear.

So, come back for the evening meeting after thinking about these topics. Come to the evening meeting after understanding the meaning of non-doing. And then in the evening meeting we will sit together. If you come after thinking about this, then you can enter non-doing. It can happen now, right now. It can happen any moment. But you need a little preparation in the form of right consideration. Then you can take the quantum leap in a moment. And that quantum leap is so extraordinary that it takes you to the center of your being, where you have always been.

We will meet in the evening for that quantum leap.

You listened to me with such silence and love, I am grateful for that. And finally please accept my respect for the godliness within you. Please accept my offerings of respect.

CHAPTER 3

darkness has no existence

THERE ARE A FEW THINGS to be discussed. The first point is that in wanting to be free of attachment and hate, we have taken it for granted that we are full of these feelings. I have already talked about this last night and this morning also: this way of approaching it is a complete illusion. If you continue believing that, in order to dissolve the feelings, you will never be able to erase them.

Hence, I don't talk about how to be free from attachment or hatred and so on. My suggestion is to realize whether you and those feelings are one or separate from each other. Just try to discover it, try to explore in your own mind whether attachment and you are one or absolutely separate. As you become clearer that "This is the feeling of attachment, this is the feeling of hatred, and this is my being – which is absolutely untouched by any feeling" – as this clarity deepens, all attachment and hatred will start to disappear. And the day the understanding that you are beyond everything becomes crystal clear, that there is neither attachment nor hatred in you, on that day you are free.

In fact, no one has ever been one with attachment, hatred.

You have assumed that you are one with those feelings, and this illusion has created the difficulty. Then you will have to find a way to get out of them.

Witnessing is the only cure for this. Be a witness to attachment and a witness to your hatred. Just witness. Neither try to avoid nor try to escape. When attachment comes, witness it, observe the whole thing: "Attachment is there and I am watching it happen. I am here, and that is attachment there." When hate arises, watch it: "Hate is arising and I am separate from it." Just observe. It is the same as noticing when it becomes dark in the evening and when daylight breaks in the morning: we just observe.

Now it is daylight here. If we go on sitting here, darkness will descend in the evening. You will not say, "I have become darkness." You say, "It is dark." Then in the morning when daylight comes, you say, "It is light; I am just separate." It becomes dark and it then it becomes light. It comes and goes.

In the same way, attachment and hate come and go: I am standing alone, standing apart. The illusion is that when attachment happens, I cling to it and say, "This is me." When hate comes, I get identified with it and say, "This is me." This very identification has to be broken. And you don't need to do something to break the identification. Just witnessing is enough to end it.

For instance, when anger arises, just watch that the anger is arising. You will be surprised to see that as you observe anger arising, and you remain unidentified with the whole thing, it becomes thinner like smoke and vanishes. You are standing aloof and the anger has disappeared.

Just be a watcher to whatever arises, just be a witness.

Osho,
Do these things arise only when we come in contact with other people?

I am not saying anything about it happening or not happening. When did I say that? I am not saying at all that it should not happen. I am saying only that whatever is happening, be a witness to it. Just by witnessing, it will disappear slowly, slowly.

Then, when you come in contact with people, nothing will arise in between. There will be one person on one side and another person on the other side, but there will be nothing in between. There will be neither any attachment nor any hatred.

So, if we understand it rightly, in our awareness there is an end to attachment and hatred. And our unawareness is the cause of falling into attachment and hatred.

We are unaware, so we immediately get identified with whatever takes place. When anger arises, you don't remember that anger is passing in front of you, rather you feel that you have become anger. If you look closely, you feel like you have become anger! The fire is burning and you have become the fire. At the moment of anger, it not just that you are beating someone under the influence of anger; rather you have become anger and are beating someone.

Hence, after anger you repent: "How could I do that! I couldn't have done that, so how did it happen?" You were not present at all, you had totally fallen asleep, and anger had become everything. Now anger is making you do everything. And the same misunderstanding that was working in anger is repeated when you repent.

At that moment you were under the illusion that you were anger and now you believe that you are repenting. That is the fundamental mistake. Now you think that you are repenting, you have become repentance. You are crying bitterly, beating your chest, and praying to God: "What has happened? It should have never happened!" Now you say that you will drop it; earlier you made the mistake of identifying with it and now you repeat the same pattern, saying that you will drop it.

That is why I say that getting identified is a misunderstanding and the effort to drop something is another misunderstanding. The wisdom is in this understanding: "I am separate and this is separate." Neither do you have to get identified nor do you have to make an effort to drop it.

You just need to gradually increase your awareness, twenty-four hours a day. Whenever something happens, just be aware whether you are separate from it or not. And this feeling of being separate must go on increasing. For instance, listening to me right now, you can listen in three ways. You can listen with appreciation or you can listen with condemnation; and if you wish, you can just listen. All three things are possible. If, while listening, you are thinking, "Yes, he is saying the right thing, let me take hold of it and do it," then you are possessed by your appreciation, and attachment has started. If, while listening, you are thinking, "What he is saying goes against what is written in my scriptures. This is wrong according to the scriptures; I can't listen to this, I shouldn't listen to this, it's absolutely wrong," then you are possessed by condemnation. In that case also you are not listening. The third way is that you are just listening, and the witness that is standing aloof has neither appreciation nor condemnation. He does not say this is wrong nor does he say this is right – he just listens, is just listening. The wisdom born out of this listening is beyond appreciation and condemnation. But we never listen this way.

Try to experiment with it in every activity, and then slowly, slowly it will not be that you become free from attachment and hatred, rather that you discover you have never been in their bondage. It is not that one day you feel you are free from attachment and hatred. If you feel like that then you are still in illusion. Instead, you will realize that you have never been in bondage.

It is as if somebody is asleep here and dreaming that he is in Kolkata or Tokyo. Now he becomes very anxious about how far away he has gone from Udaipur and he asks someone, "How can I return to Udaipur? What will happen now? I have ended up in Tokyo, and there are thousands of unfinished jobs at home. I fell asleep at home in Udaipur and ended up in Tokyo! Early tomorrow morning I have to return to Udaipur. How shall I get back? Which flight shall I take? Which ship shall I take? Will I be able to arrive there by the morning?"

His questions are logical because as far as his mind is concerned, he has arrived in Tokyo. But in reality he has not gone anywhere; he is just lying in his bed. He wakes up in the morning and is puzzled: "How did I get back? I had traveled to Tokyo, so how did I get back from there?" But immediately after waking up he will realize that neither had he gone anywhere nor had he come back. He had always been here. Going away was an illusion and returning was also an illusion; the illusion of returning was born out of the illusion of going away.

So, being bound by attachment is an illusion and freedom from attachment is another illusion. *Vitraga*, beyond attachment, means one who has realized that he is beyond both. The word *vit* means *beyond. Vit* does not imply that you have dropped something. *Vit* does not mean at all to drop anything! The meaning of the word *vit* is neither "I was attached to something" nor "I have to let go of something." I was beyond. And I was under this illusion that I was entangled.

"Am beyond" or "was beyond"?

Was beyond! Am beyond is always the case. But you will come to know that even when you were under the illusion that you were caught up in attachments and feelings, you were beyond everything – but you will realize that only when you wake up. And then it is already clear to you that you are beyond.

So, please do not ask me in the language of "dropping." The very language of dropping is the language of ignorance because it is the by-product of the ignorance that is attachment. Someone is attached to things and someone else is involved in getting rid of things. Someone is clinging to his wife – and even when he possesses his wife, even then she is separate and he is separate. No matter how hard you try, and even if you try in millions of ways, it is not possible to possess anyone. In fact, no one is attached. No matter how hard you keep hold of your wife, what are you going to cling to? What you are clinging to is not your wife; the one who is your wife is always beyond your clinging, absolutely beyond your hold. That is why there is a daily struggle, because you know that you are trying hard to hold onto something that is beyond your grip.

The man who says that he is attached to his wife is under an illusion. Then there is another type of man, who says he is renouncing his wife; the illusion of renouncing is the by-product of the illusion of attachment. Now he says, "I will not go close to my wife, I will not even look at my wife. I am going away into the forest, I have renounced my wife!"

There was a Jaina monk who had renounced his wife twenty years before. I was shocked to read his biography. He had renounced his wife twenty years earlier, and then his wife died.

He was in Varanasi when he got the news. The person who had written his biography described the monk's reaction to it as "magnificent." As he was given the news, the monk said, "Good, so even the last hindrance is gone now." The biographer has written about the incident in appreciation, writing about the great renunciation, that when the wife died, the monk had said that the last barrier was gone.

I wrote to the biographer that he was crazy. And that if the monk had said such things, then he was even crazier because the woman he had renounced still appeared to him as a barrier. He said, "The last barrier is gone!" Now this is a very interesting thing.

Twenty years earlier he had renounced his wife. But the person he had renounced was "his." The illusion is sustained because he renounced her on the grounds that she was *his* wife. She still belonged to him after twenty years. She was his renounced possession! In the inner layers of his mind, she was still perceived as a barrier. He had considered her his possession and so was attached to her; that was an illusion. Then he renounced her; that was another illusion. Now that she had died, twenty years later, he said that the barrier was gone. That means it continued for twenty years. The wife he could not get rid of through renunciation, freed him by her death! Think about this a bit. How could the wife who was not dropped from his mind by renunciation be dropped by her death? In a way, the wife was already dead for him. For twenty years she meant nothing to him, but even then he was not free of her.

Hence, I am emphasizing that the language of attachment and renunciation does not work; the language of witnessing everything that is happening will work. Just watch what is happening. And the more you move deeper into witnessing, the more you are out of everything.

But earlier you said that instead of believing, we should sharpen our thinking.

If there is a thorn in someone's foot and I say to him to bring another thorn, in order to take the first thorn out... Then the man says, "I am already bothered by a thorn, why are you asking me to bring another one? I am already dying with pain from this thorn and you are asking for another one." I say to him, "Wait, I will remove the first thorn with the other." Even if *I* bring a thorn, he will put up a great resistance when I try to use it in his foot. He will say, "I am already bothered by the first one and you are putting in another!" If I take the first one out with the help of the second one, then he will say, "I will carefully keep this thorn in my foot because it has helped me so much in taking out the first one. It was the grace of this thorn; I will preserve it." Then I tell him to him to throw away the second thorn too. Its use was just to take out the first thorn, so now there is no need of it. Do you understand?

So I ask you to remove beliefs with a revolution of thinking. And once beliefs are uprooted completely, then drop thoughts too. That is why being without thought is the third step.

Believing is the first step, the lowest rung of the ladder. The second step is thought. And the third step is being without thought, thoughtlessness. Do you understand my point? They are different levels. How can a man who cannot bring a revolution at the level of thinking move beyond thought? For thoughtlessness means letting go of thought itself. A "revolution in thinking" implies dropping wrong thoughts and cultivating the right ones. And it implies going beyond thought itself. That is intrinsic revolution. That is the ultimate revolution.

Do you understand what I am saying? We are clogged with beliefs, so I say to you to drop belief and awaken thinking. And when thinking is activated, then I say there is no longer any need for thought, let it go too: now go beyond thinking, move into no-mind. There is much more ahead to explore. I say both things; they are on two different levels. There is no contradiction in them. I say, there is no contradiction in them.

For instance, a man is climbing the stairs of a house. He can't step onto the second step if he goes on clinging to the first step. He climbs on the second step and then we tell him to move ahead of the second step, so that he can step on the third step. He says, "What nonsense! Earlier you said to let go of the first step so that I could move to the second step. Now I have hold of the second step, and you are saying to leave this too? Then I say to him that it is not a question of clinging or leaving: "I want you to reach the point where there are no steps, then neither do you have to cling nor do you have to leave. But you have to climb all the stairs." All these are steps; no-mind is the last step. The stairs end there.

Osho,
Is there anything beyond that?

That you cannot know without being there.

Can I ask you a few more things?

No, not now. We will meet in the evening. If something important remains to be asked, write it down.

Osho,
Are we not atman, souls?

You are not a soul yet. And until you dissolve what you are, you will not experience the soul. You are just mind, and the mind is a shadow.

In whose shadow are we circling around?

This is what we have to discover. We must find out exactly this! And when you start searching, you will know what madness it is that we are just going around and around. When you look in the mirror, whose reflection do you see?

There is something that is reflected in the mirror.

Whose reflection is it? Isn't it yours? And you are the observer too: you are observing your own reflection. For example, we see our reflection in a mirror; in this case the mirror is a dead thing, but even that mirror makes you happy. If it is a good mirror, that makes you look beautiful, you are happy seeing your image. And if you look ugly in the mirror, you become angry. The poor mirror does not know anything; it is neither interested in making you look beautiful nor is it concerned with making you look ugly. And mirrors do make you look beautiful. No one is as beautiful as mirrors reflect them. Those who manufacture mirrors create them in such a way that they reflect beautiful images, so that they can sell them. And you become very happy seeing your beautiful image. Who is it who is happy? And who do you become happy about seeing in the mirror?

The mirror is a dead thing. Other people's eyes are the living mirrors in which we see our images. If a few people tell you that you are good, then your ego is given such a boost. What happens when someone calls you good? It is just a good image. And if a few people call you an idiot, a stupid, bad man, then you reach home sad, you don't sleep at night, tossing and turning. Why did the opinion of a few people affect you so much? The image formed in their minds was not pleasant; what you wanted to see in their eyes was not there and you were disturbed.

What I want to show you is that we live in our images all the time. We always keep track of who is saying what, who is thinking what, and how we appear in other people's eyes. And the man who lives through images can never go on the search for the truth – because we discover the truth when we start moving away from images, when we stop being so concerned about public opinion.

Generally a man who renounces the world is called a sannyasin. But even a sannyasin is concerned with what people think of him all the time. Then where is his renunciation?

A monk came to visit me recently. He had covered his mouth with a band of cloth. I asked him, "Why don't you drop this cloth too, what meaning does it have?"

He replied, "I can drop it today, but then no one will think of me as a Jaina monk."

Then I said, "Why do you insist that people think of you as a saint? You should focus on your religious practices. What is the need to make others believe in your saintliness? That is focused on others and your being a monk is all about your life."

But without convincing others there is no thrill because that favorable image won't be formed. Then people will say, "This man is nothing." This is what I call being caught up in the image.

And please do not talk about things like the soul. These are mere words we have learned from others and they are very dangerous. We have beautiful words in our hands and beautiful explanations of the words, but those words have no relevance to the reality of our lives. We never reach anywhere close to the state of no-mind, but our words never come lower than the soul! That is why there is no agreement between our words and our lives. We live on the level of the mind and talk about the level of the soul. There is no harmony between the two.

A man living in darkness is talking about light! A sick man talks about health. And the truth is that it is mostly sick people who get engaged in talking about health; a healthy man does not bother to talk about health. What is the point? A sick man, who is suffering twenty-four hours a day through his sickness, gets obsessed with health and with talking about it. A poor man talks about money. And if a man keeps on talking about wealth, then consider him poor, no matter how much money he has. Why would a rich man talk about money? We talk about things we don't have and we tend to hide the things we have.

So, we go on hiding what we actually are. We have read things about ourselves which are not our reality, such as there is a soul within us that has no shadow. Where is that soul? What have you or anybody else got to do with that? Your concern should be with what is. And what is in our lives is the game of images; it is just a play of reflections. Our pleasure and pain are just based on that game.

If a girl is born in India with a flat nose, she will be miserable her whole life because her image in everybody's eyes will be ugly. If the same girl is born in China, she will not be miserable because a flat nose is considered beautiful there. Now, what is this misery about: is it of having a flat nose? Then it should have happened even in China. But no one is miserable in China due to having a flat nose. If people in India decide tomorrow to accept a flat nose as beautiful – and there is no real difficulty in accepting it because a flat nose serves exactly the same function as a long nose. The real issue is the function. The function of a nose is similar to the exhaust pipe in a car. Its function is to let the smoke out; it does not matter whether it is flat or round or long, it just lets out the smoke. In the same way, a nose is just a passage for inhaling and exhaling; it is nothing more than a passage. It does not matter whether the passage is long or flat. It fulfills its function anyway.

So if people want, they can accept a flat nose or a long nose as beautiful; it is just public opinion. And if they believe it for long enough, they forget whether it has any meaning or not. But reflections differ according to what people think: if someone has a flat nose, he becomes ugly! Now he will be self-conscious about his nose twenty-four hours a day. He will do whatever he can to ensure that you don't pay attention to his nose. But what is the use of acting like this? Just imagine, if someone with a flat nose lives in a jungle, where no one else is around, will he always be sad about his flat nose? He will not be because no reflection is formed, no image is created. So it is the image that causes difficulty.

One of my friends, Rahul Sankrityayan, visited Soviet Russia for the first time. Rahul's hands were very beautiful and soft; people who have never done any rough work with their hands will naturally have soft and beautiful hands. So whoever saw his hands always immediately remarked on his beautiful hands, "So feminine, as beautiful as a woman's!"

On his arrival in Russia, the first man who welcomed him at the railway station shook hands with him and then withdrew his hand immediately. He said, "Please don't shake hands with anyone here, otherwise they will hate you because in our country we consider such soft hands the hand of a parasite. You have never worked with your hands; you don't carry any marks of labor on your hands. You are a bourgeois."

Rahul said, "It was a problem in Russia because whenever I shook hands with anyone, looked into his eyes and saw how his attitude changed, I became very self-conscious that he must be thinking that I am bourgeois."

Let's consider this example. We think that when you take somebody's beautiful hand in your hand, it feels good. But if the image-building process in our mind decides that to have beautiful hands is something wrong, then there will be a difficulty.

We all are living in images, many types of images.

Osho,
Should we believe in what you are saying about our living?

I am just talking about the image-building process and about living our lives based on images. My whole effort is to make you think about these things; if you find it wrong, just throw it away. Or if it seems right to you, then experiment with it. Do you understand?

What if it creates confusion in our minds?

No, there has not been any disturbance yet. Your mind is quite solid and tough. If there was any disturbance, you would have come with doubts. Rather, you have come here full of answers; there is no confusion in you. Confusion is a totally different matter altogether. You are getting my point, aren't you? You have come with answers, so where is the disturbance?

No, after the disturbance, whatever is my own...

Has there been even a slight disturbance?

Yes, there has been.

What was the confusion?

After what you said, I wondered whether darkness can be infinite.

Until now, you have not exercised your thinking at all. If you had started thinking, you would not even bring a single word from the earlier talk. Listen to it again and try to understand a little.

In fact, anything that exists is bound to be limited. Existence will be limited. Only nothingness can be infinite, only nonexistence can be unlimited.

When we say there *is* something, that very "is" becomes the boundary. It is bound to be somewhere, sometime. It is bound to be in some space, in some boundary. Its being must have an ending somewhere and its nonbeing must have a beginning there. Existence will always be limited.

Hence, the people who say "There is God" make God limited.

That is why those who know say "God is neither in existence nor nonexistence." In order to keep it beyond any boundary, it is necessary to add nonexistence to it too.

Try to understand with the example of this room: if it is a room, it is bound to have walls; otherwise it will not be called a room. If this space is not a room, then there is no question of having walls. So the very existence of a room is bound to have boundaries. Only its nonexistence as a room can be without boundaries.

When I say that darkness is limitless, it is because darkness fundamentally has no existence, it is a nonexistence. And light is an existence, light exists. Light has an existence and darkness has a nonexistence. So, you can switch on light and you can switch off light. You can neither switch on darkness nor can you switch off darkness.

I don't understand this.

Try to understand it first. You can turn light on and turn it off. But you can neither turn darkness on nor turn it off. If we say here, "Friends, please bring some darkness into this room," you will reply that you are unable to bring in darkness. But if I say to you, "Please bring some light into the room," you will answer, "I will bring it right now."

Because light is limited, you can bring it in. How can you bring darkness in? Also, light can be brought in and taken out because it has presence, it exists. Darkness does not. The very word *darkness* means absence.

Osho,
If you hang dark curtains, it will become dark.

In that case, you will be hanging curtains to prevent the light. You are not doing anything to the darkness. You are just preventing the light from entering. You see, whatever you do is going to be with light. You cannot do anything with darkness. You are absolutely impotent with darkness.

Try to understand it a little. Whatever you can do… When you say, "I will hang some curtains," you are not bringing in darkness.

By drawing the curtains, you are just preventing light from entering. If you blow out the candlelight, you are not bringing in darkness; you are just putting the light out. You cannot do anything at all with darkness. Whatever you do is going to be with light. Light exists and it is limited, and something can be done with light. Nothing can be done with darkness.

If you look carefully at what I said earlier, you will see that you would be absolutely impotent in front of existence, so that you could not do anything. You would not be able to do anything in front of existence. If you are able to do anything in front of existence, then you are greater than existence. These are all symbolic terms. Please do not grab them literally like a crazy man; otherwise words can lead us into great difficulty. If you listened to what I said last night, you would see that it was just symbolic. And a man who says that the ultimate is light is also using a symbol.

How shall we approach your talks?

First, try to understand it as a whole; try to comprehend its totality. That is why I said that it will be difficult to understand. When I am speaking and something is going on in your mind at the same time, then my talk will not reach you. I am not asking you to agree with my talk, so there is nothing to fear. If what I am saying does not appeal to you, throw it in the garbage and go home. I don't make anyone my follower: I neither initiate anyone into a sect or religion, nor do I have any disciples, nor do I have any kind of relationship with anyone. I have shared my talks with you, you listened, and that is great kindness on your part. There ends the matter: I have no expectation more than that. If what I am saying is wrong, I do not insist that you accept it as right.

If you just give consideration to what I was talking about the other day... You will see that sometimes there is light and sometimes there is no light. Darkness is always there. There is no question of it being there or not being there. When there is light, you cannot perceive darkness. When the light is gone, you perceive darkness.

When the sun rises in the morning, you may think that the stars have disappeared somewhere. They don't disappear anywhere, they are in their place. They are just not visible in the sunlight. Now, it is very interesting that some things are visible in light and a few things cannot be seen in light. The stars in the sky are not visible during the day. When the sun sets in the evening, they appear again. The sun sets here and simultaneously they start appearing there. They were always there; the whole sky was filled with them. The sunlight has covered your eyes, so they become invisible.

Light is transient, darkness is eternal. And when I say this, I am not saying anything against light. Do not make the mistake of thinking that I am saying anything against light. When I am talking about this, I am not saying anything against those who consider God as light. When I am talking about this, I only mean that whenever we try to express the ultimate, there is no way other than using symbols.

Symbols are used to help give a certain suggestion. I want to express godliness, existence, as that which never goes, which never comes – that which is eternal. Sometimes it is hidden and sometimes it is manifest, that is another matter, but it never comes or goes. So I can express it better with darkness than with light.

When I say that existence is endless, I mean that it is nothingness because only nothingness can be limitless. Only nothingness can be without a boundary; everything else has a limit. So if one says that existence is endless, one has to add that existence is nothingness. To convey nothingness, light is not as meaningful as darkness.

When I say that existence is absolute silence, I am also trying to convey that light is a tension. Each ray of light creates a tension on you. That is why you wake up in the morning; the whole world wakes up with daybreak. The world sleeps with the darkness of night.

Darkness is a rest in deep sleep. Light is a constant movement in the depth of life. Light is movement. Darkness is no movement; it is sleep, a merger, and a disappearance.

If you want to comprehend the divine, it is less like movement and more like stillness, more like a rest. All this is just symbolic. If someone finds it difficult, then do not call it darkness. There is no conflict over it; it is just a matter of understanding what the symbols we are using to point to the ultimate are conveying.

Then again, I say that life exists today, yesterday it was not there. You are here today, yesterday you were not here. Life exists on the Earth; there is no life on uncountable stars and planets. Even on this planet Earth there was no life ten or twenty million years ago. It is possible that tomorrow the Earth will dry out and life disappear. There is no life even today on infinite stars and planets. Life is a momentary glimpse. But the nonexistence of life is eternity. In that eternity there is a glimpse of life sometimes and then it disappears again. The ground into which it disappears is much more valuable than life itself, the ground from which life originates is more precious.

Take the example of an ocean where a wave arises. The ocean existed even before the wave was formed, and when the wave disappears the ocean will still be there. The existence or nonexistence of a wave does not make any difference to the existence or nonexistence of the ocean. If someone says that the wave is the ocean, his statement is not wrong, but at a deeper level, he is not stating the truth. The truth is the opposite of it: even though the wave is the ocean, when it disappears, still the ocean remains. The ocean sometimes takes the form of a wave and sometimes it is there without manifesting the form of a wave.

Existence sometimes manifests as life and sometimes it remains unmanifest. The ultimate sometimes manifests as light and sometimes it does not. But the unmanifest is long term whereas the manifest appears as a glimpse and disappears.

What I said now is that the manifest and the unmanifest are just two sides of the same coin. But of the two, the unmanifest is deeper and more fundamental. So, being appears for a while, but nonbeing seems infinite.

I also mentioned that life is in darkness, but you did not grasp the meaning of my statement. It is difficult to understand and grasp the meaning of symbols. And it becomes even more difficult when we have fixed ideas. Then it becomes very difficult.

Life in fact exists in darkness – what are the implications of this? It means only that all the roots of life exist in mystery, where there is utter darkness, where there is absolutely no light. It does not mean that I have said there is no life in the sunlight. There is life in the sunlight; life is manifesting in flowers, in leaves, and in us. All of that is taking place in the sunlight. But why is life manifesting through sunlight? – because the roots are in darkness. Do you understand? Darkness implies the mysterious. The mysterious that is all pervading, where everything disappears. Nothing is lucid there, everything becomes diffused. Everything is obvious in light, but in darkness everything disappears.

Existence is the greatest mystery. Certainly that mystery is in utter darkness. For example, I mentioned that the roots of a tree work beneath the earth in absolute darkness. You eat your food in the light. But you are not even aware who has digested the food. All of that is happening silently in darkness. Scientists say that if we were to make a factory to do all the work which is done in a man's stomach – that is, to turn bread into blood – that factory would spread over many square miles and thousands of people would work there. And still we do not know the whole mechanism of turning bread into blood. Otherwise the whole subject of food, of digestion, would be finished. But we still don't know the whole matter: How does the conversion of bread into blood happen?

A plant takes nutrition from the earth and turns it into a flower. How is the earth converted into a flower, where exactly is it converted? It is still a mystery. And it happens in darkness, which we know nothing about. You can dissect the plant, but that does not help you to know how the earth converts into a flower. At what exact moment does the conversion takes place?

When you eat, nobody knows at what point the food turns into blood, marrow, and muscles. And what an incredible function it is: you eat a piece of bread and some part of it gives nourishment to the bones, some part of it becomes hair, some part becomes eyes, some part becomes skin, and some part turns into bone marrow. They all get nourishment from the same bread. Where does all this happen? In which space does all this take place? All of it is happening in utter darkness, quietly and absolutely silently.

Now scientists say that the effort of knowing those processes has created a disturbance. The more we try to know about human beings, the more disturbed they are getting. More troubles are arising; more roots are being uprooted and troubles are increasing.

So try to understand what I have been talking about. I am not against light. How can one who is not even against darkness be against light? In the statement of one who is ready to call the divine darkness, the presence of light is included. How can one who is saying that life emanates from darkness deny the possibility of life originating from light? Life does originate from light. So please try to comprehend my talks.

Understanding will be easier if you are not in a hurry to appreciate or condemn; there is no need to hurry for either because I have no insistence at all. Nor do you need to consider whether you should accept it or reject it. Just give it thought, that is the only a request. Just ponder over it. If you feel it is right, then it is right. If not, then you are free, you are unburdened from the trouble: "This man was wrong." The matter is finished. The only request is to think it over, nothing more than that.

Osho,
Why did life need to manifest?

Man cannot answer this question. If you meet God somewhere you can ask him why life needed to manifest. Although you will not agree with him either! It will be very difficult to agree.

My idea is...

Tell me your idea.

...this is an exchange of ideas.

No, no, this is not an exchange at all. Either I am ready to receive or to give. An exchange never happens. Do you understand?

It is not clear to me.

Try to understand what I am saying. I am ready to receive. If you want to give, I am absolutely ready. Then I will sit silently and try to understand, not bother about making you understand. Do you see my point? Let me do one thing at a time and you do one thing at a time. If both are going on at the same time – give, take – then from this side...

Both can happen simultaneously.

Yes, that is why the world is in such a mess. If give and take go on simultaneously, the result is like one train is going this way and another train is going the other way. There is a crossing somewhere, but there is no meeting. Meeting is not possible at all. I am always ready. I take no pleasure in convincing you; I take even more pleasure in understanding. So visit me sometime and we can sit for an hour, I will listen to you and try to understand you. But at that time I will not try to make you understand. That is then not needed at all.

No, but we can have a discussion afterward.

There is no need for discussion; it is a matter for your own life. There is no need for any discussion. I listened to your talk, if it is of any significance for me I will keep it, otherwise I will drop it. It ends right there. Where is there a question of discussion? Discussion should be done at the end of many lives in front of God himself. Before that it is meaningless.

That means the thing we call God is somewhere else?

Did you come and listen to the morning talk?

No, I couldn't attend the morning talk.

You didn't come this morning. Then listen to the complete recording of the morning talk; ask someone here, they will help you. The whole talk was about this topic. Listen to all the talks of the last three days. After that if you want to share anything, visit me in Jabalpur. I will listen to you for a couple of days. And I want to point out that what I cannot explain to you by talking will become clear to you by my listening to you. When you have expressed everything you have to say, then it becomes easier. It becomes much easier.

It is infinite light; it has never ended until now.

[*Osho responds to one of the many interruptions to his talk by a questioner.*] ...then it becomes very difficult.

That light has been emanating eternally and it will continue to radiate like this.

Then let it emanate, there is no harm. There is no problem.

Osho,
Do we need to learn yoga for meditation?

If you want to learn it for your physical health, it is superb. Its practice is very valuable; for physical health it is magnificent. But physical health has no direct relation to meditation, except that a healthy body can easily move into meditation; an unhealthy body will face a little hindrance.

The other yogic practices such as generating psychic powers and so on also have no relation to meditation. If you want to achieve the power of telepathy, hypnotism, or some other psychic powers then they can be useful, but even they have no connection to meditation.

I am talking about an authentic spirituality or meditation; even if you have practiced everything, at the end you have to enter non-doing.

So is all that useless?

In this sense it is futile – in this sense. For instance, a man goes to study at the university, and I say that for spirituality going to university has no meaning. If he comes to me and asks if it is futile to study at the university, I will answer no – studying at university has another meaning and another purpose. If you want to become a doctor, study at a medical college. But becoming a doctor or an engineer has nothing to do with meditation. You can meditate even without becoming a doctor or engineer. And you can become a doctor or engineer and totally miss meditation. It has nothing to do with your profession.

So when I say that any method, any yoga, is futile for spiritual growth, I am not saying that yoga is useless. I am just saying it in connection with your inner growth. Always remember this condition, otherwise you will be in difficulty.

It has other functions.

Of course, it has other functions. It has many other uses.

It is preached everywhere that yoga is meant for spiritual growth.

Yes, yes, absolutely! That is what is being taught.

All the difficulties are arising due to that kind of thinking.

Of course, it has been preached. And this preaching has created a mess, so much turmoil. Where is the spirituality in this country in which yoga is preached so much? All kinds of postures and yoga asanas are practiced, all that is going on, but where is the inner growth?

Extrasensory powers such as entering another's body are part of spirituality.

These things have no relation to spirituality.

So yogic powers do not help us in our inner growth?

Not at all. Absolutely not! In many ways they are hindrances because they take you in another direction. Suppose I want to go directly to Udaipur railway station. There are many diversions on the way; one path is going via a show at a gallery, another one via the cinema. These paths all lead to different places. If I start going toward the cinema, my trip to the railway station is hindered because the entertainment of the cinema will divert me. If I really want to reach the station directly, then I should just greet the cinema and move on toward the station. You will pass these things on the way, but they are just diversions on the side.

Now, take the example of a man like Ramamurti, the wrestler. The elements which create his body are also found in our bodies. If one of us wants to become like Ramamurti, then he can with effort. There is no problem. But when Ramamurti builds his body with tremendous endeavor, we are amazed and astonished. He is so strong that a car drives over his chest and nothing happens! You can break a stone on his chest and he does not get hurt. If he holds onto a car from the back, the engine will go on screaming, but the car will not move even an inch! All these things are hidden powers in our body. But exploring these powers has no relation to spirituality.

If someone says that first you have to become Ramamurti, only then will you be able to move into meditation, then it is difficult. It has nothing to do with becoming a Ramamurti.

It means that we all have a body. There are two ways with the body: one way goes through the body and beyond the body, and leads you toward the mind. The other way goes into the body and does not lead you beyond the body to the mind.

To understand... Let's look at these three things: the body, the mind, and the being. There is one way that goes from the body to the mind and from the mind to the being. And there is another way that goes into the body and into the deeper mysteries of the body. There is a way that moves into the mind and the deeper mysteries of the mind. There is a way that moves into the being and its deeper mystery. That is, there are vertical ways and there are horizontal ways.

Ramamurti is moving horizontally into the body. He can discover all the mysteries of the body. And it is also possible that future explorers can leave Ramamurti behind and discover more mysteries. The body itself is infinity. Even in our bodies, many mysteries are hidden that we are not aware of, which we are absolutely ignorant about.

So Hatha yoga enters the body straight, horizontally. You can go on moving deeper into it for many lives. And you will experience miraculous mysteries and master incredible powers. But it has nothing to do with your inner journey. These are mysteries which belong only to the body. You will achieve a long life and a strong body like steel. What will happen even if all that is achieved? It means nothing. Even death can be postponed, all that can happen, but no inner purpose is served by it. To enter the higher realms of consciousness, a normal healthy body is enough; there is no need to move too deeply into the realm of the body.

For instance, if you drive a car you know how to handle the steering, how to press the accelerator, how to turn the car and so on. To know these basic things is more than enough to drive a car. You will never need to bother about all the details of the car's mechanics, how it functions, what it does not do, and so on. There are mechanics for that purpose, who go deep into the world of car engines. You can drive your car without knowing all that. You have enough basic knowledge to drive a car. But for a mechanic, the basic knowledge about a car is not enough. Most car drivers do not even take a look into the workings of a car; if you ask them how a car functions, they will not be able to answer. They will say that they just know how to press the accelerator and turn the steering wheel; they do not know more than that.

When you reach the level of mind, you will find a horizontal path into the mind. If you enter the horizontal path of the mind, you can achieve all kinds of extrasensory powers, psychic powers, and miracles – there is a whole world of miracles. Things that seem impossible for ordinary people can be performed at the level of the mind. But once again you have entered too deeply into the realm of the psyche.

In order to move upward, it is enough to have a serene mind. It is more than enough; there is no need to move deeper than that.

And the third level is the realm of your being. If you enter your being horizontally, other kinds of things start happening. Those who enter the soul horizontally find a different kind of mystery. But those who enter the being vertically merge into existence itself. Hence, some people such as Jaina saints who entered the realm of the soul horizontally could not grasp the ultimate reality. The reason behind their missing is that they did not enter self-nature vertically. They could not go beyond the soul; they entered the being and could not find the ultimate there. Then they said that there is no God.

Now the same thing is happening with Western psychology.

It has gone into the mind horizontally. It claims that there is no soul. Western physiology and medical science have moved into the body horizontally. They say: "What soul, what mind? There is only the body and everything else is just part of the body mechanism." Are you getting my point?

So, all this is mystery, hence all the difficulties arise. My talks are to the point and meant to help you in moving straight forward and vertically, to take you from where you are to where you can merge with the whole of existence. I am not talking about the diversions on the way. But all those diversions do exist, they can be followed and there is a whole science of moving on those paths.

That is why Patanjali is not meaningless, Western science is not useless, and Western psychology is not futile. They are all significant, but they are hindrances for the seeker who is moving vertically. If he starts moving with those diversions, they are so long that perhaps he will never be able to return, or many lives may pass by and he cannot return to the original source.

So it is a matter of moving straight forward, vertically. Hence, I am talking very directly, so that there is no chance of going astray even an inch. I am not saying that everything else is useless, but from this point of view they are futile practices. A cinema has its own significance and a hospital has its own place, but someone who has to reach the railway station has to ignore the cinema, go beyond the hospital, and head straight toward the station. That is the significance of all this.

Osho,
I would like your guidance about taking sannyas.

The first point is, as long as you feel the need for someone's guidance about taking sannyas, then don't take it. When you have an intense feeling, so that even if the whole world says not to take it you are still compelled to take it, only then take it. Otherwise you will be in great difficulty.

What do you mean by difficulty?

When your mind is asking for somebody's guidance about

this matter, it shows that you do not have much clarity about it and that is why you ask.

No, the question arises only because I have to be in the world and look after myself, and I have to work. That may take time. I would not mind taking it this moment.

No, no. I got your point. I am saying that when things are not very clear in our minds, only then do we think about getting some guidance. To ask for guidance means to be confused. Do you understand my point? Whenever we ask for guidance from anywhere, it simply means that we are confused.

Hence, there are two types of seekers: the first type who has taken sannyas by following the guidance of someone and the second type, the real sannyasins, who never asked anyone for guidance. It is their bliss.

So the day you feel that the worldly game is over, to be a sannyasin is your bliss. Then the matter is over, do not ask anyone. Don't ask anyone at all. When you ask someone it means that you are still confused about whether to take it or not – you want some support in order to make a decision. Then you will get both answers...

I am confused about the decision because I don't know the world. I don't know where to become part of it at present.

Yes, yes that is it. That is why you will find people who will give you advice: someone will say not to take it and someone will say to take it. Still, in the end you will have to make the decision on your own.

Even if it is possible after taking sannyas as you say, to continue work... But what is the use of taking sannyas? It is only for the society. I asked one of the swamis whom I met, "What difference does it make to be a sannyasin?"

Yes, another thing you should keep in mind: the way you are observing worldly people, look at the sannyasins in the same way and see what their actual condition is. Generally people think,

"Married people don't seem to be particularly happy, then why get into the trouble of marriage?"

But I don't have any unhappiness in my life.

I understand, I understand what you are saying. In the same way you have to consider how many are blissful by taking sannyas.

But then you say that bliss is eternal.

No, no. All these words are all right, but what has your problem got to do with these things?

Supposing they are not happy, it means they don't see the happiness within them.

Yes – you can look within from anywhere; then what is the point of taking sannyas, or giving it? Then wherever you happen to be, just look within. If the whole point is to witness, what is the need of asking whether you are sitting in this room or another room? Wherever you are, just go on sitting silently and witnessing. You can go on watching your inner happiness while working as a nurse or being a sannyasin. Then there is no conflict. If it is all a matter of seeing, there is no conflict at all.

Obviously this is not all, it is not simply a matter of seeing, but it must be understood. How will you observe? How will you watch? When you are watching, there will be confusion. Then you will become aware of your confusion and wonder whether watching would be easier in this room or the other room. This is not the issue.

And the other thing is that you say you are not frustrated. This is very good. This is really good. And you also say that you do not even care about public opinion. This too is very good. Then drop bothering about any kind of guidance. And live your life the way you want to live. Remember one thing: it is very easy to become a sannyasin from being a worldly person, but it will be extremely difficult to go back to worldly life once you get used to living as a sannyasin.

Because if you become a sannyasin everybody will say, "What

great virtue!" They will applaud you, praise you, and give you their blessings. You will meet many swamis, monks, and those kinds of people. If you then say that you want to return to the world, all the doors will be closed. You will be showered with condemnation, humiliation, and abuse. So this society is very cunning. It keeps the door open to enter sannyas, but does not leave any door open for returning to the world.

So my suggestion is to always choose something that will give you freedom even in the future, and does not tie you to anything. Otherwise that will be the beginning of misery. Now, nobody is creating any bondage for you while you are working as a nurse. You have more freedom. Will you have freedom as a sannyasin? If you drop your job as a nurse, no one can say anything to you. But if tomorrow you drop being a sannyasin, you will be in great difficulty.

Hence, I am saying to you that to be a nurse is a situation with more freedom than being a sannyasin. Even being a shoemaker is a life with more freedom than being a monk or a nun, as the shoemaker can drop making shoes any moment. But a monk cannot drop this profession of monkhood. It is difficult.

But this path is a path of evolution.

All paths are paths of evolution. There is no path that is not a path of evolution. If you want to evolve, you can evolve from any path. And that is why the path that gives you more freedom also provides you more opportunities for evolution. Hence there is no need to fall into any bondage.

What else is the meaning of sannyas? When someone asks me whether to take sannyas or not I am puzzled. The very word *sannyas* means absolute freedom, someone who does not care about structures, rules, who does not accept any bondage, who does not bother about public opinion. He acts spontaneously. This is the meaning of *sannyas*.

But when someone asks whether he should take sannyas, it feels like he is asking whether to accept a particular type of bondage or not. It is a very interesting point. The very word *sannyas* implies freedom and living spontaneously: act spontaneously, do what feels right to you. Do not accept bondage.

Do you understand? Do not get tied to anything.

But we cannot stay without bondage. Someone suggests tying the knot of marriage and someone suggests not to get married. Others suggest getting tied to the order of sannyas. But don't remain untied; be bound to something or other. You are not allowed to remain in the middle, choiceless. Women in particular are not allowed to remain free at all, since society is organized through male domination. The whole social structure is inimical to women. It says: "Be a slave! Either become a wife or become a sannyasin." You are not allowed to stay free. And in my vision, *sannyasin* means to stay free.

Remain free. Continue working as a nurse as long as you wish; when you want to do something else, get trained for it. But do not get initiated by anyone. That is stupidity and barbaric. What is the sense of getting initiated by someone? Is there any initiation for freedom? All initiations are of slavery.

Stay free, then everything is all right. Search for your intrinsic bliss and move where you feel. And do not be afraid of anybody – this is the meaning of being a sannyasin. Do not fear anyone. Right now even if you take sannyas you will have to be afraid. You will be afraid of the people who initiate you. You will be afraid of the society or sect you have been trapped in. They will control your eating, drinking, waking time, sleeping time, where you should go, and where you should not go. It will be difficult. Then you will find out that it is a great misery; it has become much worse than working as a nurse.

Do one thing: whatever increases your bliss, follow that, do that. The day you become totally free, that day you are a sannyasin. It has nothing to do with others. Do you understand my point? You can become free even working as a nurse or it can happen by dropping your profession.

No, but spiritual knowledge...

Who is preventing spiritual knowledge?

My capacity is limited.

Everyone has limited capacity. Everyone's capacity is limited.

Even sannyasins have limited capability. Do you think monks don't have any worries? They also have to worry from morning till evening where to get food and where to find a place to stay. You are more carefree.

My own understanding is that the person who works six to eight hours a day is at least free the rest of the time. A sannyasin is a servant all day long. And he is a servant of utter idiots. He is a servant to those who do not even have an iota of intelligence. When you come back from your office after six hours work you are free, you can do what you want. If you want to dance, then dance, or sing, or do what you please. You cannot do these things as a sannyasin. Idiots will be watching you from everywhere – who you are talking to, who you are meeting, where you are going. If you do anything wrong, there will be no food and no respect. Everything becomes utter misery.

Whereas if you have a job, you work a couple of hours, three or four hours, so that you can fulfill your basic needs, food, shelter and so on, but the other twenty hours you are free. You can use those twenty hours as you please. Use them. And who is preventing you from knowledge? Knowledge is everywhere, search for it. Don't be in any bondage. The meaning of being a sannyasin is not to be tied.

When I say become a sannyasin, it only means do not be bound. Be free, that is right. When the people from organized religions say to become a sannyasin they have a different meaning. They mean do not be free, follow an imposed discipline: be our follower, follow our structure. Utter stupidity! That has no significance. Remain free; learn from whoever you want to learn from, there is no harm. What is the hurry, why are you in a hurry to be tied?

I visited two or three places and I observed everything. I said to the swamis there that my aim was to progress on the spiritual path and I did not find it...

Yes, yes do it. Do anything that feels right to you. Stay free and enjoy doing things. And if you feel that you have more freedom by becoming a sannyasin, then become a sannyasin. I have no objection to anything. If a woman comes to me and says that she feels more freedom in becoming a prostitute, then I will say to do it. It is your freedom and your search. Wherever you happen to be, there should not be anyone creating bondage for you. You are the master of your life. Live your life. Do what feels right to you, but don't create any bondage anywhere. Don't get chained anywhere. And please, avoid all kinds of gurudom. Gurus are wandering around as predators! There is a sannyasin sitting here; she wanted to become a sannyasin earlier, and she did so. Now she is thinking to let it go.

Did she become a sannyasin for real?

Yes, yes!

But can I grow spiritually on my own?

Of course you can. Right now you do not have a complete overview. And tomorrow you will know better than today. So always keep the door open for changing your decision because tomorrow you will have more experience than today. And if you bind tomorrow with today, you are making a mistake. Whatever I know today, I will know more than that tomorrow. And if I take a vow that tomorrow I will not turn back, and I realize tomorrow that it was all wrong, then? That is why you must keep all the freedom in your hands to turn back or not turn back. There is absolutely no need to be trapped into anything and no need to be tied to any place or country either.

But why should we think that we would want to come back?

This is not the question here at all. It is not the issue. That *can* happen: the path you are walking today, tomorrow you may find out that you have come to the end of it. Then what will you do? Will you turn back or due to your vow, will you still stand on the same path?

But it is so complicated to think about it now.

The one who is afraid of complications will be afraid of life itself. He has no other way left but to commit suicide.

That is why I ask why I should think about it more and more, because as I think, more and more complications...

Someone who is afraid of complications will be afraid of life itself. They can never discover truth.

I had never thought of all these things.

Absolutely, create more complications.

You mean we have to increase the complications?

Absolutely! Only then will you experience life, otherwise there will be no experience. If a girl becomes a sannyasin after experiencing the life of a prostitute, the richness of her experience will be greater than that of the girl who has never loved anyone. A man who has walked the path of evil, when he turns around and starts walking on the path of good, then he has a richness of experience. His life is deeper.

Complications bring more depth to your life. Why be afraid of them? And if you are afraid of complications then close the doors, sit down, and die; it is suicide.

But suppose I go on one path, then when a difficulty arises, I will see the difficulty. Why should I look at it before I start?

Do not think, do what feels right to you. All this is thinking, isn't it?

No, it is just that I am talking to you...

All this is thinking and nothing else. Where can you escape to? Where will you go? Don't think. Just remember one thing, do not escape from life. Existence pushes you into life: "Experience it and know!" but all the saints preach for you to escape. These saints are the greatest enemy of existence. Avoid the saints if you want to realize truth – that is all you must do, and nothing else!

Saints never realize godliness. [*Osho includes someone sitting in the room.*] Right, Chandresji? Have you ever seen a saint coming upon the truth? It has never been heard of! Perhaps a sinner can find godliness, but the knowledgeable saints and teachers can never realize it.

CHAPTER 4

from dreams to awakening

THERE WAS A WONDERFUL MAN called Chuang Tzu; one night he had a dream. He dreamed he had become a butterfly and was flying from flower to flower. On waking up in the morning, he looked very sad. His friends asked him, "We have never seen you sad, why are you looking so gloomy?" There had been times when others were feeling sad, and they were able to find a way out of it by asking Chuang Tzu. But no one had ever seen him sad.

Chuang Tzu replied, "What to say? What is the point of telling you? I'm confused. Last night I dreamed that I had become a butterfly."

"Have you gone mad? Why are you worrying about it?" the friends asked.

Chuang Tzu replied, "There is no problem with the dream itself, but when I woke up in the morning, I became obsessed with the idea that if a man can dream that he has become a butterfly, then it is also possible for a butterfly to fall asleep and dream that it has become a man! If a man can become a butterfly in a dream, the same possibility is there for a butterfly to become a man in a dream. And then," continued Chuang Tzu, "I am in great difficulty. Am I a man who dreamed of becoming a butterfly, or am I a butterfly who is dreaming he has become a man? How to decide what is my real identity?"

How can we too decide if what we experience during our sleep is a dream, or what we experience during our waking hours is a dream? How do we tell whether what we perceive is a reality or a dream? And until we decide whether what we are living is a reality or a dream, the meaning of our lives cannot be realized.

To search for truth, we must see the dream as a dream, know the false as false, and see the unreal as unreal, nonessential. Anyone who wants to come in contact with the truth will have to wake up from dreaming.

But when we fall asleep at night, we forget our daytime activities and everything we experience during the day. We even forget our daytime identity as a rich or a poor man, a respectable or an unrespectable person, a young or an old man. Everything is forgotten in our sleep. What we are identified with in our waking hours is all forgotten in the dream state.

When we wake up from dreaming, we forget everything perceived during our dreams. On waking up, we say that our dreams are unreal. Why? – because the waking state has wiped them from our memory. Then we should also be able to say during sleep that what we perceived during our waking time was unreal.

It is interesting: on waking up, we always remember that we have been dreaming, we remember our dreams. But while dreaming we don't remember anything from our waking hours, nor do we even remember that we have ever been awake. When we are awake, we do have a slight memory of dreaming, but while dreaming we don't have even that much remembrance of the waking state. Even the slightest memory is wiped away. It totally disappears.

In the same way, all we have experienced during our life will evaporate at the time of death. So, after death or at the moment of death, do our life experiences appear to us as reality or as a dream? There are a few things about this that we must understand, because only after knowing them will we be able to move in the dimension of truth.

You must have clarity about this: the farther away you go from yourself, the deeper you move into dreaming. And the more you withdraw from dreams, the closer you come to yourself. To come upon yourself you have to let go of all kinds of dreams.

But it is difficult for us to see life as a dream; we have been looking on dreams as reality.

I have heard – and we all know this... When we watch an actor being sad on a movie screen – where there is no one in reality, just an interaction of light and shade or light and darkness, there is nothing on that empty screen except the dance of light rays – we become sad! If someone looks beautiful on the screen, we become infatuated with them. If someone is suffering, we shed tears. And we are happy in their happiness.

During a three-hour movie, we totally forget that whatever is happening is just the interplay of light rays and nothing else; there has been only an empty screen in front of us. We got so identified with those dancing rays of light, those images formed on the screen, that we cried, we laughed. We were absorbed by it – and on top of that we also paid money for it! And we spent our time there. People come out of cinemas with wet handkerchiefs; so many tears fall, just for the sake of false images.

We seem to so easily fall into illusion. We are so used to taking dreams for reality...

There was a great thinker in Bengal named Vidyasagar. One evening he went to watch a play. In the play there was a character that was chasing a girl, harassing her – the actor took hold of the girl on a secluded path on a dark night. Vidyasagar lost his temper. Completely forgetting that he was watching a play, he took off his shoe, jumped on the stage, and started beating the actor.

The other spectators were puzzled at what was happening. Within a moment, Vidyasagar also became aware: "What am I doing?"

But the actor showed more intelligence. He took the shoe, placed it on his head, and said to the audience, "I have never received a greater award for my acting. I had never even thought that an intelligent man like Vidyasagar would take the play to be real in this way. I am blessed, and I will keep this shoe with great care. It is the evidence that my acting seemed so real.

Vidyasagar must have been greatly embarrassed.

We can even take a play for real. Why? Have you ever thought about why that happens? There is a very deep psychological reason behind it. And that is, we don't know truth and we are accustomed to believe dreams to be the truth. We are ready to accept any dream as reality; it is our habit to see dreams as reality. We accept the dreams that take place on the screen of our eyes as reality. So much so, that if in your nightmare there is a man who is sitting on your chest and you suddenly wake up, you know it was just a nightmare, but still your heart beats fast for a while. Even though you say that it was just a dream, your hands go on shaking. The impact of the dream goes on influencing you.

Even during the day, we think of dreams as reality. Or in other words, everything that we consider reality is almost a dream. For instance, a man goes on hoarding wealth. Every day he counts his money, keeps it locked in a safe, has an account of it, and is obsessed with its growth. He is having a certain dream – the dream of money – he goes on earning it and gathering it.

I have heard…

There was a rich man who had gathered lots of money. Neither he ate well, nor he drank well, nor did he ever wear good clothes. Generally it is the poor people who eat, drink, and make merry. Rich people are able only to hoard their wealth. They sell their lives and gather money. This rich man gathered lots of money.

Then his wife got sick and the neighbors suggested that she should see a doctor. The rich man said, "If my wife is to be saved then no disease can kill her. If it is God's will, who can take her life away?" What wise things he was saying! "And if it is not God's will to save her life, then no matter how much is spent on medicine, all the money will go to waste and she will die anyway. I believe in God," he added.

What people do – there are many dishonest people who hide their weakness behind theories. He had said such a religious thing that everybody kept quiet.

Finally his wife died. After her death, people asked the rich man to spend some money on her funeral. He said, "Now my wife is dead, so there is no need to spend money on her. Now that she has died, what is the point? The council cart can dump the dead body. What is the meaning in carrying the dead, making noise around her, and spending a lot of money? When I could not save her while she was alive, what can I do for her dead body?"

Some time passed after this incident and the time for his final departure arrived. Then the people said, "Now you are old and death is approaching. You are getting weaker and falling sick. So please get some treatment."

He replied, "I can't waste money. I am very fortunate to fall sick. Diseases happen because of our past lives' karma. What can money do for that?"

The people replied, "This is too much. Won't you spend money even on yourself? After your death, other people will waste all this money – you don't have any sons or other relatives."

He said, "I am not going to leave any money behind, I'm not going to let go of it."

They replied, "We have never heard of such a thing before."

Everyone believes that he is not going to leave anything behind. If it becomes clear to you that you have to leave everything behind, then all the attachment will end this very moment, right now. Your attachment is as strong as this belief that you are going to leave something behind after your death. Otherwise, could anyone fight, kill, and shed blood for every inch of land? Can anyone trade their precious life for almost nothing? The attachment is so strong that it seems as if they are never going to let go.

The rich man said the same thing – and there was nothing wrong in his statement. He said that he would not let go. The people replied, "We have never heard such talk until now, everyone has to let go at the time of death."

He said, "But I have made arrangements so that I don't have to leave anything after my death."

As the night of his death came closer, doubts arose in his mind. He gathered all his gold coins in a bag, carried them on his shoulders, and went to the bank of the river. He woke up the ferryman and said to him, "Take me in your boat to the middle of this river. I want to drown myself in the deep water of the holy Ganges. Oh, when death is inevitable, why not die at a pilgrimage site? When I started to think about what would happen to my money after my death, I decided to jump in the river with all my money."

That is the reason wealthy people make pilgrimages to holy sites before death. It is an effort to bring with them something of whatever they have been gathering their whole life. They try to find a way to bring what they've hoarded with them beyond death, by visiting a pilgrimage site, by building temples and hospices. These are devices to carry their money onward. These are tricks. They have been reassured by the priests that if they spend their money like this, donate to the religion, they will get it back on the other shore. If you donate one million here, you will get back ten million there. Hence, the misers, the stingy and greedy ones, donate money just to get back ten times more on the other side.

After he had loaded his bag onto the boat, the ferryman demanded, "I want a gold coin for the boat trip since it is midnight. I was sleeping and you disturbed me."

The rich man said, "A gold coin? Don't you feel ashamed? You don't even have compassion for a dying man. A gold coin, you shameless man! I have never given that to anyone in my whole life. And you don't even show mercy on a dying man. You are so rude!"

The ferryman replied, "In that case, you should hire someone else."

"I have to keep quiet here, otherwise people will come to know that I have jumped into the river along with all my gold coins. Then they will fish them out after my death," the rich man muttered to himself. He said to the ferryman, "Alright brother. But wait a minute, let me find the smallest coin for you."

Now, he is going to die, he is going to jump in the Ganges, but his mind… Certainly, he has lived in dreams – his whole life must have been obsessed with some particular dream, a particular madness. He must have been crazy after money.

If you see a man clinging to money, know that he is crazy. There are so many crazy people in this world that we cannot even build that many madhouses. In fact, if we were to build separate living arrangements for the mad people and the sane ones, we should build fewer places for the sane people because the majority of people are crazy.

If someone is obsessed with money, he is captivated by a dream. It makes him totally unaware of what he is doing. He does not seem to have any concern with life. But if someone is earning money and spending it to enjoy his life, that is understandable.

People are captivated by different kinds of dreams. When someone dreams about status, he has to go on climbing the ladder of status from the lower to a higher position, and from the higher to the highest. He has to go on a journey of acquiring status. He has a dream in his mind that he wants to fulfill: "I will do it!"

Alexander or Napoleon or anyone else are all engaged in the same chase. They are dreaming. Alexander is dreaming of conquering the whole world. What is the point in conquering the whole world? Let's imagine you have conquered the whole world, then what? What will happen then? Even then nothing will happen. But there is a constant chase, a mad hunt. Man goes on running.

I have heard...

Alexander the Great met a mystic on his way to India – a mystic called Diogenes, who used to live naked on the outskirts of a village. Someone had told Alexander that there was a magnificent mystic nearby and that he should visit him.

Alexander went to see him. It was early on a cold morning and the mystic was lying naked under the open sky. The sun was shining and he was sunbathing. As Alexander stood there, his shadow fell on Diogenes. Alexander said to him, "Perhaps you don't know that I am Alexander the Great. I've come to visit you."

Diogenes laughed loudly and called the dog who was sitting in his hut, saying, "Come here and listen to this man who is calling himself great with his own mouth! Even dogs cannot make such a mistake."

Alexander was shocked. A man who does not have even a single piece of clothing on him dares to say such thing to Alexander the Great? His hand reached to his sword.

Diogenes said, "Let the sword be in its place, don't waste your effort – swords are for those afraid of dying. I have reached beyond the place where death can happen; I have dropped the dreams that create death. I have died to those dreams. Now I am at the place where there is no death. Let the sword remain in its sheath. Don't waste your effort.

Can someone talk to Alexander the Great in this way? And a brave man such as Alexander had to put the sword back in its sheath! The sword was redundant in front of such a man. Those with swords are like children playing with toys in front of someone such as Diogenes.

Alexander asked, "Can I do something for you?"

Diogenes replied, "What can you do! What could you do? You can do only one thing – move a little away because I was sunbathing and you are blocking the sunlight. And remember, never become a barrier to anyone's sunshine."

Alexander said, "I will go now, but for the first time in my life, I have met a man in front of whom I feel as a camel does when it sees a mountain for the first time. I have met many people in my life, people of great arrogance, and I made them bow down to me, but in front of this man… If God grants me life again, I will ask him to make me a Diogenes next time."

Diogenes said, "Listen to my story too: if God comes to me with folded hands, puts his head on my feet, and asks me to become Alexander the Great, I would answer that it is better not to be created at all. Am I crazy that I would become an Alexander?

"I want to ask you before you leave where you are heading in such a rush, with so much noise and with such a great army."

Alexander replied with a glitter in his eyes and happiness on his face, "You are asking me? I am on my way to conquer Asia Minor."

Diogenes asked, "What will you do then?"

"Then I will conquer India."

"And then?"

"China."

"And then?"

"Then I will conquer the whole world."

Diogenes asked, "One last question. What is your plan after that?"

Alexander replied, "I haven't thought that far yet, but since you are asking, I think I will relax."

Diogenes started speaking to his dog, saying, "What a crazy man we have here. We are relaxing without conquering the world, and this man is saying that first he will conquer the whole world and then he will rest." Then to Alexander he said, "Even my dog is relaxing, even I am relaxing. Have you lost your mind? You are going to relax at the end anyway, aren't you?"

Alexander replied, "Of course, I want to relax."

Diogenes said, "The world is not disturbing your rest. Please stay with us, there is enough space in our hut. Even two more people could fit there." The hut of a poor man is always bigger than the palace of a rich man. In the palace of a wealthy man it is difficult to accommodate even one. A rich man needs greater and greater palaces. His palace is not big enough even for one, in fact not even for himself. The hut of a poor man is vast. The mystic continued, "It is a big space here and two of us can live comfortably. Please stay with us. Where are you going unnecessarily and why are you troubling yourself?"

Alexander said, "Your invitation is attractive. Your courage, your dignity, and what you are saying is penetrating my mind. But I am already halfway through my journey, how can I turn back halfway? I will try to come back soon."

Diogenes replied, "As you wish. But I have seen many people going on journeys and no one returns."

Has anyone ever returned from a wrong trip? And if you think that you are conscious, but you are unable to turn back from going the wrong way, it simply means you are not conscious yet. Suppose a man is about to fall into a well; he has taken the wrong path and there is a well ahead. He is not aware of it. If someone says to him, "Don't go that way, there is a well there," in reply will he say, "I have already come halfway, how can I return now"? No, he will go back immediately. If a man is walking close to a snake and someone says, "Don't go there, there is a snake in the darkness," will he say, "But I have already taken many steps in that direction, how can I step back now?"

Diogenes continued, "Alexander, dreams are endless, man's life is short. Life gets used up and dreams are never fulfilled. It is your choice. But anytime you come back, our home will be open for you. There is no door to the hut. Even if we are sleeping, don't worry, just come in, and take a rest. Or even if you don't find me here... There is no guarantee of tomorrow – today there is a sun in the sky, tomorrow it might not be there; we have no ownership on this hut. But you can come back and stay here. The hut will still be here."

Alexander could not see the point. In fact, for those who live in the world of dreams, great difficulty arises when they come close to a man of truth because their languages are different from each other. But Alexander must have been shaken.

On his way back from India he died somewhere on the journey, he could not return home. In fact, blind journeys are never fulfilled; the man comes to an end. And the truth is that for so many lifetimes we have gone on blind journeys, we have died again and again and then we start chasing those unfulfilled dreams again.

Once a man comes to know what he has done in his past lives, this life would come to a standstill because he had done exactly the same before. The same stupidities, the same enmities, the same friendships, the same chase after wealth, fame, status. No one knows how many times each human being has gone through death. That is why nature has arranged it so that you forget your past lives – so that you can participate in the same circle of affairs in which you have been moving many times. If you come to know that this has happened many times, that you have all this done many times, everything will become absolutely meaningless.

Alexander the Great died. And that same day, Diogenes died. And an incredible incident happened... A story became popular in Greece after their death. The story that an ordinary man, a mystic, had told many things to Alexander had already spread over Greece – then both of them died the same day. Someone spread another story after their deaths, that they met at the gates of heaven...

Alexander was ahead of Diogenes, since he died an hour before. Alexander, nearing the gates, heard a loud laugh. His heart trembled. This laughter was known to him; this must be the laughter of the same man, of Diogenes!

No one else could laugh like Diogenes. In fact our laughing is not real laughter. For a man who is always miserable and crying, his laughter is bound to be phony. Laughter is on the surface and crying is beneath. Even in his laughing, tears are mingled. His laughter is always phony. Only a man whose laughter has penetrated his very being can really laugh. Someone whose heart is full of suffering and trying to laugh on the surface is just making an effort; he is just trying to forget his misery.

Laughter belongs to people like Diogenes. Alexander started shivering. And he sensed that there was going to be trouble that day. In their last meeting, Alexander had been in the robe of an emperor and Diogenes was naked. Today it was a different situation – Alexander too was naked. They were both naked. Diogenes had always been naked, so it was not a matter of shame for him to be naked now. Alexander looked back to encourage himself, to boost his self-confidence and he also laughed.

But Diogenes said, "Stop laughing! Just phony laughter. All your life you have been doing false things and even after your death your laughter is phony. Stop this laughing!"

Alexander became very nervous. He said, "I am happy to see you again. How wonderful it is. It happens rarely that an emperor meets a naked fakir after death at the pearly gates. This must be the first time."

Diogenes said, "You are right. But you are making a mistake about who is the emperor here and who is the beggar. The emperor is behind and the beggar is ahead in this situation. You are coming here after losing everything, for whatever you desired was an achievement only in a dream. And I am coming here after total fulfillment, because I have ended all dreaming and I have found that which remains beyond dreams."

All our running belongs to the world of dreams. What will be gained if someone achieves great fame and high status? What will happen? What is the point if a few people worship, honor, and respect you? Nothing will happen. And something that is significant, which can happen through inner search, gets postponed because of this mad rush.

When people visit me they say, "What you are saying is right, but we have no free time, where is the time to meditate? Where is the time to search for the truth? Where is the time?" Their time is consumed by their dreams. They are saying, "Where is the time for truth?"

What a strange and incredible statement. Dreams have occupied the mind so strongly that they command you not to spare even one moment of time. And why do dreams act like this? Because if even a single ray of truth enters your life, then not just a single dream but the whole dreaming mind will disappear.

It will evaporate. Hence, do not give it even a slight chance. Keep on being occupied with the race, go on running. Even before one race is finished, start the next one. The mind says, "Before this desire is fulfilled, provide another one!" Even before one desire ends, another grows. The mind says, "Before one search ends, get engaged in another search." The mind says, "Before one dream is broken, awaken another dream." For, if even a single ray of truth enters the gap between two dreams, everything will change. Everything will be transformed. No matter how deep our dreams are, even a little hit of awakening cannot save them.

So in this third meeting of today, I want to tell you that if you want to move inward toward the truth, first you have to recognize your dreams as dreams. And you will have to ask whether you're giving nourishment to your dreams. You will have to search within to see whether you are cultivating the roots of your dreams. Whether you are strengthening your dreams. Whether you are living in dreams for the sake of dreaming. You will have to ask this. If the search moves in the right direction, the mind comes to a realization and the consciousness becomes aware of what is dream. The moment the awareness sees the dream as a dream, the race ends.

To be identified with dreams, you must have the illusion that they are reality. In fact, dreams are so weak that they cannot dominate you unless they pretend to be reality. If you want a lie to prevail, then it has to dress in the clothes of truth. Even if dishonesty wants to prevail in the market, it has to put up a sign: Honesty is our policy. Even if you want to sell fake butter, you have to start a shop for real butter!

Dreams, lies, and nonessentials are so weak, so impotent that they always have to borrow the legs of truth.

I have heard a story...

When the earth was created and things were descending to earth from heaven, God created the goddess of beauty and the goddess of ugliness. The two goddesses from heaven came down to the earth. On the way, their clothes and their bodies became covered with dust and sweat.

When they reached the earth, they took off their clothes, left them on the banks of a lake, and stepped into the water to take a bath. The goddess of beauty swam off across the lake, but the goddess of ugliness went back to the shore, put on the clothes of the goddess of beauty and left.

When she returned to the bank, the goddess of beauty found herself in a difficulty; the goddess of ugliness had stolen her clothes. She wondered what to do – she was naked, it was almost dawn, and the village people were beginning to wake up. The only clothes available were those of the goddess of ugliness. Seeing no other way, she put them on, thinking that if she found the goddess of ugliness along the way, she could exchange clothes with her.

Since then, it is said that the goddess of beauty is roaming around in the clothes of ugliness, and the goddess of ugliness is wearing the clothes of beauty. And the two never meet. The goddess of ugliness never stays anywhere. She is constantly on the run, just keeps on running. Now so many days have passed that beauty has even dropped the very idea of finding her own clothes.

The unreal is doing the same – dreams are doing the same. If they want to move, they need the feet of truth and the clothes of truth. Dreams can circulate only as long they are thought to be true. The moment they are seen as dreams, they immediately disappear.

Have you ever thought about it, that when you are dreaming, you are not aware that it is a dream? And if you become aware that it is just a dream, immediately the dreaming state is over and you are awake. Once you have awakened, only then do you realize that it was just a dream.

A seeker who sets out in search for the ultimate truth has to explore what are the dreams in his life. What in his life belongs to dreams? The more consciously he thinks about it, explores it, and identifies something as a dream, that very dream will evaporate. And the more his understanding deepens and clarity expands, in the same proportion, dreams lose their intensity. Consciousness relaxes back to its original source, turning inward where there is truth. A consciousness turning inward, away from dreams, finally reaches truth.

Our whole consciousness is occupied with chasing dreams. We are running toward dreams. And the whole society emphasizes chasing dreams from the cradle to the grave. When a child starts going to school, his parents tell him to come first; they have started cultivating dreams in him. The teacher says to come first – blessed is the one who comes first! All the others who could not make it to the number one position are the unfortunate ones.

The race has begun. They have poisoned the mind of a small child. Now he will make an effort his whole life to come first. Wherever he goes – number one: "I have to be number one!" A race has begun.

If someone asks, "What is the point in becoming number one"... It would be understandable if someone said, "Wherever you happen to be, stay blissful." But you are taught that you can't be happy until you become number one. And the amazing thing is that the person who is number one is hardly ever seen to be blissful. We are such blind people!

When has anyone who is at the number one position been seen to be happy? And the truth is, who has managed to be number one? Wherever you reach, there is always someone ahead of you. There is always someone ahead and always someone behind, as if the whole humanity is running in a circle. It is just as if we are moving in a circle: no matter how much you run, still someone is going to be ahead of you and someone is bound to be behind you. And you are aiming to become number one!

Jesus said, "Blessed are those who are able to be last." He must have said the wrong thing, since all our teachers, our entire society and civilization preach that we should become number one. Whether in the field of wealth, or knowledge, or enlightenment: become number one.

Even the saints are in the same race: how to become a world teacher, how to get to the throne of the Shankaracharya. And sitting on their thrones they become as arrogant as any political minister. The saint swells up with arrogance in exactly the same manner. He has his own attitude; an attitude toward others as if they are just creeping insects and he is the world teacher. And the interesting thing is, how do they become a "world teacher" without even asking the world? No one bothers to ask the world, he just declares himself as a world teacher.

Conceit is behind all this, dreams are behind it. They have ambition to become the emperor of the world, the desire to become a guru. It is exactly the same thing. It shows their effort to climb over others' chests. But what will really be gained by that? It is a race of ambition, and ambition implies a dream.

We are all ambitious people. And the more ambitious someone is, the more he will move away from himself. He will move away from truth. Truth is discovered only by those who are non-ambitious; a non-ambitious mind, a mind that has no ambition at all. A mind that neither wants to become anything, nor wants to find anything, nor wants to dominate anyone, nor wants any mastery over anyone, nor wants to become anyone's guru. Someone who has dropped all becoming, someone who does not want to become anything. Someone who just wants to know, to live, and to be with that which is. Someone who has no moving ahead and no running away from himself. But everyone is running.

Just observe a saint in his race. If you ask him where he is heading, he will reply, "Until I reach ultimate liberation, I cannot relax." Where is ultimate liberation? He will say, "The faster I run, the quicker I will arrive there." But you should ask him where he will run, where he will go, and where exactly this ultimate liberation is. He will reply, "Don't waste my time, let me run faster. The faster I run, the sooner I will arrive." But he does not know where the thing is that he is running after. Where are you running? Is the ultimate liberation located outside you, so that you can run and arrive there?

When a man says that he wants to be wealthy, he joins the race for wealth and goes on running. But he never asks whether the real wealth is outside. Yes, there *is* a wealth of money and riches. But no matter how much a man hoards, has anyone ever become rich by that? The inner poverty still remains. The riches pile up outside but the inner poverty remains.

An Indian emperor Akbar had a friend called Farid. One day, the people of Farid's village said to him, "Go to Akbar, he loves you so much. Please ask him to open a school for the village."

Farid had never gone to Akbar before. He replied, "I have never gone to see him; I have never asked anything from anyone. But you have put me in a great difficulty. If I refuse to go, you will criticize me for not doing a small favor for the village. And if I go, what will Akbar think? He always comes to ask my blessings, and now I have to beg him for something? But if you insist then I will go."

So Farid went to visit Akbar. He arrived early in the morning, so that he could see him before his court started. The people in the palace told him that Akbar was praying in the mosque. The mystic went in. Akbar was just finishing his morning prayers and was praying to God with folded hands, "Oh God, please give me more riches! Please increase my wealth, expand my empire."

On hearing this, Farid immediately turned back. When Akbar got up, he saw Farid descending the stairs. Akbar called out to him and asked, "Why have you come to visit me, and why are you leaving without even greeting me? Have I done something wrong?"

Farid replied, "No, you have not done anything wrong. I have committed a mistake."

Akbar asked, "What mistake? You, doing something wrong?"

Farid said, "I came to the wrong place. The village people said that Akbar is an emperor, but by coming here I found out that even Akbar is a beggar. He too is begging. So I don't blame you for anything. Please forgive me, I have come to the wrong place. If I have to beg then I can beg to the same God you were begging to. There is nothing wrong with you, but it would be very difficult for you to build a school for my village."

Akbar did not understand and asked, "What school? What is the matter?"

Farid replied, "No, it doesn't matter now. You need not build any school. It would reduce your riches; you already don't have enough, you were begging to God. I don't want to disturb you more. I am a monk myself and unknowingly I approached another beggar for alms.

Even an emperor like Akbar is not rich. In fact, rich people never really manage to become rich. The riches accumulate only outside, but the inner beggar remains the same. He demands more and more. Nothing changes through outside wealth; our poverty does not end by it.

There is another kind of wealth. That richness is not in the currency of the outside world. There is status – status of the outside. No matter how high a position you achieve, it does not matter at all; it is just a child's game and nothing more. It is like a small child climbs on a chair at home and says to his father, "Papa look at me, I have become taller than you." The father just laughs and says, "Of course you have become taller than me." And he puts the child on his shoulders so that the child feels bigger than him. And the child becomes very happy, feeling proud that he has grown bigger.

If the child feels bigger by climbing on the chair, then someone who feels that he has become bigger by climbing the ladder of status must be known as childish. It cannot be anything else. How did you become greater by sitting on something taller?

There was a British magistrate in Chennai. He was very particular about the people in court being given the right chair according to their status. We all have that concern inside us, but we are not that crazy. He was consistently mad, he was mad in an organized way.

We too bother about this kind of thing: when a servant comes, no matter how old he is, nobody asks him to take a seat. The old servant stands and the young employer sits on a chair. And the young man talks to the old servant in a disrespectful way: "Go do this or do that" and so on. Nobody asks the old man to sit down. The old servant is almost invisible to the people of the house – but he too is the father of somebody. The father of a poor man is not regarded as a father. Then a wealthy man comes; he is a worthless person, but possesses a lot of money. And you immediately stand up in his honor, start buttering him up and saying, "Please take a seat, please sit down!" So we also have the same kind of mind.

This was the condition of the magistrate, but he was very organized about it. He had seven chairs with numbers on them and when someone came to him, he asked his servant to fetch a chair according to the status of the man. For instance, he wouldn't even ask someone with no status to take a seat; he would just let him stand. In his court, the magistrate would sit on a chair.

When someone came in, he would order the servant to go and fetch either number-one chair or number-two or number-three or number-seven. He had seven chairs with seven numbers.

Chair number seven was for the man with the lowest status. And there was no chair with number eight. That kind of low-class person had to stand in court. And even the number-seven chair was nothing more than a stool.

It happened that a man came to visit him one morning. And this is not a story, this incident is real. Dr. Pattabhi Sitarmaiya has mentioned in his autobiography that he was acquainted with that magistrate. And his court was a topic of gossip in the whole village.

So the man came into the court; an old man walking with a stick and wearing old clothes. The magistrate calculated that keeping this man standing would do, and he let him remain standing. But when the old man looked at his watch, the watch looked expensive, so the magistrate immediately ordered his servant to fetch chair number three.

While the chair was being brought, the old man said to the magistrate, "Perhaps you don't recognize me. I am the landlord of the village." The magistrate immediately asked the servant to put back the number-three chair and bring the number-two chair. Meanwhile the old man added, "No, you still did not recognize me. I donated one million rupees to the government during the Second World War."

By that time the servant had brought the number-two chair, but the magistrate ordered, "Put it back and get the number-one chair immediately."

The old man said, "Now I am getting tired just standing here. Please ask him to fetch the highest number chair you have, since I have come here with the idea to donate one million rupees to you."

We measure human beings in such a way. If it was the same man without money, would he be a different man? If he did not have a good watch, would he have a different soul? If he was not going to donate one million rupees to the magistrate, was he then nothing? Was he then nobody, was he nothing, was he worthless? Did his existence then mean nothing?

This is our evaluation. Are we weighing dreams or are we measuring truth? Truth is inside the man, it is his very being, that which is. These are just dreams: who has what kind of watch, or what kind of house, or what status. These are dreams through which we are connected to others. But we recognize only dreams because we live in those dreams ourselves. We insist on, we demand those dreams and we want to follow through with them.

A dream world is a world of outer clothes. The world of dreams is the world of the outer eyes. There are no dreams in the inner world; all dreams belong to the outside world. And the person who finishes with dreams, who wakes up and gets unidentified with them, is the one who turns in.

So you have to discover for yourself; it has nothing to do with anyone else. Each and every person has to enquire within: "Am I a dreamer, am I a dream cultivator, am I nurturing dreams?"

We all are cultivating dreams. And how many dreams do we have? How many things do we desire to happen? How many ideas of becoming somebody do we possess? And sometimes we even have strange desires about this becoming and happening! It is hard to find a man who while walking in the street isn't dreaming of becoming the president of the country. Many times we feel, "Aren't my neighbors going to think of me? Isn't somebody going to propose my name in parliament for the position of the president?" This kind of idea does occur to us. Who doesn't have this happen? In our minds, how many things take place? Somebody wins the lottery in his mind while walking on the road – just as if he has actually won a million.

A friend of mine was a doctor. Day and night he was occupied with playing the lottery. Day and night! And he never went for those lower than in the millions. His clinic was doing such poor business. How could it do well, with his obsessed mind? Whenever patients visited, he was preoccupied with his lottery. He would say to his patients, "Wait a little because it is a matter of millions." Who wants to be bothered about a fee of a few rupees from the patients?

I also visited him occasionally. Every month he was dreaming of getting millions from the lottery, but he never actually won anything. As soon as it went past the closing date, he would start all over again with the same game. One day he told me, "This time it is definitely happening, I am absolutely certain to win one hundred thousand rupees."

I said to him, "If you win one hundred thousand rupees, can you donate some of it to the village library? It needs some support."

He started pondering on how much he should donate. With great difficulty he said that he could make a contribution of five thousand rupees. He was supposed to win one hundred thousand rupees. Just five thousand! It seemed so painful for him.

I said to him, "No, five thousand will be too much for you. It feels too heavy for you."

"You are right when you say that I am a poor man, five thousand will be too difficult, but two and half thousand is certain. I will donate two and half thousand," he replied.

I said, "Then give it to me in writing, you might change your mind later."

While he was writing it down, he said, "Two and half thousand! And who else has donated? Who else is giving in this village? How much is the wealthiest businessman of the village donating?"

"He is donating only two hundred and one rupees," I replied.

Then he said, "And you are asking me to donate two thousand, five hundred! If he is donating two hundred and one rupees, you should take the same amount from me."

He still has to win the lottery, he hasn't won yet. He is supposed to win one hundred thousand and the win is absolutely certain…

I said, "As you wish, just give it to me in writing."

"Why do I need to write it down? I have promised you, and that means I will certainly give it," replied the doctor.

I went home laughing after talking to him, and thinking what kind of a man is this? What kind of a man and what a mind!

I was sleeping on the roof of my house as it was summer. About eleven o'clock at night, he shouted from the ground floor, "Listen!"

I asked, "What is the matter?"

"Please drop the idea of getting a donation from me this time, I will donate next time I win," he said.

He came to my place at eleven o'clock at night after thinking it over. It must have been half a mile between our homes.

I told him that he could have told me about it in the morning. Then he said, "I could not sleep. Be sure, I will certainly donate next time."

He has not yet won the first time, so there is no question of the next time.

But how this man lives! And we all live like that. Please don't laugh at him because he is nothing special; he is just like us, he is a man exactly like us. We all live in that way. We live exactly like that.

Can this kind of mind, a mind that lives in this way, ever come across the truth? And is there anyone who has not built up dreams? How far have we cultivated our dreams? Is there anyone who has not sailed his boat made of dreams in the ocean?

We say that a boat made of paper is too weak, but a boat of dreams is even weaker than that. Even the paper boat sinks. The dream boat does not even float – but everybody is sailing them! And when the boats sink, we suffer and quickly build other boats made of the same stuff. Even before one boat sinks, we start building a new one.

We have to observe each and every dream within us with tremendous awareness. The moment we perceive something as a dream, it disappears. The moment you become aware that something is your dream and you are moving in a dream, that very moment the dream will evaporate. But while you are sitting on your sofa, your mind starts dreaming – and daydreaming starts.

This state of mind is the greatest hindrance in meditation. The dreaming mind is the greatest obstruction in meditation. Only one who comes out of the dreaming state of mind can move into meditation.

But we are not aware of our own state. We can easily see another person's state: "Yes, this person is dreaming." But when we turn toward ourselves, we are not able to perceive that we are dreaming.

Everybody looks at himself in the mirror to improve his looks, to prepare himself before going out of the house. He does all this with the idea that the whole village will notice him – although who has the time to observe anyone in a village? He is going out with so much preparation! When I see someone make so much preparation, the village people seem so hard, because no one will notice what a great effort this man is making. He will just pass by; the village people have no time to see all that. And they have also been preparing themselves. They also want that someone should notice them. Now there is a great difficulty: Who is going to watch who?

A father was telling his son, "God has created you so that you can serve others."

In earlier days the son would have easily accepted that. Nowadays, even children are very wise. The son replied, "I see your point that God has created me to serve others. My question is, for what purpose did God create others? I also have the right to know what for purpose others are created. If they are also created to serve others, then a great network is formed – that we have to serve them and they have to serve us. It would be better to each serve ourselves."

Everybody is leaving the house with the idea that others should notice him – each and every one. The other has also gone out with the same idea. He is also out to be noticed by others. It would be better if we just keep our mirrors with us and whenever we want, we can look into them. A few clever women have started keeping their mirrors on them. Man is not that clever or he does not have that much courage.

Who is going to watch who? Who has spare time? But what a pointless dream we are occupied with. Even if a few people took a look at us, what is the point? What will it bring? It is a dream that the whole world should watch you. But for what? And what is the need? What is the point? What is the purpose? What is the gain? What will it bring? We are not even aware while we are tying our shoelaces or putting a necktie on that no one knows in which imaginary world we are living, imagining that someone will watch us.

We don't wear clothes just to cover our bodies. Even our clothes serve some other purpose. Any clothes will cover the body, but it not just a matter of covering the body at all. The question is something else – covering the body has become secondary. It is something else. The truth is that very few people are wearing clothes just to cover the body; our clothes are used to exhibit the body. Clothes that exhibit the body are considered to be fashionable.

Hence, clothes tend to become tighter. This fashion is sucking the breath out of people and clothes go on becoming tighter and tighter on the body. The tighter the clothes are, the more the body is visible; otherwise it will not show much. And life is getting sucked out of the body in the tight clothing. If you observe people, you will see that when clothes are tight, the man is choking inside. But he is self-restrained. He is practicing great abstinence! Actually he is practicing austerity. India is a warm country and men are going around wearing ties! Why don't they just hang themselves? It is a hot country and men go around wearing shoes and socks. Are they living in reality or somewhere else? Perhaps some other values are functioning in them.

It happened…

Galib, a famous poet, was invited by emperor Bahadurshah Jaffar. Galib was a poor man, so he was wearing old clothes – poets have not yet managed to become rich. A poet has no chance of becoming rich; only thieves can become rich. How can a poet become rich? Yes, if the poet is a thief too, that is, if he steals others' poems, then he can become rich.

But Galib was a poor man. One is hardly paid anything for poetry. Now the emperor had invited him. His friends said, "Have you gone crazy, are you going to meet the emperor wearing those clothes? The guards will not even allow you entry."

Galib said, "I have been invited, not my clothes." Anyway he did not agree with his friends. Some uncomplicated men don't agree with society, and Galib must have been such a straightforward man.

The clever people – or better to say the cunning people – were right when they said, "Nobody will realize it is you in such ordinary clothes. The emperor has listened to your poetry, he has heard about your talent but what do the guards know about you?"

Galib didn't listen to them. He went. At the gate he said, "Please let me in, I am a friend of the emperor. He has invited me for dinner."

The guard did not answer him. He just gave him a push and said, "Yes, you are right, all the beggars of the village are friends of the emperor. The whole day we face this trouble! Once again, someone has come. Everybody wants to enter the palace. Go on your way!"

This was beyond Galib's understanding. He thought that his friends had been right. He returned and said them, "You were right, please find some clothes for me."

They borrowed clothes from the neighbors. A good shirt, a coat, a turban, and nice shoes – all borrowed. Galib wore those borrowed clothes and set out to visit the emperor. Now he was looking proper. Borrowed people look quite proper! On the same road, everybody was looking at him and wondering, "Who is this man?"

The same guard bowed down, greeted him, and said, "Please come in sir, welcome. Who are you, sir?"

Pointing to his clothes, Galib said, "This!"

The guard did not understand what "This!" meant, but just out of fear that he must be some great man, he let Galib come in, saying, "Alright sir, please come in." The gatekeeper thought that he must be a great man since he was wearing a gold chain. Now, it was difficult to know that the gold chain was borrowed and did not belong to him: "It must be his, since it is hanging on his neck. What can be stronger evidence than that?"

Galib went in. The emperor was worried because he had arrived so late. He asked him, "Why did you get here so late?"

Galib replied, "My apologies. I got into a little trouble. I got entangled in my foolishness and made a mistake because I didn't listen to the clever people. So I was delayed."

The emperor did not understand what he was talking about. Anyway he said, "Good. Take a seat. It is already late so the food is here."

Galib took the food and said to his turban, "Dear turban, please eat this food." Then he said to the coat, "Dear coat, eat this food!"

The emperor asked, "What are you doing? You have strange eating habits. Why are you behaving like this?"

Galib replied, "I arrived here much earlier, but I wasn't allowed to enter because of my poor clothes. Now, due to my good clothes, I was allowed in, so they are your guests and only they are going to have dinner with you. Forgive me, it is not a question of habit. I do not exist – in fact, I was sent back by your guards. This time only these clothes are visiting you, so they will eat. Please say hello to them, talk to them, and welcome them."

Galib said the right thing. It is only the clothes that matter. We all are living in clothes which are false. The inner truth is buried under them.

The clothes of dreams are of different kinds – of respectability, of honor, of knowledge, of knowledgeability, and even of renunciation. Observe a man who has renounced a little, how arrogantly he walks! Why are you walking with such arrogance, just because you have fasted for seven days? It was your bad luck that you had to starve, then die of hunger – do what you want to do! But why are you so arrogant about it? If you are fasting for seven days, it is nobody else's fault. Why are you going around with an announcement of your fasting accompanied by drums, music and so on, even disturbing small children who are studying for their exams? What is this arrogance all about? Whether you eat seven times a day or don't eat for seven days, it is your choice!

No, but he is going to announce to the whole world that he has fulfilled a seven-day fast and he has become somebody special. What a life of dreams! Can anybody become special by starving?

We have become attached to all kinds of things that have nothing whatever to do with discovering truth. Rather, they function as a device to escape and falsify life. If we are attached to these things, our journey into meditation is not possible.

Hence, the second thing I want to say to you is that, when we are sitting in meditation, observe with awareness what dreams keep you occupied. Forgive them and let them go.

The mind will feel bad, for it hurts immensely when dreams are uprooted because they have been everything to us. They are our assets, our vital force, and in fact we have become one with them. So when dreams are uprooted, it feels like death to us. They are everything to us. When they vanish, we will be reduced to nothing. Naked, no-thing-ness, nothing left to lose. What do we have except clothes? What do we have except thoughts? What do we have except our minds conditioned, chattering all over the place? That is our wealth; that is our life. It has become our soul. That is what I am asking you to let go of. And then you will be gone, you will disappear.

But one who is ready to disappear is entitled to discover ultimate fulfillment. One who dissolves himself becomes entitled to be himself.

What does it mean to dissolve oneself? Only that which is temporal can end. Only dreams can disappear. That which *is* can never come to an end. Truth cannot be erased. So, go on uprooting each and every dream inside you; go on tearing down and demolishing all the buildings of imagination you have erected, clean your whole interiority from everywhere.

Children gather on the banks of a river and build sandcastles. And they fight and keep everyone away from their sandcastles saying, "Keep your feet away from my house, otherwise it will fall down." On the one hand they are building castles made of sand, on the other hand they are warning others to keep a distance. "No one should come to my sandcastle because it might collapse."

When you are building a sandcastle, why are you afraid of its collapse? Then you try to make sure that others don't come close to it. When some other child steps on someone's sandcastle, quarrels, fights, tearing of clothes, bleeding, and injuries follow.

Someone should ask, "What are you doing? You are injuring someone's head for sandcastles! Tearing their clothes and beating someone up."

And as dusk descends and the sun sets, and the mother's voice calls them to come back, it is time for dinner… Then the children kick down their own sandcastles and run home. Everything is left lying on the sand; whatever they were fighting for is left behind on the sand. What they fought for is all just dropped there.

But grown-ups act exactly the same as children. They build houses of dreams on the beach of life and then they fight with their neighbors, with this person, with that person. There are courts and court cases and such tangled webs! What are all these webs about – that I have built a sandcastle, and you have built one, and someone has trespassed somewhere. My house is overlapping your house or your house is intruding on my house, and the roof of your house is encroaching on my house a little – this is trespass! Dreams have intruded into each other's dreams. People are killed for them. The courts are involved. What a remarkable pretense; some fools are fighting and other fools are sitting there in court with their special outfits and giving judgment.

And the interesting question is, what are you fighting for? Why are you fighting? If the consciousness is awakened a little... And no one else can awaken it. You have to examine your life on your own, inch by inch. What am I living for, what am I fighting for, what am I building, what am I searching for, and what do I desire to become? And if this enquiry continues, suddenly tremendous silence starts descending within you and in that clarity you can see this is a dream, it is arising, and disappearing.

Dreams disappear and truth comes into being. Truth is eternal; it is just buried under the dreams. And can truth ever remain hidden under dreams? It gets caught in the same way as the reflection of the moon was trapped in the well. In reality it can never be trapped – how can truth ever be buried? Yes, in the well of dreams, the reflection of the moon can be trapped. But the moon is moving in the sky.

What we actually are at the innermost being – that which is – is always untouched. But all around us is the interwoven web of dreams; and the reflection is formed in that web of dreams. The image is trapped. And we are caught in trouble.

The meaning of meditation is to end this creation of reflections, to withdraw from images, and to discover who is reflected.

Now we will prepare for the evening meditation. First, for a couple of minutes try to understand what we will be doing. In fact, it is a non-doing. In that state of non-doing, let go of everything.

For ten minutes, let go of everything and sit silently. Feel your body to be totally frozen, close your eyes. And try to see only one thing: everything is outside of me. And whatever is outside is a dream. I am within, I am alone, pure consciousness, my being and the witness is the only truth.

And slowly, slowly you have to settle down in that witness. This settling down happens when clarity begins. And this clarity will happen. Then I will be silent for these ten minutes. And you will just remain a witness.

Please take a little space away from each other. No one should be touching anyone. No trespass at all! No one should intrude on anybody, nor touch anyone. Please move away from each other. And no talking at all. Absolutely no talking!

Even if someone wants to leave, then leave after ten minutes, so that there is no disturbance for others now. Even if you don't want to meditate, just sit quietly outside, but don't leave immediately because others will be disturbed by that. As long as you are leaving, the disturbance will continue. So just for the sake of caring for others, please sit down. Even if someone is in a hurry to leave, even then, sit outside quietly.

Sit with enough space between each other. Sit wherever you can find a place…

CHAPTER 5

losing suffering, attaining bliss

MY BELOVED ONES.

Man lives in suffering, and fantasizes about happiness; man lives in ignorance, and fantasizes about knowledge. Man is not even alive in the true sense, he only fantasizes about life.

Today, I want to tell you that because of living in fantasy, we are unable to become that which we could have become. If a sick man firmly believes that he is healthy, he will stop taking steps toward health. If he believes himself to be healthy, there is no question of his becoming healthy. If a blind man assumes that he knows about light and what it is, he will stop searching for a cure for his eyes.

A blind man must know that he knows nothing about light. A sick man must know that he is not healthy. And a man in suffering must know that he is not blissful. But to comfort and console ourselves we imagine that which we are not.

Man is unhappy, but living in a dream of happiness. And remember, suffering does not end by fantasizing about happiness. Fantasizing about happiness means only that suffering continues and goes on increasing.

In order to end suffering, the fantasies about happiness have to be dropped – you must know your suffering. For someone who knows suffering, his suffering comes to an end. But for someone who imposes happiness on himself, his suffering gets covered up. It doesn't cease to be; instead, it continues underneath.

If you want to make ignorance disappear, you don't need to imagine wisdom – rather, see the very ignorance itself. Someone who sees their ignorance attains wisdom. But for the one who clings to knowledge, false knowledge, imaginary knowledge, his ignorance does not end, it just gets covered up. He never attains knowing because imaginary knowledge has no significance.

It would be good to understand this from two or three angles. I want to ask, are we blissful? Have we ever known happiness? If you look at your life clearly, you will find out that you have never known bliss, all you have known is just suffering.

But we try to forget the suffering; we imagine a bliss we have never known and try to impose it on ourselves. We hope that we will experience bliss one day but we hope only for that which we have not experienced. We have not experienced bliss; hence we continuously think that we will find bliss tomorrow, in the future. People with more imaginative powers think that they will find it in the next life. And those with an even more fanciful imagination think that they will find bliss after death in heaven, in some ultimate liberation.

If human beings had known bliss, they would never have imagined heaven. Heaven is imagined by those who have never experienced ecstasy. What they have not experienced, they hope to find in heaven.

Have we ever experienced bliss? Is there any moment in our lives when we can say that we have experienced bliss? Be careful, don't be in a hurry to answer – because one who has experienced bliss once cannot have any suffering. One who knows bliss becomes incapable of suffering; he never experiences suffering again. He is absolutely incapable of being miserable. Because one who comes to know bliss also realizes that he *is* bliss. It is a very interesting thing. And since we have been constantly experiencing suffering, that is evidence that we have never known bliss. There is hope and imagination.

Sometimes we impose happiness too. A friend comes to visit

you, you hug him and say, "What a great pleasure!" You experience great joy in embracing your friend. What a great delight you feel in hugging your friend! But have you ever thought that if the friend who is embracing you continues hugging you for ten, fifteen, or twenty minutes and does not let go of your neck, you will feel like calling the police to get rid of him: "What is this person doing?" And if your friend continues hugging you for an hour or two then their hug will feel like the noose of a gallows.

If it was bliss, it would have increased. The bliss you felt for one second should have been multiplied ten times in ten seconds. So it was not bliss, it was all just imagination; it disappeared in a moment. Only imaginary things disappear from one moment to the next; that which is truth is eternal. That which is imaginary is temporary. That which is fleeting, know it as imaginary. And that which *is*, is endless, is eternal – that which is not just for the moment is timeless, it can never die. That *is*, that is and that is. That was, and will be, and will be. There will never be any moment when that ceases to be.

Pleasure that turns into pain, know it as something imaginary. It was not pleasure at all. And all the pleasures we know of are capable of turning into pain.

When you have your meal and you think that the food is delicious... If you were to continue eating, then after some time, the pleasure of eating would turn into pain. And if you still continued to eat more – as many people do, they cannot stop eating – then their whole life would be tortured by the pain of eating.

Doctors joke sometimes that only half of what you eat is used for your nutrition; the other half of your meal is the nutrition for your doctor.

If you reduce your food intake to half then you will not need a doctor anymore. Many diseases happen to you due to overeating, which is then followed by a visit to the doctor. If we continue overeating, food turns into poison. One can die of overeating.

Someone sings a song to you and you say: "What a joy. Sing it once more!" Then he sings the same song once more and you do not say, "What a pleasure," you remain silent. If he sings it a third time, you will say, "Now it is enough." If he sings it for a fourth time, you will say, "Excuse me please." If he does it a fifth time, you will try to escape. And if the doors are locked and you are forced to listen to it for a sixth time, your head will get dizzy. And if he still continues, then you will go mad. The same song that was a pleasure to listen to the first time will drive you crazy.

If it was pleasure, then by listening to it ten times, it should have been multiplied by ten. Take this as a criterion for bliss. Consider it a criterion that the pleasure which is momentary, and its repetition brings about pain, is not a pleasure at all. You must have imagined it as a joy. You imagined it once, but the second time it was hard to keep that imagination going, and the third time it became even more difficult to imagine, and after ten times the imagination was uprooted: things started to appear clearly as they are. All our pleasures turn into pain.

Our pleasures are pain; we just imagine pleasure, assuming it to be pleasure from the outside. How long can an imagined pleasure be sustained? We have not experienced any bliss, we have just imagined it. All we know is suffering. But why have we imagined in this way?

We have used our imagination because without it, suffering will kill us. If we do not imagine pleasure, how will we live with the suffering? So, by creating a web of false pleasures we try to push the misery away, we try to forget it. Our whole life is an effort to forget our suffering and nothing else. A long effort to forget misery.

Friedrich Nietzsche used to laugh a lot. Somebody asked him, "Why do you laugh so much, are you very happy?"

Nietzsche replied, "Don't ask me this, please don't ask. The reason for my laughing is totally different."

His friends enquired, "What other reason could there be, except that you are blissful?"

Nietzsche said, "Just drop the subject. The reason is certainly other than bliss. Bliss is not the reason at all."

His friends insisted, "Please tell us what the reason is."

"I laugh in order to avoid crying. If I don't laugh, I will start crying. Crying is going on inside; I keep myself engaged in laughing to stop tears from flowing," answered Nietzsche.

So the more someone is absorbed in a search for pleasure, you should know that they are suffering to the same extent. They need pleasure around the clock because they are suffering twenty-four hours a day. That is why we go on inventing new devices for entertainment. It is evidence of a miserable world. Someone who is not miserable never seeks entertainment.

People spend their time in the movie theaters, but if they were happy then they would have enjoyed being at home. They are miserable and that is why they are found in the movie theaters. People who are drinking alcohol in bars are there because they are miserable. Those who are watching prostitutes dance, if they were blissful then they would have closed their eyes and would be sitting somewhere, absorbed in their inner bliss. They are watching those dances because they are miserable and they are trying to forget their suffering. All around, the effort to forget suffering is going on.

And you should not think that only someone who is sitting in a cinema is trying to forget his misery, only someone who is drinking alcohol is trying to forget his suffering, and only someone who is sitting on the doorstep of a prostitute is trying to forget his pain. No, even the man who is worshipping and chanting in the temple is equally engaged in an effort to forget agony. There is no difference. Why would a blissful individual go to a temple and participate in chanting and prayers? Has he gone mad? Why would a blissful man stand in front of a statue with folded hands? A miserable man is trying to forget, and trying to find a way to do it. He gets absorbed in chanting mantras such as "Rama, Rama" and forgets his misery. Then again the suffering comes back. As long as he goes on moving the prayer beads through his fingers, he forgets his suffering. He gets occupied with something and it helps him to forget misery.

Whether you are watching a movie or watching a religious drama such as Ramleela makes no difference. It is all an attempt to forget suffering. It is all an effort to forget oneself. Alcohol and prayer serve the same purpose. One of them is a morally correct way and the other is morally wrong, but both ways belong to forgetfulness. Man has to forget himself somehow. The man who is miserable wants to forget. Someone is doing it by playing cards, someone by playing chess, and someone is reading the Gita. What are you doing?

We don't know how to be blissful. We are miserable. We want

to escape this suffering somehow, just want to forget it. We want to forget it any way we can. If you read the ancient scriptures such as the Vedas, then you will find that even in the Vedic times, people were drinking soma, an intoxicating drink. If the seers and sages drink it then it is called soma. And if an ordinary man drinks it then it is called an alcoholic drink. All the way from the Vedic times to modern America – from soma to mescaline and LSD! Now all over America, LSD, mescaline, and marijuana are consumed. And even people such as the great American thinker, Aldous Huxley say that man's suffering is so great that we need ways to forget it. We want to forget suffering.

Are all our ways of getting pleasure perhaps ways to forget misery? And that is why all our ways inevitably fail. When a man is crazy after a woman, he thinks he will be happy if he manages to get her. The day he gets her, that same day she becomes useless. A man looks at the face of his lover, but does he look at the face of his wife? The woman he has married and brought home becomes worthless. The fantasy disappears in a second. The wife has arrived home and she is forgotten. Now the neighbors can enjoy looking at her and get some pleasure, but the husband does not seem to get any joy.

Lord Byron got married. He was an incredible man. He was so crazy about this woman before he married her that he used to think that his whole life would be meaningless if he could not marry her. He married her and was going down the church steps, holding the hand of his newly-wedded wife. The church bells were still ringing and the wedding guests were saying good-bye. The marriage ceremony had just finished; the wedding candles were still lit. Byron was going toward the coach, holding his wife's hand, and at that very moment he saw another woman on the road.

Byron must have been a very honest person. As they sat in the coach, he said to his wife, "What a wonder! Till yesterday I used to think that if I could get you then I would have found everything in my life. And just now when we were coming down the steps of the church, a woman who was passing in front of us charmed me completely. I forgot you and I wished I could get this woman! I totally forgot you because you are available to me and now you have become insignificant to me. Now you are mine and worthless."

All the attraction is for the unavailable. All the attraction is for that which is not available yet. What is available becomes meaningless. Why? Because our fantasy of pleasure can continue in what is unavailable. But our fantasy of joy ends in what is accessible, because it is already available. Just a glimpse of pleasure happened and then it was lost. The fantasy was finished.

A poet has expressed this as: "Blessed are those lovers who could never get hold of their beloveds, because they can imagine the pleasure of uniting with their beloveds for rest of their lives. And unfortunate are those lovers who get their beloveds, because they come to know that they have gone to hell."

All our pleasures at any level are imaginary. And our suffering is absolutely real. No one imagines suffering. Who will bother to imagine suffering? We try to avoid pain and our pleasures are imaginary. This is the difficulty of life. And the man who spends time with imaginary pleasures becomes lost.

We can end up imagining so many things...

The head of Majnu's village called him and said, "Have you gone mad? The girl you are madly in love with, Laila, is a very ordinary girl. We will find much better girls than her for you. We have called many girls; come with me and see. You have gone crazy because her father is not letting you meet her. Just let her go, there is nothing special about that girl. She is very ordinary looking."

You might be also thinking that Laila must have been a beautiful girl, but then you are mistaken. Laila was a very ordinary girl, a homely girl. But do you know what Majnu's reply was? He said, "No, no. You don't know; only Majnu can perceive the beauty of Laila."

The king asked, "What do you mean? Am I blind?"

Majnu replied, "No, you are not blind. I am blind. But what is visible to me can be seen only by me and no one else. I see everything only in Laila! I do not see anyone else."

Now, no one else is able to see what Majnu perceives. Hence lovers seem to be crazy. The whole village will call them crazy, except themselves. Only the man who is infatuated with his beloved would not be able to see his own craziness. The web of his imagination is so interwoven that he is not able to see what you see; he perceives something else.

What a lover sees in his beloved is the projection of his imagination; it is not necessarily found in the beloved. What a beloved sees in her lover is the projection of her imagination; it is not actually there in the lover. The pleasure we think we take from others is our imagination, which we have spread over them and projected onto them. And how long will it take for that projection to disappear? It vanishes in a moment; it dies out with proximity. It already starts fading away with acquaintance; it evaporates with intimacy. It disappears with familiarity. It was nourished by remoteness, distance made that fantasy happen.

People have not only cultivated fantasies of pleasures in ordinary life; when they find no pleasure and cannot avoid pain in ordinary living, they start with even greater fantasies. Someone has a vision of Krishna playing on his flute and he closes his eyes and becomes absorbed in that image. Someone else has a vision of Jesus Christ. Someone else has visions of Rama with his bow and arrows. All these fantasies are not going to lead you to the truth. No matter how deep a fantasy you create. Whether someone is having a vision of Krishna playing on his flute or Rama with his bow and arrows or Jesus hanging on his cross, or of Buddha and Mahavira makes no difference. These people have nothing to do with your visions. There is nothing there other than your own imagination.

But you can forget yourself in that imagination. And remember, a fantasy can be sustained for a long time because there is nothing solid there which can be destroyed. It is just imagination, and imagination can live for a long time.

So, someone who loves an ordinary human being has the possibility to become free from his fantasy, but the devotees who create a fantasy of God cannot be freed from it so easily. Their imagination is vague; it is in their hands to put it together the way they like. If you are in love with a real human being, that person is not going to always behave the way you like. If you ask a man to lift his left leg, hold a flute in his hand, and stand for an hour, he will say, "Excuse me please, good-bye!" But the Krishna is your imagination, so you can keep the poor guy standing on one leg and holding his flute. He cannot do anything. And you can make him behave the way you wish; if you order him to put the other foot down, he has to follow your orders. It is a projection of your imagination, there is no one else there. Hence, the devotee is very happy to find God in his hand. You can make him dance the way you please: God is in your hand! But the entity that is in your hand is made of your imagination.

What will be gained by getting lost in fantasy? What will be achieved? Bliss cannot be attained by forgetting about suffering. If you want to just forget suffering, imagination is a significant device. But if you want to attain bliss, imagination is a fatal mechanism. Then you must stay away from imagination.

This I want to point out to you: we have tried to forget suffering in every way. And someone who is trying to forget suffering is creating such a trap for himself by his own hands that it will be difficult to come out of it. He will have to create a new web of fantasy day after day, then he will have to manufacture new lies every day in order to guard the original lie. Finally it will be such a long series of lies that he will not even be able to figure out where the truth is.

We have built so many lies! We have created a long procession of lies, and we are all lost in those lies. We are not aware of it. Our family is a lie; it is based on our fantasy, not on truth. Our friendship is a lie; it is based on our imagination, not on truth. Our enmity is a lie, our religion is a lie, our devotion is a lie, our prayer is a lie; they are founded on imagination, not on truth.

We have spread the net of lies so widely that it has become very difficult to know from where to break it today. A man is standing with folded hands in front of a temple – to whom is he praying? He does not know anything about God. If you are standing with folded hands to one who is unknown to you, then your prayers are false. What are you praying to?

I have heard...

A group of merchants were returning home by boat. They were coming back from earning a lot of money, so they were loaded with diamonds and gems. There was a mystic among them, who had asked to join them on the way back. It was the last day of their sea journey, and it seemed that the shore was not far away. But a great storm approached; clouds covered the sun, strong winds started blowing and wild waves were crashing against the boat. The boat was about to capsize.

All the travelers brought their hands together, knelt down, closed their eyes, raised their hands toward the sky and started praying, "God save us! Save us, please. We will do anything to save our lives." They prayed to survive and reach the shore, one saying that he would distribute all his wealth among the poor, and someone else praying that he would donate all he has earned in the service of humanity. Someone was praying, "I will do anything you ask me to do, but please save me!"

But in the middle of all this chaos the mystic was sitting peacefully and laughing. The people said to him, "What kind of man are you? Our lives are in danger, your life is also in danger, so please join us in prayer! As you are a mystic, your prayers will be heard sooner."

But the mystic said, "Continue your prayers by yourself." And when they were engaged in their prayers with closed eyes, he shouted, "Stop! Do not give a promise to God that you will donate everything. The land is close by. I can already see the shore."

Immediately all of them stood up, leaving their prayers unfinished. They started laughing and packing up their belongings. And they said to the mystic, "It was good that you warned us in time. Otherwise we could have made a promise to God and got in trouble."

But one man had promised. And everyone had heard his promise. He was the wealthiest man of the village and he had said that he would sell his house and distribute the money earned from it to the poor. Everybody said to him, "Now you are in trouble." He looked a little worried.

But the mystic said to the people, "Don't be worried, he is so cunning that he will manage to deceive even God."

And this is what happened. Fifteen days later, the people of the village heard drums being beaten. The rich man had declared that he was selling his house, and the money earned from the sale would be distributed to the poor.

The whole village gathered because he had the best house in the village, it was worth millions. When everybody was there, he came out of his house. He had tied a small cat to the door. People started asking him, "Why have you tied a cat there?"

He said, "I have to sell both my cat and my house. My house costs one rupee and the cat costs a million. Whoever wants to purchase will have to buy both together."

The mystic was among the crowd. He said, "Aha!"

The house was sold. It was worth a million. The people said, "What do we care? We would buy the house for a million and the cat for one rupee! It does not matter either way." Someone bought the house.

The rich man had sold the house for one rupee and the cat for a million. He put a million rupees in his pocket and donated one rupee to the poor.

He had promised to distribute the money from the sale of his house to the poor.

These are our prayers, this is our devotion, and finally all these things are part of our dishonesty. We don't even spare God from our deception! And it is natural, since we have nothing to do with God. He is just an escape from our misery. What have we got to do with God?

When the boat was about to sink, the rich man made the promise. Did he have any concern with God? Had he any concern about the poor? He was only concerned with escaping his own suffering. After his survival he was confronted with a new grief of losing a million-rupee house, so he invented a way to escape that suffering.

There is no contradiction between these two. The promise made on the boat was a measure to escape suffering and the cunningness of selling his house for a rupee was also an act of avoiding misery. Whatsoever a man does in order to escape suffering cannot be a religious act.

Religiousness is not a way to avoid suffering. Escaping suffering will only take you on a wrong path because in escaping suffering, you have accepted the fundamental lie that you are suffering. "I am suffering" – this fundamental lie has been taken for granted. Then you have to escape suffering.

My suggestion is that there is another way to approach suffering. That is, not to escape suffering but rather to try to know what suffering is. And where is it?

The man who enquires what is suffering and where is it, is

surprised: "Suffering is outside me and I am apart from it. I have never suffered. I am not suffering, so what is the need to escape?" Hence, escape from what? And the man who comes to realize that he is not suffering, what condition does he end up in? The man who comes upon the realization, "I am not suffering" also realizes simultaneously, "I am blissful."

But we believe that we are suffering – I am miserable, I am suffering, I am in grief. This very assumption leads us to another lie, the lie of: How do I escape this suffering?

A man went to visit a mystic and asked, "Please show me how to escape death."

The mystic said, "Go to someone else because I have never died. Death happened to me many times but I never died. Now I am out of this trouble. Now I know that I cannot die. Hence, I don't know any way to avoid death. Go to someone who has died. Ask him, perhaps he can tell you a way to escape death. What can I say, since I have never died! And now I also know that I can never die. So death is not a question for me."

The first issue is that we have accepted death as a matter of fact. Then the second fallacy is that we ask how to avoid it. The first fallacy is that we have accepted that we die. And then the second lie we will have to invent is how to escape death. And the series of lies will continue. But a building that is erected on a foundation of lies, no matter how high it reaches, can never be permanent. A building on a false foundation is bound to collapse any day. When it starts to collapse, we will have to build up other false support to save it from disintegrating. And in this way, we will be caught up in a never-ending circle. Just lies upon lies will line up.

But we are not aware that if we follow the mind, which has taught us one lie, then it will train us in more lies. If you understand it rightly, then the mind is a lie-manufacturing machine; lies are manufactured there.

Just the day before yesterday, I was telling a story…

There was a poor mystic in a village. Day and night he was occupied with prayers to God. His wife got fed up with it. The wives of God-worshipers generally get irritable. She was very worried, worried about bread and butter. She was concerned that the man was thinking about nothing but God.

Finally one day she got angry and said, "Now enough is enough! You constantly say that you are a servant of God. Even a public servant can earn his bread, but what do you get as a servant of God?"

The mystic said, "Don't talk about that please. It's another matter that I have never asked for anything. If I ask then everything is deposited in an account. I have served God for so long; all my good deeds are saved there. I have not asked for anything, that's a different issue."

"Then show me what you got by asking today," she replied.

The man went out, raised his hands toward the sky, and shouted, "Send me a thousand rupees immediately!"

A rich man lived in the neighborhood. He was listening to the whole conversation. He decided to joke with them; he put a thousand rupees in a bag and threw it outside their house, just for fun. When he had seen the man coming out of his house and ordering God to send a thousand rupees immediately, and heard him shouting that he had not asked before for anything from God in return for his services to him, he thought, "This is too much! Let me fool around with them."

The bag of a thousand rupees fell on the ground. The man grabbed it and said, "Thanks! Keep the rest safely. I will take it when it is needed."

He went inside and put down the money in front of his wife. The wife was surprised. She was impressed too, that a thousand rupees were lying in front of her. Now it was better to stay quiet.

The rich man thought that after having a little joke, he would go to them and ask for his money back. But then he saw that a lot of things were being delivered to their house. Then he muttered to himself, "Oh, this is going to be difficult. My joke will be an expensive one. The man has already sent someone to buy things. Things are on their way. Expensive items have been purchased."

The rich man came running. He said, "Sorry brother! I was just joking with you. I threw the money to you!"

The mystic said, "Enough! Didn't you hear me ask God to

send me a thousand rupees? And I thanked him too. Didn't you listen?"

The rich man said, "I heard that. But it was me who threw the money."

"I cannot accept that. My wife is my witness."

"This is a deception! Then let's go to the village court right now, let's go to the magistrate," replied the rich man.

The mystic said, "I won't go with you like this, because I am a poor man, you see my old clothes. You will be riding a horse in your majestic clothes and the magistrate will naturally favor you. Has any magistrate ever favored a poor man? He will take it for granted that you must be saying the right thing. A man with money is always right. Just seeing my poor clothes, he will ask me to drop the bag and return your money."

"No, first give me some good clothes and your horse. If I can go there with honor, only then will I go. Otherwise everything will go wrong," he added.

The rich man had to get his money back. So he gave the poor man his horse and his clothes. He was on foot himself. The mystic rode the horse with honor.

He tied the horse in front of the court, shouting, "Take care of the horse," so that the magistrate could hear inside. He went inside wearing the magnificent clothes.

Then the rich man entered the court and presented his case. He said, "This poor man was praying to God and just as a joke I threw a bag of my money in front of him. Does God ever send money? Have you ever heard that God has sent money? But this crazy man has taken it as his own money. I want my money back!"

The magistrate asked the mystic what he had to say.

The mystic said, "I have nothing to say except that this man has lost his mind, he is mad."

The magistrate asked for evidence.

He replied, "The evidence is that you are just talking about money, but if you ask this man whose clothes I am wearing, he will claim that they belong to him. And if you ask him about the horse, he will say that it is his horse."

The rich man immediately said, "Be quiet! The clothes are mine and even the horse is mine."

The magistrate said, "Case dismissed! This man has gone mad."

The rich man could not understand that it was dangerous to give his clothes and horse to such a mystic who could tell such a great lie. He could tell even more lies.

If we follow the mind, which trains us in the basics of lying, then whatever arrangements we make in our lives are bound to be false.

But we don't even give it a thought that we have accepted the first false assumption provided by our mind: "I am suffering." It is a fallacy. No human being, no soul has ever been suffering. The suffering surrounds, it is on the outside, and the mind says, "*I* am suffering!"

The very identity of "I am suffering" is a fundamental lie. After accepting this lie we have to step into other lies to "forget this suffering." – by drinking alcohol, by prayer, by worship, by dance, by music and so on. How to forget suffering? There is suffering – so how to forget it? And the man who moves in the direction of forgetting suffering can never take a journey toward truth.

Then what is the way? This morning I say to you, don't try to forget suffering. No one has been able to end suffering by forgetting it, because someone who is trying to forget it has assumed that he is suffering. Now, whether he tries to forget it or whatever he does for it, there is no end to suffering.

The way is to know: Where is suffering? What is suffering? Is it really there? First of all, recognize the suffering. For someone who tries to recognize suffering and has focused his eyes on suffering, his suffering disappears like the dewdrops disappear when the sun rises in the morning.

When a man starts observing the suffering with immense attention, the sunrays of witnessing encounter the suffering, and it disappears like dewdrops evaporate, leaving no trace behind. What remains is bliss.

Bliss is not the opposite of suffering. No one can ever be blissful by fighting with suffering. Bliss is the absence of suffering. When suffering is gone, what remains is called bliss.

You must understand this rightly. No one can become blissful by fighting with suffering. Bliss is not the opposite of suffering

– it is not that you have to conquer suffering and bring bliss. Bliss is not the opposite of suffering. Yes, if suffering ends, if it disappears, if it evaporates and the realization comes that there is no suffering, then the state that remains is bliss. Bliss is our nature; we do not have to bring it about.

Suffering is a cloud that covers our inner sky; we have got so attached to it and are so occupied with it that we have totally forgotten what is hiding behind the cloud. We have forgotten that which is beyond the cloud – just as the clouds cover the sun. Let the clouds cover the sun, what difference does it make to the sun? Does the sun lose its light when it is covered by clouds? Does the sun vanish by being surrounded by the clouds? Does being surrounded by the clouds make any difference to the light of the sun? Does it make any difference to the nature of the sun? But if the sun has a mind and is conscious of itself, it will be afraid and start saying, "Oh, now I am dying, the clouds have covered me. What am I supposed to do to get rid of these clouds?"

Then the sun will be in difficulty. How can the sun avoid clouds? How can the sun fight clouds? And the more it fights, the more it escapes, the more it will be obsessed with clouds. It will forget that it is the sun and who it is fighting with – the clouds! But if the sun takes a careful look and discovers: "The clouds are over there and I am here – and there is a great distance between me and the clouds. And no matter how close the clouds come to me, still there is a great distance. And the distance is always infinite..."

No matter how close I try to bring my hands together, still there will be a space between them. The space is infinite. The space between two hands does not disappear by bringing them closer. If the space disappears, then the hands will become one. As long as they are two, a space will be maintained. No matter how close you bring them to each other, a distance will remain.

No matter how close clouds come to... Now the scientists say that two molecules are very close to each other but there is infinite distance between them. The distance is great. It cannot be erased.

No matter how intimate two lovers are, or how closely they sit together, still there will be a distance between them. And this is what hurts lovers – that no matter how intimate they are to each other, still a distance is felt between them. They get married; still the distance does not disappear. They can register their togetherness in court; still the distance does not go away. They suffocate each other; still the space does not cease to exist! The gap exists.

Distance can never be erased. No matter how close the clouds come to the sun, the sun is the sun, the clouds are clouds. And the distance is infinite. But if all the attention goes to the clouds then the difficulty arises. The sun forgets itself and starts bothering about the clouds. Someone who forgets himself, slowly, slowly gets identified with the thing he is focused on, thinking, "I am that." Just like when the sun starts saying, "I am the cloud! I am the dark cloud!" we will say to the sun that it is a condition of ignorance. So is the condition of man's ignorance.

The innermost being is bliss. It is surrounded by the clouds of suffering. It is experiencing suffering all around and has forgotten who it is. We have become identified with our experience so much that we assume, "This is me, this is me, this is what I am! Now how am I going to avoid it? How to escape it? How to get rid of it? Shall I pray? Drink alcohol? Where to go? Suicide or live? What to do? Stand on my feet or do a headstand?" Do whatsoever. As long as you believe in this assumption that you are this suffering that you are experiencing all around, then you are going to be in great difficulty.

One has to withdraw from this phenomenon and examine what suffering is. Where is it? Who am I and where am I?

When a man starts this search, a gap is created between him and suffering. And immediately a transformation takes place. He instantaneously comes to know: "Suffering is over there and I am here. Suffering is that, I am this. Suffering is being experienced, I am the experiencer. Suffering is observed, I am the observer. Suffering is known, I am the knower. I am separate. I am not miserable; I am not one with suffering." And for the man who discovers this, his whole energy gathers at the center of his being. At the innermost being of man there is sun, there is bliss, there is ecstasy. And the man who has even a glimpse of that bursts into laughter, and his laughter continues for infinite lives. Then he is puzzled how crazy people are: "Why are they suffering?"

When Buddha became enlightened, people went to him and

asked, "What did you achieve?" He looked drowned in bliss. They asked, "What did you get?"

Buddha replied, "I got nothing other than that which was always mine. I have discovered that treasure." Buddha said, "Nothing is achieved at all, but what eternally belonged to me and was forgotten has been discovered. Yes certainly, I lost much. I lost suffering, I lost agony, and I lost escape. Much is lost, nothing is gained. What is gained was always there – always there as the most intimate and always available, unconcerned with my being aware of it or unaware of it. That is discovered. Much is lost that did not belong to me but I had believed to be mine. That which was not me but I had taken to be me, all that is gone. Nothing is gained, much is lost."

The man who wakes up from within finds out that there is nothing to gain; whatever is to be achieved is already given to us. There is much to let go of. What we cling to, what we think about. And what are we attached to? What can we cling to? The capacity of man is incredible. The madness of man is unbelievable. The capacity of man to be auto-hypnotized is endless. We are auto-hypnotized by our own suffering. We can be hypnotized by anything.

I will tell you a few incidents, so that you can understand this, and with that I will finish my talk.

During Nehru's lifetime, there were a few people in India who believed that they were Pandit Jawaharlal Nehru. One of them was in my village. He somehow had the idea that he was Jawaharlal Nehru. He was even signing his name as Nehru. He would send a telegram to the guesthouse in Nehru's name, making reservations, and then he would arrive. When people saw him there they would be puzzled and ask him, "Who are you?"

He was Pandit Nehru! After a while he was admitted to a mental asylum. There were many Pandit Nehrus at that time that had to be admitted to asylums.

Once, Pandit Nehru had a chance to meet such a man who thought that he was Nehru. Nehru went to visit a mental asylum. The officials thought that the man – who had been admitted as Pandit Nehru three years ago, had been cured, and was about to be released – should meet the real Pandit Nehru. They also thought that it would be good for him to get the release papers directly from Nehru, but everything went wrong.

The man was brought and they introduced him to Pandit Nehru. Nehru asked him, "Are you totally cured now?"

"I am totally cured. Now I am absolutely fine. Thanks to the asylum authorities. My mind was completely cured in three years. Now I am going back home after being healed," he replied. "By the way, I forgot to ask your name" he enquired.

Pandit Nehru said, "Don't you know who I am? Pandit Jawaharlal Nehru!"

The man started laughing and said, "Don't worry, stay here for three years and you will be also cured. I too came here in the same condition, but in three years I was totally cured. You should have absolutely no worry. The doctors here will give you great treatment. They will cure you in three years."

The man was so identified with the idea of becoming Pandit Nehru that he had lost his own identity.

A similar incident took place in America a few years ago.

Abraham Lincoln's centenary was being celebrated. A look-alike of Abraham Lincoln was found. They created a play that was put on all over the country in the big cities. The man was playing the role of Lincoln. He traveled around the country from town to town, playing the role of Lincoln. His face resembled Lincoln, and through all the constant practice, he forgot his own identity. He started saying he was Abraham Lincoln.

At first people thought that he was joking. But when people were leaving the show as the drama company was to be dissolved, he refused to take off the Lincoln outfit that he wore for the drama.

The members of the company said to him, "Those clothes have to be returned."

The man said, "These clothes belong to me. I am Abraham Lincoln!"

Even then people thought that he was joking. But he was not. He had gone mad. He returned home in those clothes. His family members tried to explain to him that wearing the outfit was all right for acting in a play, but if he was going out on the road wearing them, people would think he was crazy.

The man said, "There is no question of being crazy, I am Abraham Lincoln."

At first his family also took his behavior as a joke, but when he continued like this day after day, they realized he had gone crazy. Even when he was having an ordinary conversation, he was talking in the manner of Lincoln: Lincoln stuttered, so he also stammered in his speech. He was walking like Lincoln. He was repeating the same dialogues that he had learned during the play. Those expressions had become stronger now. He was repeating exactly the same dialogue!

Finally the doctors were consulted. They said, "It is a difficult case. How did he get this idea so strongly that he is Abraham Lincoln?"

For a year he had been surrounded with the cloud of becoming Lincoln – morning, evening, night. He took great pleasure in becoming Lincoln and was given so much respect.

When somebody dresses up like Rama, observe what happens. All the crackpots start offering him flowers, bowing down and washing his feet with great devotion. Then it is natural for that man to go crazy. What is the use of becoming an ordinary man, why not become Lord Rama?

In the same way, this man went mad. He was brought to the doctor.

They had made a device in America, a lie detector. It is a small device, used in court for detecting lies. When someone comes to testify, he has to sit at that device. They will ask for example, "What is the time by your watch?" He will tell them the time by looking at his watch. Why would he lie about such things? The machine measures his heart rate. Then he is asked, "What is two plus two?" and he will answer, "Four." Why would he tell a lie? The machine shows his heart rate. Then he will be asked if he had been stealing. His heart says, "Yes I did," because he has done it, but from outside he denies it. His heart rate becomes elevated with a shock and that shock is registered by the device.

So the man who had become Abraham Lincoln was brought to a lie detector. He was nervous because everybody was asking him whether he was Abraham Lincoln. He was fed up with the questions. So he decided, "No matter how much people ask me, I am going to deny completely that I am Abraham Lincoln." He sat at the lie detector. The doctors were standing around him and they asked him, "Are you Abraham Lincoln?"

He replied, "No, I am not Abraham Lincoln." But the machine detected that he was lying! He was convinced in his heart that he was Abraham Lincoln, so he was lying outwardly. The machine reported that the man was Abraham Lincoln and he was lying!

One can be identified at such a deep level. This is what I call auto-hypnosis. It is to be hypnotized by a certain thought or feeling.

We are hypnotized by suffering; we are living in suffering around the clock, trying to escape it twenty-four hours a day. The hypnotic effect has gone deep by seeing nothing but suffering day and night. And this is the hypnosis of endless lives. That is why we go to someone asking how to get rid of suffering: "How can we avoid disturbance? How to avoid darkness? How to escape ignorance?" And as long as we are searching for a way, we will never be free because the basic thing is a lie. Neither are we in ignorance, nor suffering, nor bondage nor non-liberation. We are not in all that, so there is no question of escaping.

But how can we become aware of this? You will have to focus your attention on your suffering. Don't escape. Let the suffering come, just observe it, recognize it, and know where you are. And as you start knowing, recognizing, you will be amazed to discover that "I am always separate, I am always a witness. Suffering comes and goes away, it surrounds and disappears. Me? I am separate. I know I am the knowing itself."

The very being of man is knowledge, just knowing. All suffering is false. All suffering is untrue. Only knowing is truth. This is what I call meditation. If there is awareness of suffering, meditation begins.

When we sit for the evening meditation, remember this. Try to have this remembrance with you the whole day – are you suffering or are you a witness of suffering? Come for the meditation with this knowing and with this enquiry. And if it becomes absolutely clear to you that "Suffering is over there and I am here," then that is it. The transformation begins which takes you on the inner journey and takes you into truth. We will experiment with this during the evening meditation. We will try to find out how to use this and how to turn in.

I am grateful that you listened to me with such silence and love. And to end this talk, I salute the buddha within you. Please accept my respect.

CHAPTER 6

prayer is love toward existence

FIRST, I WILL TAKE A QUESTION from a friend, who has asked:

Osho,
The other day, you talked about dropping all search. If we drop all search, how will scientific development happen?

I talked about dropping search in the context of discovering the truth within us: it is not only futile to search for that truth, it is a hindrance. But there is also a reality that exists in the outer world. And that outer truth cannot be discovered without search.

Hence, there are two directions. One, which is outside of us: if we are to search for the reality of the outer world, which science does, then we have to search. No truth of the outer world can be discovered without searching.

And there is an inner world: to discover the inner truth, you have to drop all search. If you search, the very search will become a hindrance and the inner truth cannot be discovered.

These two truths are parts of a single larger truth. The inner and outer are both part of a single existence. But someone who wants to start from the outer has to go on an endless search – he has to search, search, and go on searching. And someone who wants to start searching for the inner truth has to stop searching this very moment. Then the inner journey will begin.

Science is a search, and religiousness is an end to all searching. Science discovers by searching, and on an inner journey one attains by dissolving himself, not by searching.

So what I said was not in the context of science. It was in the context of the meditator, of meditation, and the inner journey. I said for the meditator that someone who wants to attain the inner truth should drop all search. Someone who wants to search for scientific reality must search. But remember, no matter how great a scientist someone becomes, and how many truths he discovers in the outer world, he will still be as ignorant about inner truth as any layman.

The vice-versa is also true. No matter how enlightened a man is, no matter how wise he is about the inner world, he may be as ignorant about science as any layman. If you approach Mahavira, or Buddha or Krishna to mend even a small engine, his enlightenment will not work. And if you approach Einstein and enquire about the mysteries of your innermost being, all his scientific knowledge will be of no use.

Scientific research is one kind of search, one dimension. The inner search is another dimension, a totally different direction. That is why there has been a destructive outcome. The countries of the East like India became involved in the inner search; hence, science could not grow because the way to approach inner truth is just the opposite of the outer. On that path, one has to drop logic, thought, and desire, and finally even the search. One has to drop everything. The path of the inner search is letting go of everything. Hence, science could not develop in India.

Scientific search took place in the West. If a man wants to do research in the outer world, he has to apply logic, thinking, experimenting, and searching. Only then is a scientific fact attained. Hence, the West could discover scientific knowledge, but about the inner world it remained primitive.

If a culture is to be complete, then it needs a few people who can devote their energy to the inner search and drop all outer searching. And it also needs people who can go on an outer search and discover the outer reality.

But it is also possible that a man can simultaneously be a scientist and a religious being. No one should think that he cannot have a scientific mind because he is on an inner journey. And there is no need to think either that if a person has become a scientist, he cannot meditate. But if someone wants to do both types of work, then he has to work in both dimensions. When he pursues scientific research, he will have to use logic and experiment. And when he moves on the path of meditation, he will have to put aside logic, experiment and so on. One man can be both; a total human being has to work in both dimensions.

If the people of a country decide to drop all scientific research and not to search for anything, the country will become very peaceful but very weak. It will become peaceful and content, but it will be surrounded by many kinds of suffering. Inwardly it will be blissful, but outwardly it will become a slave, oppressed and downtrodden.

And if a country decides to focus on the outer search, it will become rich, it will become powerful, it will become wealthy, it can become free from physical suffering, but inner turmoil, grief, and madness will cloud the people of the country.

So, for a nation to cultivate the right culture, it would have to work in both dimensions. And if the individual wants to, he can work in both dimensions. But the ultimate purpose of life is religiousness. Science can only make the path of life more beautiful, more powerful, and bring more richness. But ultimate peace and ultimate bliss is attained only through religiousness.

Another friend has asked many questions. I will answer a couple of them today and the rest of them we can discuss tomorrow.

Osho,
To whom should we pray?

If you pray to anyone, it is not prayer. But the very word *prayer* gives us the feeling that we have to pray to someone and we have to beg for something. There must be a demand behind the prayer – the beggar and the begged. So we feel that without a demand and someone to pray to, there can be no prayer. If you simply are left alone, what you will do, how will you pray?

What I am saying is that prayer – if you understand it rightly – is not an activity; it is a mood, a prayerful mood. Praying to someone is not the question, but a prayerful mood. Praying is not the issue, but a prayerful heart. It is totally different approach.

For instance, someone is passing along a road. He has a prayer-less heart. He sees someone has fallen on the side of the road and is dying. That prayer-less heart will go on as if nothing has happened there. But if he is a man with a prayerful heart, then he will do something. He will try to save the injured man, he will be concerned, he will run around getting help, and take him somewhere for treatment.

If there are thorns on the path then the prayer-less heart will pass by just avoiding the thorns, but he will not remove them from the path. A prayerful heart will try to pick up the thorns and remove them from the path. A prayerful heart means a loving heart. When someone loves another individual, it is called love. And when someone's love is not attached to a certain individual, it is toward the whole, I call it prayer.

Love is a connection between two individuals and prayer is a relationship between the individual and the whole. Someone who is loving toward all that is spread all around us – trees, birds and all – that person is in prayer.

When someone is sitting in a temple with folded hands it does not mean that he is prayerful. This is not the meaning of prayer. Prayer means a loving individual. Wherever he looks, he moves, he breathes, he is full of love, each and every moment.

There was a Muslim mystic: all his life he had been praying in the mosque. He became old and one day, people did not see him in the mosque and they thought that he must have died – it was impossible that he would miss coming to the mosque, as long as he was still alive. They went to his house and found him sitting outside. He was playing on a small drum and singing a song.

People asked him, "What are you doing? Have you become an atheist at the end of your life? Are not you going to pray?"

The mystic said, "I could not go to the mosque because of my prayers."

They asked, "What do you mean? You could not go to the mosque because of your prayers? How can you pray without visiting the mosque?"

The mystic showed his chest and said, "I have an ulcer in my chest and there are worms in the wound. When I went to pray, as I knelt down, some worms from the ulcer fell out and I thought that they would die. How would they survive without the ulcer? So I cannot kneel down today when I pray. Hence, I could not come to the mosque today because of my prayers."

Very few people will be able to understand this kind of prayer.

But when I talk about prayer, my meaning is: a prayerful mood, a prayerful attitude. The point is to become prayerful toward all that surrounds us in life.

It is not about worshipping any God or deity. I consider prayer as another word for love, and I say that love is the only prayer. If we get attached to one person, the flow of love stops and love turns into attachment. If we spread our love, and the flow of love is unobstructed, then love becomes prayer.

Think about this. If love stops at one individual, then it becomes attachment and creates bondage. But if it goes on expanding and spreads over all, slowly, slowly becoming unconditional, we have no condition on it that we will love only this person, then it remains just as a state of being so we can only love and nothing else…

There was a Muslim mystic called Rabiya. Somewhere in the Koran it is written: "Hate Satan." She erased that sentence from her Koran. One of her friends who was visiting asked, "Who made this correction in the Koran? Can anyone make a correction in the Koran? No one can make a change in the Holy Koran!"

Rabiya replied, "I had to make that change because it is written in the Koran that we should hate Satan and I have become unable to hate. From the moment my prayers were fulfilled, since then I cannot hate. Even if Satan stands in front of me, still I am bound to love him. It does not matter who is standing in front of me. It is about me, because I have nothing but love. So I had to erase this statement. This sentence is not right. Now whether God comes in front of me or Satan, I can only pray, I can only love.

Hence, it is difficult for me even to recognize who is a god and who is a devil. And there is no need to differentiate either because I will do the same no matter who is there!"

When love stops at one person, it becomes bondage, it becomes attachment. As if a river stops and turns into a puddle. Try to understand this, that when a river stops flowing, it becomes a puddle of water. If it stops flowing and starts circulating in one place, a pond is created. It will become stagnant and will not flow. If the river stops, it turns into a pond. And if the river flows and spreads, then it becomes the ocean.

If the current of love within you makes a pond around one person or around a few people – around your son, your wife, your friend and so on – then the flow of love becomes rotten. Then nothing comes out of that love except stink. That is why all families have become the center of stench. They all have become ponds and a foul smell is bound to arise from a stagnant pond. All our relationships are rotten because the moment love stops, it starts stinking. There is nothing between a husband and wife except stink. There is nothing between father and son.

Where love stops flowing, it loses its incorruptibility, its innocence, its freshness. And we try to stop love because of our attachment and our fear that it should not spread onto others. We all try to prevent it with the idea that if it no longer spreads, we will get more of it for ourselves. The interesting fact is that the moment it stops it becomes stagnant, and then nothing is gained. It should grow; it should expand and should continue to expand. The more it expands, the more it reaches its maximum expansion, the more it is transformed into prayer. And finally, if love goes on expanding, it reaches the ocean and that love becomes prayer.

So, "To whom?" is not the question. When you ask "To whom?" then you are asking "To whom can I attach my prayers – to Rama, to Krishna, to Mahavira or to Buddha?" So the love we have attached to a certain individual gets projected even in our prayers. If a devotee of Shiva is crazy enough, he will refuse to go to a Rama temple. If someone is a devotee of Krishna, he will not worship Rama. Even prayer is attachment!

There are so many temples at the sides of the roads but everyone has their own temple where they worship. Even temples are divided among devotees. A temple should belong only to the god. But everybody has their own temple. There are sects even in those temples. Even the devotees of Mahavira constantly fight court cases because someone's Mahavira wears clothes and someone's Mahavira stays naked. So the one who believes in a naked Mahavira would not allow clothes on the statue and the believer of a clothed Mahavira will not allow nudity on his statue. And the conflict continues! It is so ridiculous.

I have heard…

There was a festival in a village and a procession to celebrate Ganesh was happening. In the village, people from each caste made their own statue of Ganesh. The brahmins had their own Ganesh, the blacksmiths had their own Ganesh, the merchants had their own Ganesh, and the sudras had their own Ganesh. All these statues took part in the procession. The brahmins' Ganesh was always in the front. That was the rule of the village.

But that day the brahmins were late in taking their Ganesh out into the procession and the Ganesh of the oil seller arrived first. When the brahmins came and saw this, they could not tolerate it. Is it possible that the god of the oil seller goes ahead of the brahmins' god? They started shouting, "Take this bastard oil-seller Ganesh away!" Now even Ganesh became low caste! "Take this statue to the back. It has never happened before – the Ganesh of the brahmins should come in the front." And the oil seller's Ganesh was forcefully pushed back. The brahmins' Ganesh was brought to the front.

If there is any god called Ganesh somewhere, he must be hitting his head after watching this. Does any of this have anything to do with Ganesh: "My Ganesh"? Even with that, there are differences.

Even prayer creates bondage, it asks "To whom? Who should we pray to?" Don't pray to anyone. The very meaning of prayer is to the whole of existence; prayer is love toward existence that is spread everywhere, the ultimate which is ever expanding.

It is not a matter of folding your hands, that you just fold your hands together in prayer, and finished. It is a matter of living it around the clock. Live in a way that your love continues to flow toward the whole, only then is prayer fulfilled. But the cunning people have invented tricks to avoid real prayer. They go to the temple for a few minutes with folded hands and say that they have done their prayers. These are dishonest tricks to avoid real prayer.

Love is prayer. Love for the whole is prayer. Live your life in such a way that your love does not become confined. Create such a way of living that your love expands. Live your life in such a way that your love does not cease at anyone, it does not stagnate. Live in a way that slowly, slowly your love becomes unconditional.

Our love is always conditional. We say that if you are a certain way, then I can love you. If you act like this, then I will love you. If you love me, then I will love you. When a condition is applied to love it turns into a trade, a thing of the marketplace. When I say that I will love only if...

I have heard...

There was a great saint in India – I will not mention his name because mentioning a name in this country is inviting great trouble. A great saint who was a devotee of Rama was brought to a Krishna temple.

He said to the statue, "Please appear to me in the form of Rama with bow and arrow in your hand, otherwise I will not bow down my head to you!"

What a ridiculous statement! He is putting a condition even on his love, that he will bow down only when the statue appears with a bow and arrow in its hands. It means that he will bow down his head with a condition. First his god has to follow his order, only then will he pay his regards. This devotee is even trying to become the master of his god; he is trying to be possessive. He is saying: "Behave the way I want, then I will bow down to you. Otherwise the matter is finished, our relationship is finished!"

This kind of mind cannot be prayerful. A conditioned man can never be prayerful. Unconditional! My love is not based on how you are, I love you because I can give only love to you. I want to share only love; only love can be shared by me. I have nothing except love to share. How you behave is not an important question for me.

I will finish my talk with a short story and talk about the remaining questions tomorrow.

Early one morning, a man came to Buddha and spat on him. Buddha wiped his face with his shawl and said to the man, "Do you want to say anything more?" If someone spits on you, would you be able to ask, "Is there anything more you want to say?"

The monks who were sitting around Buddha became furious. They said to Buddha, "What are you asking him! 'Do you want to say anything else?'"

Buddha replied, "As far as I know, this man has so much anger in his mind that he is not able to express it through words, so he expressed it through spitting. I understood that he wants to say something and that his anger is too much to be expressed through words. So he expressed it by spitting. When love is too much to be expressed through words, you say it with a hug. What he expressed by spitting, I understood. So I asked him, "Have you got something more to say?"

The man was puzzled because he never imagined that somebody would respond to his spitting in that way. He got up and left. He could not sleep the whole night and the next day he came back to beg for forgiveness. He fell at the feet of Buddha and started crying. When he got up, Buddha asked, "Do you have anything more to say?"

The monks around him said, "What are you saying?"

Buddha replied, "Look. I told you yesterday. Now this man again wants to express something, but he is so overwhelmed by his feelings that only tears are flowing. He is not able to find words, so he is touching my feet. Words are not enough. I understood it."

Buddha asked the man, "Do you want to express something else?"

The man said, "Nothing else. I just wanted to say that I could not sleep the whole night because I felt you have always loved me, but by spitting on you I don't deserve your love anymore. Now I will never receive your love."

Buddha replied, "Look! What a wonder! Did I love you because you were not spitting on me? Was this the reason for my love toward you? You were not the reason for my love. I love because I am helpless, I cannot do anything other than love."

When a candle is lit, whoever passes nearby receives the candlelight. The candle's sharing of light does not depend on how you are. Light is the very self-nature of the candle, it showers. Whoever passes by, it does not matter whether he is an enemy or a friend. Even someone who wants to extinguish the candle receives its light when he comes close by.

So Buddha said, "I love because I am love. How you are has no meaning for my love. Whether you spit on me or throw stones on me or touch my feet, all this has no significance. It has no connection with my love. How you are is not the context of my love. You can do whatever you feel; let me do what I feel. I am love, so I will continue loving. You continue doing what you are bound to do. And see for yourself whether the love is victorious or the hate."

This man is full of love; this man is prayerful. Such a consciousness is called prayer.

I will talk about the remaining questions tomorrow.

CHAPTER 7

belief: the greatest obstacle in the search for truth

THIS EVENING, I am going to talk about the search, and how to know the truth. Once you come to know the truth, there is nothing left to know. Until we attain that truth, we live in agony, like a fish thrown out of water onto the sand. And when we attain the truth, we become as peaceful and blissful as the fish when it manages to return to the ocean. Tonight, I will talk about one more direction and door to search for that bliss and nectar.

How to search for the truth? What is the way? What are the means? Man seems to have only one instrument – thought. There seems to be only one kind of energy: man seeks through thinking. But no one has ever attained the truth by thinking and pondering. No one ever reaches anywhere by thinking. You may be able to know something about the outside world by thinking, but that which abides within can never be known that way. And we spend our lives just thinking and thinking.

No one knows how man got caught in this illusion that by thinking he will be able to know everything. There is no relation between thinking and knowing. The truth is, only someone who drops thinking can know. Thinking and contemplating clouds the mind like smoke; it covers the mirror of the mind with dust. The mirror of the mind is transparent and innocent only when there is no thought in the mind.

But you will ask, "Shall we then believe, have faith, in order to attain the truth?" Even that will not do. Faith is an even lower state than thinking. Faith means blindness. Neither faith can make you attain the truth nor can thinking give it to you. You have to rise higher than that. If you understand this, only then will it be clear to you how to search.

So, first let us try to understand what belief is. Belief is blind acceptance. Faith implies: neither do I think, nor do I search, nor do I meditate, nor do I move into thoughtlessness; I just accept what others say. The inner being of someone who believes in others in this way remains hidden. He does not even take the challenge to wake up. And we all live our lives believing in others.

You must have heard a story… But the story is incomplete – it always happens that people are told incomplete stories. And if a half truth is told, it is more dangerous than a lie. Why? Because a lie is perceived as a lie, but an incomplete truth does not appear false. It appears as truth. And remember, there is nothing such as partial truth. Either truth is total or it is not there. If someone says to you that he loves you a little, you will exclaim, "Partial love?" Have you ever heard of such a thing? There is nothing like partial love, either you love someone, or you do not.

Anything important is never partial; the moment it is divided it is destroyed. But many partial truths are widespread. This story is also widespread in an incomplete form. It is taught in every school – you must have read it in your childhood. And your children too will read this incomplete story. We all know the story…

There was a merchant who sold hats. He was going to sell his hats in a fair and, getting tired on the way, he took a rest under a tree. He fell asleep. The monkeys came down from the tree and saw that the merchant was wearing a hat. So they took the hats from his basket and put them on. When the merchant woke up, he saw that his basket was empty. He laughed because he was familiar with the habits of monkeys. He looked up and saw that all the monkeys were wearing hats, sitting on the tree with great pride! Other than monkeys, no one feels such pride in wearing a hat. How can pride increase by putting on a hat? And if it is a Gandhi cap, the arrogance enhances greatly!

Those hats must have been just such hats, since the monkeys were sitting with such superiority. Then the merchant took off his hat and threw it. All the monkeys threw their hats. Monkeys are imitators, they are ready to imitate anyone; they never think or consider for themselves. After all they are monkeys – why would they think, they believe. When the merchant threw his hat, they followed him.

The merchant collected the hats and continued on his journey. You must have read the story up to this point. I want to tell you the rest of the story.

The merchant's son grew up and started working in his father's business. Unintelligent children always follow the footsteps of their fathers. It is evidence of their lack of intelligence. A son should move ahead of his father. But neither do most fathers like their sons to move ahead of them nor do most sons have the courage to move ahead of their fathers.

So the son also started selling hats. He too went on his way to that fair. And he stopped under that same tree where his father had stopped for a nap, saying to himself that he should rest just where his father had. He put his bag under the same tree as his father had. The monkeys were watching from the tree. They were not the same monkeys – they must have been the children of the earlier monkeys. They saw the hats and they too must have heard the story about their forefathers wearing the hats. The merchant's son fell asleep. The monkeys came down, put on the hats, and climbed back up the tree.

The merchant's son woke up and laughed. But his laughter was phony. It was based on the story of his father. His father had told him, "Don't ever be afraid. If the monkeys take the hats, don't worry. It's not difficult to get them back. Just throw your hat."

The son took off his hat and threw it. But a miracle happened. None of the monkeys threw his hat. One of the monkeys couldn't get a hat earlier, so he climbed down the tree, took the son's hat, put it on, and climbed back up the tree.

The monkeys had learned the lesson. But the man had not

learned. The monkeys had been deceived once. They were not going to be deceived again and again. This part of the story is not mentioned in any book. And until this half of the story is written, the story is dangerous.

There are a few people who follow others; they never walk on their own. Some people just learn readymade answer from others; they never search for any answer by themselves. Some people always bring borrowed solutions; they have no solutions of their own. And new challenges appear every day, but our solutions are old and great difficulty arises.

Even in the search for the truth, imitation will not work. In the search for the truth, readymade answers will not work. Things memorized from the Gita, the Koran or the Bible will not be of any help in the search for the truth. One has to search by himself.

And all believers are nothing more than imitators. They lose the dignity of being human and become monkeys. Anyone who blindly follows others loses his right to be a human being. Only the gurus benefit from the phenomenon of a man becoming a monkey instead of a man. Hence, there is a big crowd of monkeys gathered around every guru.

People who don't have courage to do anything themselves and start following others are bound to be easily exploited. But being exploited is not the worst thing which happens to them – they are also forever deprived of knowing the truth, because the first step in the journey of truth is to stand on your own feet. Your own guts, your own courage, your own capability, are essential for your search. Someone who is not ready for that – saying he will borrow it from others, will touch someone's feet, hold someone's tail, or just follow someone and everything will happen – he is mistaken. Nobody reaches anywhere by believing.

Belief is borrowed thought. But does it mean that if we start thinking, we will reach somewhere? If we go on thinking on our own, we will reach somewhere? Now, if you look a little deeper into it, you will see that even your thoughts are not actually yours. The believer is a secondhand phenomenon and it seems that a thinker does not believe, but if you examine his thoughts deeply, you will find out that all his thoughts are borrowed. There is just a little difference; the difference is that he has gathered his thoughts by applying logic. He has not collected his thoughts blindly, he has exercised thinking. But what can a man think? What can he think? Can that which is unknown be thought out? Can you think about that which is unknown, that which is unknowable? We can only think about the known. We cannot think about the unknown. What is unknown is unknown. How can we think about the unknown?

Believing will not work because beliefs are borrowed from others. Thinking will give a little strength and courage. It will help you to stand on your own feet. But even thinking alone cannot take you there because thoughts can reach only to the limit of the known. Beyond the known, thinking ends, it gets lost.

Can you think about something which is absolutely unknown to you? You might say – often! You might say that often we think or imagine such things, for instance, sitting on a golden horse and flying in the sky. In this example, the golden horse is unknown to us. Neither have we seen a golden horse nor does a golden horse fly. All of this is unknown, still we can think about it.

But no, this is not thinking about the unknown. You have knowledge of a horse, you know about gold, and you have seen birds flying. Your mind puts these three together and creates a flying golden horse. There is nothing new in it at all. It is a new product assembled from three things.

So, in the process of thinking, one can accumulate many thoughts and cultivate a thought which will appear to be new. But that newness is just apparent, not actual. It will not help you to discover the truth. If you spread out all your thoughts and examine which ones are your own, you will find that all thoughts are gathered from others, heard from somewhere, read and accumulated – and then a new collection is generated. The new compilation will appear to be unique, will seem to be original.

But no thought is original. Thoughts cannot be original. Thoughts too are borrowed. A believer is a scrounger, but he borrows blindly. A thinker is also a scrounger, but he applies reasoning, he uses reasoning and logic. But what can be gained from reasoning? What has been achieved by it?

The believer becomes a theist and the logician becomes an atheist. Neither of them is religious. Neither the theist is religious nor is the atheist religious. A theist is a believer, he has caught hold of others' beliefs. An atheist also grabs other people's thoughts, but using the process of reasoning. But what can be proved by logic? Logic does not prove anything. Reasoning is a game played by grown-up children. Grown-ups can play a game called reasoning.

I have heard…

A man went to a big city in America and announced that he had brought such a unique horse that no one would have ever seen a horse like it. Such a horse had never existed before. It was absolutely unique. The unique thing about the horse was that its tail was placed where its mouth should be, and its mouth was where its tail should be.

The man starting selling tickets at ten dollars each to see the horse. Thousands of people gathered. If you had been in that city, you would also have gone there. Everybody from the city without exception was there, it was so important to see the horse. The hall was full and people were yelling, "Hurry up! Bring the horse out."

The man said, "Wait just a little. It is not an ordinary horse, it will take time to bring him out." After a while, it became even more difficult because the place was totally packed. Then the horse was brought onto the stage and the curtains lifted. Immediately everyone could see that the horse was absolutely ordinary, just like any other horse. They shouted, "Why are you deceiving us? Are you joking? The horse is completely ordinary."

The man said, "Be quiet! Try to understand my argument. I had declared that the horse's mouth is where the tail should be and its tail is where the mouth should be. Look carefully!"

They looked carefully; it was an ordinary horse, its tail was where the tail should be and its mouth was where the mouth should be. But then they realized and burst into laughter… The bridle was fastened on the horse's tail instead of its mouth.

The man said, "Remember what I announced: the mouth is where the tail should be and the tail is where the mouth should be. The bridle is strapped onto the tail. Can't you see it?"

There was no way to say anything. The argument was right. People left quietly.

But logic can play only up to a limit. Nothing more can be achieved by it; the most it can do is to place the tail where the mouth is and the mouth where the tail is. Logic can do no more than that. Things remain the way they are, logic does not make any difference. Hence, logic is a double-edged sword – you can use it for or against anything, if you wish. It does not make any difference.

I had a very close friend who was a great lawyer. He was overloaded with work, with a law practice in India and in London. He was stressed by it; often he was not even able to prepare for his cases.

One day, he went to court to fight a lawsuit. And he got confused between the clients and forgot which side of the argument he was defending and which side he was going to oppose. He began to speak against his own client. His client became very nervous: "What is this man saying?" For half an hour, the lawyer pleaded against his client. His client almost stopped breathing, thinking that he was about to die because his own lawyer was trying to plead him guilty!

The lawyer pleaded so forcefully that even the other side's lawyer was stunned, that there was nothing left for him to prove: "What is going on here?"

Then my friend's clerk went to him and whispered, "What are you doing? You are pleading against your own client!"

The lawyer said, "Is that so? Wait a minute." And he turned toward the judge and continued, "Your honor! I have said everything the lawyer for the defense would be presenting to you. Now I will refute it all."

Logic has no meaning at all; it is just a game. It is just a game! The pundits are playing the game, the lawyers are playing the same game, and the politicians are playing the same game. Logic is just a game. And as long as people are engaged in the game of argumentation, there cannot be any decision about the truth. Logic has no significance; it speaks for this side and it can also plead for the other side. The arguments which prove the existence of God can also be used to disprove God.

The believer, the theist, says, "How can this creation come into existence without a creator? This world, this creation does exist, so then there must be a creator because everything has a creator. There has to be a creator for any creation." He says, "This is my argument to prove the existence of God. There must be a creator of this world and God is the creator."

The atheist says, "We accept your argument, but it does not prove the existence of God. It actually disproves the hypothesis. It is all right to say that everything needs a creator: God exists, so who created God? If you say that without a creator God, the world cannot come into being, then we accept that God created the world. Now we ask you: Who created God? How can God exist without a creator? Since without creation nothing is created…"

This game can continue and you go on playing it. The theist and the atheist have been playing it for thousands of years.

Once it happened…

There was a great theist and a great atheist in a village. And the village was in great difficulty. Wherever scholars happen to be, difficulty arises; the theist was preaching that God exists and the atheist was preaching that there is no God. Day and night they were harassing people. People got bored and said, "Please leave us alone. We don't care whether there is God or not. Let us do our work."

But they were not ready to give up. First one would go and preach to people and then the other would go and try to convince people in his way. Finally the villagers said, "It is so difficult. We have to make a decision."

The whole world is in the same situation. Muslims, Hindus, Christians, Jainas, Buddhists, all are bothering the whole world. The representatives of each different religion visit people: one religion sends its monks, the other sends its saints, and another sends its priests. They all preach different things and create a disturbance.

The villagers suggested, "Both of you should sit together one evening and argue with each other. We will follow whoever wins the debate. We always follow the victorious. We don't care whether there is God or not."

The debate took place on a full-moon night; the whole village gathered. It was a unique debate. The theist presented such strong arguments that he proved the existence of God. The atheist also presented strong arguments and he proved that there is no God.

Finally the theist got so influenced by the atheist that he became an atheist. And the atheist got so convinced by the arguments of the theist that he converted into a theist!

The villagers were in the same difficulty because they still had a theist and an atheist. They said, "What did we gain? Our trouble remains exactly the same!"

Logic does not have much significance. Logic does not have much meaning. What logic proves, it can also disprove. Logic is just a game, just fooling around. Hence, nothing has ever been proved by logic. Has it been proved that the Hindus are right? If it had been proved, the whole world would have been converted to Hinduism. Has it been proved that Jainism is right? If it was so, the whole world would have been converted to Jainism. If it had been proved that Muslims are right, the whole world would have been converted to Islam. Nothing is proved. Nothing can be proved. Nothing is ever proved on the path of logic; the game just goes on.

And we do not even understand the game that the pundits play because it is very subtle. It is such a subtle game that they go on arguing and people don't know anything about these things. People just accept.

Hence, people have decided that an individual's religion is determined by his birth. It is a cheap trick because if it is to be decided by logic, it would never be determined. Your life would have come to its end, but you would not have been able to decide whether you are a Hindu or a Mohammedan or a Christian. That is why we have invented a cheap solution, that the religion will be decided by where you were born. Now, do you have any choice in where you are born? If a Muslim man has a child, his son becomes a Mohammedan. Why? If the son wants to determine his religion by rational thinking, his life will pass by, but he will not be able to decide whether he wants to become a Hindu or a Muslim. It can never be decided. Hence, we have invented a trick whereby there is absolutely no need to decide.

Now, what relation does birth have with being a Hindu or a Muslim? It is a very crazy idea! Tomorrow someone from the Indian Congress Party can start saying that his son belongs to his party because he is from that party. The son of a Communist can say that he is a Communist since his father belongs to the Communist Party. Such stupidity is not prevalent yet, but it will happen because the same logic applies. And when nothing can be decided, people will come to the conclusion to decide it by birth.

Can a principle be proved by birth? Can truth be determined by birth? But for thousands of years we have been caught up in logic and belief systems. Some people get lost through following faith. Some people get lost through following logic. And nothing has ever been decided because it is just groping in the dark, so what can be decided?

It happened...

An emperor decided that he would expel all untruths, that he would not allow any kind of lie in his country. If anybody told a lie, he would be hanged! And that every day someone will be hanged, it will happen regularly, so the whole city can watch what happens to a liar.

He was unaware of something. All law experts are aware of the fact that crime is not stopped by capital punishment or flogging or by locking someone in jail. Nothing is stopped that way. Crime goes on increasing. We send thieves to prison; still there the number of thieves increases. We lock the corrupt in jails, still corruption increases. The people who are employed to check the corruption prove to be doubly corrupt themselves. And the security guards who are supposed to catch the thieves prove to be master thieves. They are bound to end up that way.

About a hundred years ago in England, thieves were whipped publicly in the marketplace, so that the people of the village should see what happens to a thief. But it had to stop – and do you know why they had to stop it? Whenever the thieves were whipped in London, thousands of people gathered to watch. And it was found that while thousands of people were busy watching the flogging, pickpockets were in action. A thief was whipped and the crowd gathered to watch, and while they were watching the show, their pockets were picked.

Then they realized that it was a futile madness; public punishment had no significance. It was creating a good condition for the pickpockets. When the crowd was gathered, the pickpockets picked their pockets!

But this emperor said, "I will stop the lies!"

The elderly people of the village said, "It is difficult even to detect a lie, how will you stop it? How will you decide what is untruth and what is truth?"

He replied, "All will be decided." But then he got worried about how to determine it.

There was an old mystic in the village. The emperor decided to call the mystic and ask him about it, because the mystic talked so much about the truth. He called him and said, "I have decided to hang a liar on the gate tomorrow, since it is first day of the New Year, so that the whole village can watch."

The mystic asked him, "How will you determine truth and untruth?"

The emperor said, "Is there no logic which can determine what truth is and what is untruth? I will employ all the scholars of the country for that."

The mystic said, "All right. I will meet you tomorrow morning at your gate."

The emperor asked: "What do you mean?"

He replied, "I will be the first one to enter the gate. You should be there with your team of scholars. I will tell a lie. If you want to hang someone then I will be the first."

The emperor said, "I just called you for advice! What are you talking about?"

He said, "We'll talk tomorrow at the gate. Be there with your scholars."

The emperor arrived at the gate along with his scholars. The gate was opened and the mystic entered, riding his donkey.

The emperor asked, "You, on the donkey! Where are you going?"

"I am going to hang on that gallows," replied the mystic.

The emperor asked the scholars, "Please decide whether he is telling the truth or a lie."

The scholars said, "We give up. This man is very complicated. Nothing can be determined in this case. If we say that he is telling the truth then we have to send him to the gallows. And we are not supposed to hang a truthful man. And if we say that he is telling a lie, we will have to hang him. And if he is hanged, what he was telling becomes true."

The mystic asked, "Tell me what truth is and what is untruth. Decide it by your reasoning. And if you cannot determine that now, come to me when you are able to decide and then you can make the law."

That law was never enforced because it is difficult to decide what truth is. It is difficult to determine by logic because logic cannot determine anything, it is just a game. When one of the two logics wins, that does not mean that the victorious one is right. It only means that the victorious one is more skillful in playing the game. It means nothing else. When one of the two logical arguments wins, that does not mean that the victorious one is the truth; the victorious is more skillful in playing the game, that's all.

When two people are playing chess and one of them wins, does he become the true one? No, he is just more skillful. Does the loser become the untruthful one? No, he was just not as skillful. Victory or defeat does not prove truth or untruth; it only proves whether the player is more skillful or less skillful. Does the more competent one win and say, "What I am is true"? Logic is also a game of chess, played with words and thoughts, nothing more than that.

Hence, no one should think that when I say you cannot attain the truth by believing, it means that you can attain it by logic. I am saying, neither you can attain it by logical argument nor by thinking. Then you will say to me: it cannot be attained by believing and when you don't want to believe, you have to apply thinking; but then you say again that it is not even attained by thinking. This is exactly what I am saying.

It is as if a man gets a thorn in his foot and we take another thorn in order to pull this thorn out. And he replies, "What are you doing? I am in pain with one thorn and you are going to use another thorn!" You would say to him, "Don't worry, I'm going to use this thorn to pull the other thorn out. If the first thorn was not in your foot, there would be no need for this thorn. But since the first thorn is already there, we have to use the second thorn."

You take the first thorn out with the help of the second thorn. Then the man starts worshipping the second thorn and asks you to put it back in his wound because it has done a great kindness to him; it has helped to remove the first thorn. You will say to him, "You are crazy. That thorn has taken out the first thorn, and now it is useless. Throw this one away too."

Rational thinking has a utility and that is to free you from belief. It has no more utility than that. Thinking is useful to liberate you from believing. If the thorn of thinking has removed the thorn of believing, its work is done. Then both thorns are equal; then both have to be thrown away.

But then where to go? Then move into thoughtlessness. Then you have to move into the dimension where there is not even a single thought, the mind is absolutely silent and serene. There is not even any thinking. Where you are not thinking, "What is the truth" and where you have dropped all thinking. Where you are just silent, just being. If there is any truth it will be perceived; if there is nothing, that nothing will be perceived. You will perceive that which is. You are so silent that you are just witnessing. You are just like a mirror, witnessing that which is.

You are not thinking; the mirror does not think. When you are standing in front of a mirror, it does not think that you are beautiful or ugly; you are good or bad; you are black or white. The mirror does not think. You see in the mirror only that which is, because a mirror just reflects.

But there are some mirrors which do not show what you are but show what you are not. You must have seen some mirrors in which you look much taller or fatter or more bent than you are. There are mirrors like that. Those mirrors don't have a flat and clear surface and the image is slanting, rounded or upside down. The more crooked the surface of a mirror, the more distorted a reflection it will create.

There are two keys for the search for truth: one, drop thinking; and the other, have a straightforward and clear mind. The surface must be clean and straightforward, not uneven. That's it! In such a mind, the truth is reflected. We come to know that which actually is and are liberated from that which is not.

Thinking works as dust on the mind because thoughts get stuck and cover the surface. Such a thick curtain of thoughts is formed that when you try to look through them, you don't see that which is. This curtain which is in between functions as a barrier.

Suppose a man believes there is no God. It is a thought. He

has assumed there is no God. Now wherever he will look, he is bound to perceive the nonexistence of God.

If someone is dying on the road, he will say, "How can there be a God in the world when people die like this?" If someone is poor, he will comment, "How can there be a God in the world where poverty exists?" This kind of man will count the thorns when he comes close to a flower: "There is one single flower, thousands of thorns – where one flower is surrounded by thousands of thorns, how can there be God?" He is prejudiced that there is no God. Everywhere he will invent tricks, ways, arguments, and thoughts in order to deny God. He is prejudiced and prejudice makes the mirror of the mind uneven.

Now take the example of another kind of man, who says there is God. If his shop is running well, he will say, "The shop is doing well because of God." It is very funny – poor God has nothing whatever to do with your shop. Otherwise he will also suffer with you. But the man will claim, "See, with God's grace everything is going well." If someone is sick in his house and then gets well, he will say, "See, God's grace." As if the other sick people who did not get well were enemies of God. God has special grace on your patient. You are so privileged. If someone has lost a penny and he finds it again, he will say, "See the grace of God, I found what I had lost." As if God is running a lost and found business. As if God is your accountant who keeps an account of your every cent.

A prejudiced man extracts his own meaning from whatever is happening around him. Then he becomes incapable of seeing that which is.

I have heard...

A poor man bought a cow from the king of the village. He thought that a cow from the king must be a very good one. But he forgot that it was very easy to buy the king's cow, but to look after it was very difficult. Many people get into trouble by buying a king's cow...

There are many kinds of king's cows that later on prove to be very expensive. Now, this man brought the king's cow home with him. He put some hay in front of it. It was dry hay; how could the poor man afford green grass? And the cow would have been grazing on soft grass from Kashmir. When it saw the hay, the cow started a hunger strike. Since Gandhi started the tradition of hunger strikes, even cows, bulls, horses, donkeys are all going on hunger strike. The cow launched a hunger strike immediately. It said, "I won't eat any more," and stood meditatively with closed eyes. It just stopped opening its eyes.

The poor man tried hard to persuade the cow: "I consider you my mother. I am a disciple of the Shankaracharya: we really consider you our mother. O mother, have mercy on me! I am your poor son. There are rich sons and there are poor sons and mothers don't discriminate between the rich and the poor sons. A mother treats them equally."

But why should the cow listen? No cow has ever called any man her son! Until now, no cow has made the mistake of calling a man her son. The Hindu goes on shouting that the cow is his mother. And no cow has testified until now that it is true, because no cow would think a man compatible to being her child!

The cow was not convinced. The man got very angry, but what could he do? He asked the old men of the village what he should do. One of them advised, "There is no need to do anything. Just buy a pair of green glasses and put them on the cow."

He bought the glasses and put them on the cow. The cow looked down, saw the green grass, and started grazing. The grass was dry but the glasses were green. The cow was deceived.

We all get deceived. We see according to our spectacles. And anyone who is wearing the spectacles of prejudice can never know that which is. We all are wearing glasses. Someone is wearing the spectacles of Hinduism, someone of Islam, someone's eyes are covered by communism, someone's eyes by atheism, and so on; there are thousands of spectacles of different kinds available in the market. And there is not even a single person who is going without glasses. Everyone has their own glasses. They look through their glasses and then everything is distorted. That which is, is not perceived and what is perceived is colored by our glasses. We are not able to see more than that.

The revolution happened in Russia in 1917. There was a small school in a village, with just one student and one teacher. Later, after the revolution, there were two students in the school. Still there was only one teacher. The Soviet newspapers reported that there had been such progress in the field of education in every village that education had almost doubled. There had been a one hundred percent development: the number of students had doubled in the school in that village.

An American journalist went to the village and he reported that there was no limit to lies: in the school there used to be only one student and now there were two students. They still had only one teacher.

The journalist reported that there was no growth in education in Russia. There were still schools with only two students, with only one teacher. Russian newspapers were reporting that the education has doubled, multiplied, that the number of students had doubled. But no one is telling a lie. Everyone has their own glasses and their own way of looking through them.

We must understand that as long as we are full of prejudice, the mirror of consciousness cannot be clean. So, freedom from all prejudice is absolutely essential. Liberation is needed. Without being free from prejudice, no one gains the right to reflect the truth as it is. The truth is constantly being reflected, but the thoughts and beliefs we carry in our minds distort the reflection, the emotions completely distort everything. Our very feelings are projected and we start seeing exactly what we want to see.

When you pass by a Muslim mosque, you don't see anything there worth folding your hands in respect. But if a Mohammedan passes by without paying his regards, he will feel as if he has done something wrong and he will regret it.

When you pass by a statue of the monkey god, then you automatically fold your hands. Someone else standing there sees your actions and thinks, "What a strange person who is worshipping a red stone with folded hands. What is there to worship?"

We perceive only that for which we are prepared. And we go on projecting it. This applies on all levels. When a man understands that he is full of prejudice, then there is no difficulty for him to be free of that prejudice. There is absolutely no difficulty for him to drop his prejudice and start seeing things as they are. And at the same time, he also drops the illusion of thinking, the illusion that he will know what is by pondering over it.

We can never know what is by thinking about it. If it was possible to know by thinking, we would have known it by now, since we have been thinking so much. We have been thinking for many lives. We have created a mountain of thoughts. We have been thinking all our lives. We are all thinking, but where has anyone arrived by thinking? We go on thinking and thinking. We pile up great mountains of arguments, words, and thoughts. Knowledge is gathered, yet we stand still.

Ask any pundit what he has known. He will repeat the Upanishads, the Brahma Sutras, and so on. Then you ask him, "No, I am not asking you to repeat what you have learned, rather I am asking you what you actually know. We are not asking you what you have been thinking about; we are asking what have you experienced. What is your direct perception? We are not asking about philosophy."

And remember, the word *philosophy* and the word *darshan* do not mean the same. These words have become synonyms in India and people like Dr. Radhakrishnan write about Indian philosophy. There is no other expression as wrong as this one. *Darshan* does not mean *philosophy* at all. *Philosophy* means thinking and *darshan* means seeing. There is a great difference between *darshan* and *philosophy*. *Darshan* and *philosophy* are as different as earth and sky.

A blind man thinks about light, he does not see it. Hence, whatever a blind man says about light is his philosophy. A man with eyes can see light, so whatever he says about light is his *darshan*, it is not his philosophy.

There is no such thing as "Indian philosophy"; it is an absolute lie. Indian *darshan* is a valid term. A Western thinker has coined a new word for *darshan*: *philosia*. He says it is a matter of seeing, not thinking.

If we are blind, what can we think about light? A blind man can try and try and try to read... There are books for blind people – and the truth is that all the scriptures belong to the blind. They are trying to read those books, trying to extract meaning out of them and making an effort to understand them. And the interesting thing is that the light is showering all around.

A blind man will read in a book, "What is light? What is the meaning of light? What is the definition of light? What is light made of? What is it not? Who are the people who perceive light? Who are the people who do not see light?" A blind man will read all about light. But a man with eyes will see. Light can only be experienced by perception. What can be experienced by reading? Even a blind man can remember the definition by repetitive reading. And if someone asks him to say what light is, he can explain what he has read. Light is this and this. It is written in the Upanishads like this. It is mentioned in the Gita in this way. Mahavira has said it so. The Buddha has said it so. "I know all the scriptures; light is like this." But after a while the blind man will ask, "Where is the door? I need to leave." Then you can tell him, "If you know light, you can go out on your own." And he will say, "No, I don't have eyes, I don't know light, I know *about* light. There is a difference in knowing about light and knowing light."

I have heard...

Ramakrishna used to say that there was a blind man whose friends invited him for dinner. They cooked *kheer* and after eating it, he asked, "What is *kheer*? What is its color? What is its form? It is very delicious."

His friends said, "Let's explain to him." They started explaining, "It is white. It is made of milk. Have you ever seen milk?"

Those friends must have been crazy. If a blind man can see milk, then he can also see *kheer*. They were asking him, "Have you ever seen milk?"

The man replied, "Milk? What is milk? What is it? Please tell me! Please explain it to me. Don't confuse me more. I don't even know *kheer*, and you have raised a new question about milk."

They started saying, "*Kheer* is made with milk."

The man replied, "Alright, please explain milk first, then I will understand *kheer*."

The friends said, "Milk? Have you ever seen a heron which flies in the sky and catches fish on the banks of the river? The crane is snow white, have you ever seen it?"

The man asked, "What are you talking about? Now you have created more trouble for me! What is this heron? Now first you need to explain a heron to me, then I will understand milk, and then *kheer* will be clear to me. You are puzzling me more. Tell me something which I can understand. Explain something about the heron in such a way that even a blind man like me can understand."

One of his friends came forward. He must have been the clever one – the more cunning ones are always the dangerous ones. He came forward and gave his hand to the blind man and asked him to touch it.

The blind man touched his hand and asked, "What does this mean?"

The man said, "The neck of a heron is as soft as my hand. What you feel when you touch my hand, you will feel the same when you touch the neck of a heron – long and soft.

The blind man replied, "Got it, got it! Now I understand that *kheer* is as soft as a hand. Milk is as soft as a hand. Got it, I completely understand it."

The friends said, "You have not understood anything. It is even more difficult now. It would have been better for you if you had not understood at all. At least one thing was certain, that you did not understand. Now another difficulty arises. Now, don't go out and say to people that milk is as soft as a hand. Otherwise not only you but we will also be considered fools."

The blind man said, "But you are the ones who told me that."

No matter what you explain to a blind man about light, what is he going to understand? He needs eyes. And we think about the truth. What can we think? The more we think about it, the more difficulties will arise; the more definitions like a soft hand will take hold of our minds.

Ask someone, "What is God?" He is bound to answer something or other. You will not find anyone with such courage that he can say, "I don't know, I don't have eyes to perceive the ultimate, so how can I explain? I don't know whether he exists or not. I don't know anything."

No, he will answer, "God has four arms; he is holding a lotus in his one hand, a conch shell in another hand, and a club in another hand!" Is God involved in some kind of theater play, holding a lotus, a conch shell, and a club?

The poor man has learned this from somewhere. It is similar to those soft hands. God is standing on a lotus flower. He must be tired of standing there by now and the lotus must have been crushed. Or if it was a fake plastic lotus, then it is a different matter… But why is he standing on a lotus? Some painter has painted his image and the blind man has got hold of that image. He is saying that God is standing on a lotus.

Is God going to be according to the image we have caught hold of? He is bound to be like that because from where are we going to form an image of him? We have not seen anything. We have thought, read, and pondered. We have not experienced; the knowing is not our own and we don't care to know either. We are never concerned with knowing at all. We just hold on to these kinds of ideas. Then the blind will fight the other blind men.

Different people have different kinds of Gods. A Mohammedan has his own God and a Hindu has his own and so on. And they all are fighting with each other: "Yours is wrong and mine is right." And so the fighting of blind men with one another goes on. They are fighting to such an extent that human beings are murdering other human beings. Nations are destroying other nations. They have divided the whole earth into pieces. Now even in our nation, two types of blind men have divided the country – Hindus and Muslims.

I have heard that when India and Pakistan were being divided, there was a madhouse on the borderline. Now, it was a problem where to place the madhouse – in India or in Pakistan? So someone thought that it was better to ask the people in the madhouse which country they want to belong to, India or Pakistan.

The mad people said, "We want to stay here, because after hearing about the kind of madness which is going on in the name of India and Pakistan, we feel that we have become sane and others have gone mad! Please spare us from this madness. We want to stay right here. We don't want to go anywhere else because what is happening outside this madhouse has made us firmly believe that we are inside the walls with God's grace. If we were outside, we would have been in great difficulty. Everyone has gone mad outside these walls."

But the officials said, "This is not good enough. You have to say clearly where you want to go. You will stay in the same madhouse, but according to your decision you will belong either to India or Pakistan."

The mad people said, "You are puzzling us. You are saying that we will remain here, but still if we want, we can either go to Pakistan or to India. When we will stay here, how can we go to India or Pakistan?"

Then the officials said, "If this issue is not solved this way, the Hindus will be sent to India and the Muslims will be sent to Pakistan."

The mad people said, "We are just mad and we don't know whether we are Hindu or Muslim! The most we understand is that we are human beings. More than that we do not know; whether we are Hindu or Muslim..."

Now there was no other way. There was no other way left, what to do? It was decided that half of the madhouse would belong to India and the other half would belong to Pakistan. Divide the madhouse. Divide the madhouse in half. What else could be done!

So a dividing wall was erected. The madhouse was divided: half of the mad people went to India and the other half went to Pakistan. A wall was raised in the middle. Now the mad people were climbing the wall and shouting, "We will have victory over Pakistan," and others were shouting, "We will occupy India."

There were some intellectual mad people there also. They were shouting from beyond the walls, "What is the matter? What is going on over there? We are exactly where we were, and you have gone to India and we have gone to Pakistan!"

Our divisive thoughts, ideas, and prejudice have divided the whole world into small sections – thought has divided the whole of humanity and the whole being of man.

Thoughts will always be divisive. Thoughts never unite, they always divide. Hence, the moment a man clings to one thought, he becomes the enemy of the opposing thought. When you cling to one particular thought, you become the enemy of the other and the conflict begins. The conflict all over the world is because of thoughts.

Then thoughts change. Sometimes Muslims fight and other times Hindus fight. Then capitalism and communism fight. Faces change, but the ideologies go on fighting, the thoughts go on fighting.

Truth has no relation to thought. Thoughts can generate beliefs, but the truth can never be discovered by thought. Only one who drops all opinions can discover the truth. He drops all dogmas. He says, "Neither I am a Hindu, nor a Muslim, nor I am this nor I am that, neither I am a theist not I am an atheist. I have no prejudice. I want to know the truth without any prejudice." One who drops all prejudices, drops all thoughts, and dives into silence, attains the truth. The truth is ever present there. We are occupied with our prejudices and closed; hence, we have no experience of the truth.

But there are two kinds of people in this world: either they believe or they think. No one wants to move beyond thought. And when there is an individual who lives in thoughtlessness – whether he is Krishna or Buddha or Mahavira, or Christ or Mohammed or Moses; whenever that individual dives into nothingness, into isness, immediately he finds that the truth is knocking at his door. Truth is always waiting there. If we empty ourselves, the truth enters. If our door opens, the truth can come in. But our doors are closed.

The truth can be attained neither by believing nor by thinking, but only by thoughtlessness. Thoughtless consciousness is the door to truth. This is what I call *dhyan*, meditation. *Dhyan* means to be absolutely thoughtless.

Now we will sit together for our evening meditation.

Enter thoughtlessness for ten minutes – where you drop all prejudice and all thoughts.

During the meditation, no one should leave, so that no one is disturbed by your leaving. Even those who don't want to sit down should sit silently for ten minutes, just for the sake of others. The lights will be switched off. Before that, take some space from each other. No one should touch anyone else, everyone should be alone.

Sit down peacefully. Turn off the lights. First of all, relax your body with ease and sit down. There should be no tension in the body. No talking please.

Feel your body to be frozen. Close your eyes. Now I will give suggestions, feel with me. First, feel your body to be frozen. The body is relaxing, the body is relaxing. Feel that your body has totally relaxed and frozen, so that you can move away from the body. Relax your body so you can move beyond it. Someone who is clinging hard to the body, how can he move beyond it? He will stop at the body. We stop at that which we cling to.

Let go... Let go of the body from the mind... Move beyond it. The body has totally relaxed... The body is totally frozen as if it is not there.

The breath is relaxing... Feel that the breathing is relaxing... The body is relaxing, the breath is relaxing... The breath is relaxing... The body is relaxing... The breath is relaxing...

Let go of the body, let go of the breath – let the breath come and go on its own, relax it absolutely.

And for the next ten minutes have only one feeling: I am a witness, I am only the experiencer, I am only the knower. The winds are blowing, I am just experiencing it. The wind is touching me, I am just experiencing it. The coolness is surrounding me, I am just experiencing. If there is a sound, I will just listen. Whatever is happening, I am just witnessing it.

The legs may hurt, I will just experience it. The body is relaxing, I am seeing it. The breath is relaxing, I know it. The breath is slowing down, I know it. Any thought is moving in the mind, I am noticing it. The mind is becoming peaceful, I am witnessing it. There may be some explosion of bliss within, I will witness it. I am just the knower. I am just the witness.

This remembrance: I am the witness, I am just the witness, I am just experiencing, I am nothing other than a witness, I am just the energy to know. I am a witness... I am a witness... The more this awareness deepens, the more profound the peace and silence surrounds. The more this remembrance deepens, the more a coolness of bliss surrounds. The more this awareness settles, the deeper you enter within.

Deepen this awareness – I am a witness, I am just a witness, I am just a witness...

Now I will be silent for ten minutes. Go on deepening this remembrance – I am a witness... I am a witness... I am a witness... I am a witness...

CHAPTER 8

losing the urge to hurt others

FRIENDS HAVE ASKED many questions about the three days' talks. Someone has asked:

Osho,
If the soul is beyond all pleasure–pain, what is the use of saying prayers for the peace of another's soul?

It is a very important question and it will be very useful to understand. The first thing is that the soul is certainly beyond all pleasure–pain, all peace–disturbance, and all attachment–hatred – basically all kinds of duality and polarity. The soul neither gets disturbed nor is it peaceful, because only one who is disturbed can become peaceful. Only the mind gets disturbed and only the mind becomes serene. And if you understand it rightly, the very existence of the mind is disturbance. No-mind is silence. Self-nature in itself is neither peaceful nor ever disturbed; it is neither in pleasure nor in pain. Self-nature is the name of a third state, which is called bliss.

Bliss means where there is neither suffering nor pleasure; bliss does not imply pleasure. Suffering is a tension and pleasure is also a tension. A man can die of suffering and of pleasure. Suffering creates anxiety and pleasure also becomes an anxiety. Suffering is stimulation and pleasure too is an excitement. Self-nature is excitement-free; there is neither the excitement of pleasure nor that of pain.

We know that pain makes us suffer; for example, in countries like India where there is poverty, starvation, hunger, and all kinds of suffering, there, people are stressed. On the other hand, in countries like America where there are all kinds of pleasures, all the facilities, and all the riches, wealth, and affluence are possible, even there people are stressed. Poor nations are suffering from stress and rich countries are suffering from stress as well! What does this mean? It means that suffering is a kind of stress and pleasure is also a kind of stress.

Poor people are suffering and rich people suffer as well. Their sufferings are different. For example, someone can suffer from starvation and someone else can suffer from overeating.

Self-nature accepts neither this kind of stress nor that kind of tension. The soul is tensionless, no tension exists there.

I have heard…

A man won a million-rupee lottery. His wife heard the news over the radio and was worried that if her husband came to know he had won a million-rupee lottery, he might die of pleasure because she had never seen him having even ten rupees at once. She was afraid, and went to the church to see the priest who used to talk about the meaninglessness of money; she had heard his sermons on wisdom and peace.

She said to the priest, "I am in difficulty. My husband has won a million-rupee lottery. The good news might prove fatal to him. Please do something so that he does not have a shock from it."

The priest said, "Don't worry, I'll come. I'll gradually reveal the news to him."

The priest went to the house and said to the man, "Have you heard the news that you have won a lottery of twenty-five thousand rupees?" He thought that if the man could tolerate the shock of twenty-five thousand rupees, he would tell him twenty-five thousand more, and then twenty-five thousand more, and so on.

The man replied, "Twenty-five thousand! If I have really won twenty-five thousand rupees, I will donate twelve and half a thousand rupees to you."

The priest fell down on the spot and had a heart attack. Twelve thousand, five hundred rupees! He was shocked by the good news.

It is comfortable for priests, saints, and holy people to preach to others. When they have to face trouble themselves, then they realize exactly what they were preaching to others!

Pleasure gives a shock, a jolt. Pain is also a shock, an impact. And if someone constantly feels the impact of suffering, he gets used to the shock of misery. He becomes habituated, it becomes habitual, and then suffering does not shock him any longer. Then he develops a tolerance for that much tension. That is why if you continue to live in misery, it doesn't feel like misery anymore. The opposite is also true. When a pleasure shocks you for the first time, you feel it. If the same impact goes on happening every day, you don't feel it any longer. Then you become habituated to that pleasure and you no longer get pleasure from it. Someone who constantly lives in suffering stops feeling it; and someone who continuously lives in pleasure cannot feel pleasure because if you become habituated to a particular stimulus, its sting and impact dissolves.

I have heard...

A fisherman went to the city to sell his fish. He sold everything, and before going back, he decided to take a tour of the capital. He went to the street where there were many perfume shops; perfumes from all over the world were sold. The fisherman knew only one kind of aroma, that of fish. He didn't know any other smell, nor could he distinguish other smells. Only fish seemed to him to be perfumed.

When he entered the perfume market, he covered his nostrils with a handkerchief, saying, "What kind of mad people live here? What a foul smell they have spread here!" As he went farther along the street, he started suffocating because all those unfamiliar perfumes were penetrating and shocking him. Finally he panicked and ran. But the more he ran, bigger shops appeared ahead.

How could he know – he thought that he would get out of the market, but instead he ran into the middle of it. There were shops all around, where great emperors used to buy their perfumes. He fainted, falling down with the shock of the perfumes.

The shopkeepers rushed to him. They knew that when someone is unconscious, you make him smell a strong perfume and he comes back to consciousness. So they brought out the perfumes from their safes, which were not even available to the emperors, in order to bring this poor man to consciousness. They went on making him smell the perfumes. He was throwing up his hands and banging his head in an unconscious state. His condition became worse.

A crowd gathered. A man who used to be a fisherman said to the people, "Friends, you will kill this man. You think that you are helping him, but you are actually murdering him!" Often helpers have proved to be murderers – it is just a matter of them getting the opportunity. "Move away! You will kill him. As far as I understand, he has fainted because of all these fragrances."

The perfume sellers said, "Have you gone mad? Has anyone heard of someone becoming unconscious from perfumes? A man can faint due to a foul smell. But because of a fragrance?"

The fisherman replied, "You don't know... There are perfumes which you will consider as a foul smell, and there are bad smells which someone else will consider a perfume. It is just a matter of habit."

He moved the people away. The fisherman's basket had fallen next to him: dirty clothes and a dirty basket in which he was selling fish. The foul smell of fish was emanating from them. The old fisherman sprinkled some water on that dirty piece of cloth and placed it on the fainted fisherman's nose. The man took a deep breath, as if the life force was returned to him! He opened his eyes and said, "This is real perfume. Those devils would have killed me!"

What had happened to that man? When one becomes used to a foul smell, it turns into a perfume. That is why toilet cleaners and cobblers don't revolt against their condition. They are never going to revolt; they have become habituated to it. For how long have sudras existed in India? For thousands of years, India has been treating millions of sudras so badly, and still it claims to be religious. Still it is called the holy land. Millions of people have been treated in a way that no one else has ever been treated anywhere on the earth. But the sudras have never revolted.

Why? – because they have got used to it. That very suffering has become part of their life. If any revolution *has* happened, it has come from the non-sudras because they can see that this cast is carrying human excretion from morning till evening. The others feel pain because it is beyond their imagination to carry human excretion all day long. They would rather die than carry it.

But they don't know that the person who is carrying it is not aware of it. Hence, no revolution came from the sudras. Revolution came from the brahmins, the vaishya, the kshatriya. They felt the pain and saw that such a thing should not happen.

You will be surprised to know that the poor and the downtrodden never revolt; there is no question of revolt for them. They become habituated to suffering. There is so much poverty in India and nothing bothers us. If an American tourist visits India, he is unable to understand: "Why do these people silently tolerate all this? So much poverty cannot be tolerated!" He is able to see it because he is not used to it. Habit makes people capable of doing anything, absolutely anything.

There are two kinds of tension: of pleasure and of suffering. Both are stress. And the one who rises beyond both can experience self-nature.

We will go into this a little more, then we will try to understand something else.

Buddha once visited a city. On his arrival, people asked him in wonder, "We have heard that the prince of our town has been initiated and become a monk. Has our prince been initiated?" The whole town was amazed because the prince had never even come out of his palace or walked on paths that were not covered by soft carpets. Now he will be begging with a bowl in his hands, from village to village, and he will walk barefoot. It was beyond imagination. They said to Buddha, "It is a miracle the prince has been initiated!"

Buddha said, "There is no miracle in it. When the human mind becomes habituated to one thing, sometimes it becomes desperate to change it. The prince had experienced the tension of pleasures, now he wants to experience the stress of suffering. He is finished with his previous experience. He is tired of his earlier experience and now he wants to see the other extreme. I say unto you that before he was on the extreme of pleasure, and now he will move to the other extreme of pain."

That is exactly what happened. Within six months, the prince left all the other monks behind in torturing himself. While other monks were walking on the well-paved roads, the prince would walk on the paths which had thorns on them. While other monks were eating one meal a day, he was eating every other day. Other monks were sitting in the shade, he was standing in the heat of the midday summer sun. His feet were pierced with thorns. His body became dehydrated and sunburned. After six months, it was difficult to recognize him. He used to have a very beautiful body, a golden body. People from faraway places used to visit him and admire his beautiful body. Now, seeing his physical condition, no one could believe that he was the same prince.

Buddha went to see him after six months. He was lying on a bed of thorns; that was his way of resting. His name was Shron. Buddha said, "Shron, I have come to ask you something. I have heard that when you were a prince you used to be very skillful in playing the *veena*. Can I ask you something, will you answer?"

He replied, "Yes, people used to say that there was no one better at playing the *veena* than me."

Then Buddha asked, "If the strings of the *veena* are too loose, can they produce music?"

Shron replied, "How is that possible, master? When the strings are loose, they will not even produce any notes. How can they produce a melody?"

Buddha said, "And if the strings are too tight, can you produce a melody?"

Shron replied, "The strings will break if they are too tight. Then too, no melody will be produced."

Then Buddha asked, "When is a melody created then?"

Shorn explained, "I don't know if you will understand, but those who understand music say there is a state where the strings are neither too tight nor too loose. There is a point between tight and loose; at that point, the string is beyond being tight or loose, it is beyond both. At that point, music is born – when the string is neither tight nor loose."

Buddha said, "This is exactly what I came to say to you: that the rule for producing music from a *veena* also applies to creating a melody of life. The *veena* of life also has a state of balance, when there is neither excitement on this side nor on the other side. No tension either this side or the other side. The strings are balanced in the middle. Then there is neither suffering nor pleasure, because pleasure is a tension and pain is a tension. And when the strings of life are in the middle, one is beyond pleasure and pain. In that state, the dimension called self-nature, life, bliss, is experienced.

Certainly self-nature is beyond both. And until our eyes focus beyond both, we cannot experience self-nature.

But the questioner has asked, "...then what is the use of saying prayers for the peace of another's soul?" There is a purpose, but not what people understand – that is not the purpose. There is another purpose. When we pray for the peace of another's soul, the other's soul cannot become peaceful by our prayer; but when we are prayerful, our souls become peaceful.

When you think about hurting someone, it is not certain that the other will be hurt, but the person who wishes to harm others sows many seeds of agony for himself. The one who wishes for the other to suffer creates suffering within himself. Whatever we wish for others, knowingly or unknowingly, the same happens to us.

So, when we talk of praying for the peace of others, it has many meanings. The first meaning: someone who is praying for the peace of others cannot also do anything to create a disturbance for others. And if he does, then he is a hypocrite because he is praying for the peace of others together with doing something to disturb them. That man is highly dishonest. So, the first meaning is that a man who prays for the peace of other souls will slowly, slowly stop creating disturbances for others. The desire to hurt others will slowly, slowly diminish within him.

And remember, we all have the desire to see others suffer. And we have no wish at all to see others happy. When a big house is built in your neighborhood, you go to the owner of the house and say, "This is a great house, very beautiful," but have you looked within at what is happening there? Inside, you are thinking about when the house will fall down: "Oh God, make this house fall down. What has this devil done to deserve it?" This is what happens within you.

A kind of satisfaction is derived from others' suffering and a kind of disturbance is felt from others' happiness. Knowingly or unknowingly we are desperate to make others suffer.

A man was dying, and he called his sons close and said, "I am dying now. Will you fulfill my last wish?"

The elder sons were wise so they kept quiet. The youngest son was naïve. He said, "Tell me what you want and I will do it."

The man called him closer and said, "All my older sons are unworthy. See, they don't want to fulfill the desire of a dying man. You are a good son. I will whisper in your ears… When I am dead, cut my dead body into pieces and throw the pieces in the neighbor's house, then send a report to the police."

The son asked, "But why?"

He replied, "My son, you do not know. I have always derived pleasure from seeing my neighbors suffering. And while my soul is on the voyage to heaven, I will watch my handcuffed neighbors going to court and it will give me immense pleasure. At my last moment, please arrange some pleasure for me. For the sake of your dying father, arrange some happiness!"

There was a German poet called Heinrich Heine. He wrote that one night God was standing in front of him and saying, "I am very happy with your poems. You can ask anything and your wishes will be granted. Whatever you want, I will give you. I will grant you all the pleasures you want."

Heinrich Heine said, "It was a strange dream because when God told me I could ask anything for my happiness, I thought that it was no pleasure to ask only for my happiness. I said to God, 'Forget about my pleasure. Whatever suffering you can cause my neighbors, give me that as your blessing!'"

He continues, "On waking, I was very shocked by what I had said in my dream!"

But the truth often comes out in dreams. People tell lies in their waking hours. A son strangles his father in his dream and touches his feet in the daytime. A man runs away with the neighbor's wife in his dream, but in his waking time he says, "All women are like my mother, my sister." The real man is revealed during dreaming, the one who is within. We all are desperate to see others suffer.

Hence, by praying for the peace and bliss of others, it is not guaranteed that they will get peace and bliss, but we will rise upward; one who wishes happiness on others stops doing them harm. Someone who starts wishing good on others brings about a revolution in his own life. There is no greater revolution than feeling happy in someone else's happiness. Feeling sad in others' sadness is very easy, but to be happy in the happiness of others is difficult. Feeling sad about the sadness of others is not difficult – rather, you get a kind of juice from it, you get a kind of enjoyment from it.

Just watch – when someone dies and people gather to express their condolences, watch their faces, and listen to what they say. They talk about suffering, even shed tears, but if you observe their whole attitude, you will notice that they are getting pleasure from it. And if you go to someone's house to express your condolence – someone's father has died and you go there to shed your tears – and he says, "What nonsense are you saying? What's the point, dead is dead!" you will return home very unsatisfied.

I was staying with a family. The lady of the house did one regular activity, and that was to go to funerals and express her condolences. I asked her, "Please tell me the truth. When you go to express your condolence, if you feel that your being sad is not valued in that family, do you feel good or bad?"

She said, "I feel bad. I feel very strange that I have come to express so much sadness for them and the family members don't care about it at all."

Try to look within whenever you go to express your sadness in someone's sadness and find out whether you are taking pleasure from it.

When two people are fighting on the road, a crowd gathers – people who were on their way to the courtroom or to their office or to college. They drop a thousand activities and stand there to watch. Two people are fighting and you are watching! What are you watching? People will even be telling them, "Friends, don't fight!" But in their minds they are thinking that the fight should continue, otherwise the joy will be gone. And if you have stopped to watch a fight and the fight finishes quickly, you go back sad that nothing happened, the time was wasted. In our minds... All these things are not visible on the surface, but our minds are like that.

In the First World War, almost three and half million people were killed. And during the war, a strange thing was noticed: as long as the war continued there were fewer diseases in Europe, fewer mental disorders, murders decreased, and fewer people went mad. There were fewer cases of robbery and suicide. Psychiatrists were puzzled: "What is the connection between war and all these things decreasing?" They could find no relation between the two happenings: the war could just go on and if someone wanted to commit suicide, he could do, or if someone wanted to murder, then he could do so. But all crime decreased.

Then in the Second World War, the level of crime fell even lower. About seven and half million people were killed. And crime decreased so much that it was beyond the understanding of psychiatrists: "Why does this happen during a war?" Slowly, slowly they understood that people become joyful during a war; they derive a lot of pleasure from it. So many people are being killed and then no one wants to murder someone on his own. He gets so much joy from the killing in the war that he is satisfied.

Where there is so much damage happening, why would anyone want to commit a small destruction? He joins in the great destruction and gets satisfaction. Where the whole society has gone mad wholesale, no one bothers about private madness. Then there is no need for one's own private madness. When all are mad, it is all right!

You must have observed: when the Indo-China or the Indo-Pakistan conflict was happening, the aura around people's faces was different. Their faces were shining, which is rare to see in India. People were waking up early in the morning, before sunrise, to read the newspapers and listen to the radio about what was happening in the war. A man who never woke before seven would wake at five and ask about the latest news. There was movement, and shining and joy were seen in everybody.

It is very puzzling to see that when there is a war going on, and people are being butchered, killed, buildings are on fire, bombed, so much joy is derived from it. The sadist within us, the one who gets pleasure through causing pain to others, gets great satisfaction. On the inside he says, "What joy!" although on the outside he says different things. He talks about patriotism, the nation, religion, and all kinds of bullshit. All this talk is nonsense. What he means on the inside is different: the real meaning is that he wants to torture others. We get satisfaction from torturing others.

So, praying for the well-being and peace of others may or may not give peace to others, and that is not important. The important point is that in saying that prayer, in evoking that feeling, you will be transformed. The sadist within us dissolves. And in that sense, praying for others is valuable.

Someone else has asked:

Osho,
There is no shining, no charm, no elegance, and no aura on the faces of Indian young people. The reason behind it is certainly that their celibacy has been destroyed. Please explain to us the importance of celibacy.

I would like to say a couple of things. The first thing is that there is more shine in the eyes of the American youth – does that mean they are more celibate than you? There is more life energy in the eyes of English young people, more vigor. Great vigor is seen in the eyes of Russian young people, which is not found anywhere else in the world – are they more celibate than you?

The first thing is that it is not a question of celibacy. And the interesting thing is, the more celibacy is preached in this country, the more ill effects have happened. It has not been beneficial, rather it has been harmful.

The truth is that the amount of life energy wasted due to the preaching of celibacy is hard to calculate. In this nation, for thousands of years we have been preaching wrong things, unscientific things, and unnatural things. And we want to depend on them: people don't have enough to eat nor does their food have enough nutrition, but there are those who want to preach that the vigor and shining is missing due to a lack of celibacy! People are dying of starvation, the whole nation is dying of starvation. From where will they have vigor? From where will they be shining? You are not ready to deal with the real issue.

There is a very strange condition in this country. The saints say such dishonest, hypocritical things that no one can compete with them. The real issue is that the nation is starving. There is not enough blood in their veins, not enough food to eat, not enough milk to drink, no clean water; there is nothing. And what do people say? The cunning people will talk about how celibacy has been destroyed and that is why there is no vigor: "Preach celibacy!"

The preaching of abstinence cannot make bread. Neither can it become milk, nor can it make food. And you will be surprised to know that the weaker your body is, the more non-celibate it will be. The unhealthier your body is, the more sexual it will be. The healthier the body is, the less sexuality there will be. Hence, poor people create more children and the rich people produce fewer children. Often it happens that the rich man has to adopt a child and the poor man goes on creating a crowd of children. Do you know the reason behind it?

The richer a country becomes, the more the population decreases. For example, it has happened in France. People are living in comfort, and comfortable people are not so sexual. Miserable people become very sexual. Why? Because for a miserable man, sexuality is the only pleasure left. It is the only entertainment that remains for the poor.

A rich man can afford to listen to the *veena*, he listens to music, goes swimming, takes trips into the forest, has a holiday on a hill station. There is neither any hill-station holiday, nor any *veena* or any other music, nor any literature, nor any religion for a poor man. The poor man has only one door open and that is sexual pleasure. Just that is his only hill station, his only *veena*, and his only pleasure. After being exhausted, downtrodden, tired, he returns home and has only one way to relax – sex. He has no other relaxation. He goes on producing children. Remember, an unhealthy body is highly charged and full of tension. The more the body is charged within, the more it needs to release tension through sex.

Sex is actually a desperate effort of an excited body. The body is stimulated, feverish, it releases some of its energy so that it can become peaceful and relax. The more healthy, relaxed, blissful, and peaceful a body is, the less is the need for sex.

A poor society can never be free from sex. But the saints and holy men preach that there is a lack of celibacy and that is why everything has gone wrong. There is no lack of celibacy.

And the second thing you must consider is, if the teaching of abstinence becomes repression, it helps less and harms more. If it supports suppression... And what is the meaning of preaching celibacy in India? The teaching of celibacy in India means: keep men and women separate, far away from each other. And when man and woman are kept apart, they constantly think about each other. The more their thinking is obsessed with each other, the more sexual perversion increases. The more sexual they become, the more impossible celibacy becomes.

I have a doctor friend who lived in Delhi. He traveled to England to participate in a medical conference. Five hundred doctors gathered in Hyde Park for the conference – food, drinks, and meetings were arranged there and my friend, who is a sardar from the Punjab, was also there.

In the park, where five hundred doctors had gathered, eating, drinking, gossiping, meeting each other, a couple were hugging each other and lost in a different world. My friend felt uncomfortable; he was talking to others, but his eyes were focused on the loving couple. And he was thinking, "Why aren't these people arrested by the police? What indecent behavior! It could never happen in my country. What is going on? What kind of culture is this? What kind of uncultured behavior is this?" He was looking again and again, unable to focus anywhere else. All his attention was absorbed there.

An Australian doctor put a hand on his shoulder and said, "Sir, don't stare at them again and again, otherwise the police will arrest you."

He said, "What are you talking about?"

The man replied, "It is between those two, it is not a matter of anyone else. You keep on looking over there; that shows your sick mind. Why are you staring there again and again?"

My doctor friend said, "But this is bad manners! In the presence of five hundred people, these two are sitting in an intimate embrace. It is unmannerly."

But the man replied, "Out of five hundred people, who is looking at them except you? Who is bothered about them? Those two people know that five hundred educated doctors are gathered here. They don't expect any rudeness from them, so they are sitting peacefully. Whether they are sitting here alone or among five hundred people does not make any difference. But why are you disturbed?"

My friend said to me when he returned, "I was very upset. And when I looked inside myself, I found out that it was my own perversion that was projected there. Otherwise it was none of my business."

In a country where women are kept apart from men, trouble is bound to happen. People will read pornographic books, hiding the book inside a holy book like the Gita. Inside the Gita there will be dirty literature hidden, just the cover will be the Gita! Where women and men are kept apart and suppression is preached, trouble is inevitable.

The day before yesterday, I was reading in a newspaper that in the city of Sydney, which has a population of two million people, a European actress was going to play a nude show. They expected a great audience to come for the show. But from a population of two million, only two people showed up in the theater. Only two people came to see the naked woman. And she caught a cold due to being naked; it was a cold winter there. She was furious: "What kind of city is this!"

In India, in Udaipur, if you put on a show of a naked woman, how many people will show up? Two people? Everybody will go to watch the show. Yes, there will be a difference; the courageous ones will come through the front door. The saints, the holy people and the priests, and the politicians will come through the back door. But everybody will come. No one will miss the opportunity.

It could also happen that a few will go saying, "I am going to see who has been to the show." It could also happen. He is just going to observe who has gone to the show. That could also happen.

What kind of disaster has happened in this nation? This calamity has happened in this country because of forcing celibacy on people; it has not been a natural growth. The natural, innate growth of celibacy is a different matter altogether. And if there is to be an innate growth of real celibacy, there should be a complete education about sex, not preaching about celibacy. A holistic sex education has to be given to every boy and girl, so that every child can know what sex is. And boys and girls need to be so close to each other that they should not feel that they are two different species of animal, that they are not the same kind of animal, that they are not from the same species.

If there are a thousand men sitting here and a woman enters, every man becomes conscious that a woman has come in. This should not happen. Women sit separately and men sit separately, leaving a gap in between. What kind of madness is this? Why is there a constant feeling of being man and woman? Why is there such a wall? We should come close to each other, we should be intimate. Children should play together and grow up together. If they get familiar with each other, there will not be such madness.

What is the situation today? It is difficult for a girl to walk through a market; it is difficult for a girl to go to college. It is impossible for a girl to go out without being abused, molested, pushed, or eve-teased. Something or other will happen to her on the way. Why? The sons of saints and holy men are behaving in a very strange way!

But there is a reason behind it, and the reason is the preaching of the saints and holy men. We are constantly making men and women enemies of each other and that is what causes this damage. The thing you try to prohibit becomes very attractive; negation is an invitation. If you say that something should not be talked about, it will be talked of even more, but underground. The thing you prohibit will become more attractive in people's minds and curiosity about it will grow. The mind is no longer healthy and it becomes perverted.

You must have noticed that if a veiled woman passes by, more men are attracted toward her than toward a woman without a veil. If a veiled woman is passing by, everybody wants to see what is behind the veil. What is there to see in a woman without a veil? She is openly visible and the matter is finished. The more we hide, the more difficulties arise. The more difficulties arise, the more distortions are invented. And then everything becomes perverted.

Celibacy is miraculous. Its power is limitless; its bliss is incredible. But celibacy is attained only by those who comprehend, know, and recognize all the states of mind. Through right perception they become free from the mind.

Celibacy is not attained by those who don't understand anything and who just suppress their minds. So much steam is gathered by the repression and then that steam starts coming out through perversions. It is bound to be released; there is no way to avoid it.

Celibacy is marvelous. But the experiment which has been done in this country has not helped the nation to become celibate. Rather, it has made the whole country very sexual. It is difficult now to find a more sexual society than ours. Absolutely impossible! But we go on repeating the song of celibacy. And the whole mind is becoming pathetic.

I was working in a college for a while. One day I was passing the principal's chamber and I heard him shouting at a boy. I went in and asked, "What is the matter?"

The principal was happy I had come in. He said to me, "Please take a seat and try to make him understand. He has written a love letter to a girl."

The boy said, "I have never written any love letter, someone else must have written my name."

The principal said, "You are lying. You have written this letter – many complaints about you have been reported to us earlier. You have even thrown pebbles at girls. We know all that. You should look upon every girl as your mother or your sister!"

The boy replied, "I do think that way, what are you talking about sir! I have never thought otherwise. I think of every girl as my mother or my sister." The more he denied, the more the principal was shouting at him.

I said to the principal, "Wait a minute. Can I ask a few questions?"

The principal said, "My pleasure!" He thought that I was going to ask the boy.

I said to him, "I am not going to question the boy. I want to ask you something. How old are you?" He was fifty-two years old. I asked him, "Can you put your hand on your heart and say that you have reached a state where you consider every girl as your mother or your sister? If you have reached that state, you have the right to say something to this boy. If you have not attained that state of mind, you have no right to say anything."

He said to the boy, "You can go now."

I said, "He will not go. We will talk in front of him."

And I said to the boy, "Have you gone mad? If you think of all girls as your mother or your sister, it is something to be worried about. Then you are sick, unwell, there is something wrong with you. If you have written love letters, you have not done anything wrong. If twenty- and twenty-four-year-old boys and girls stop loving, this world will become hell. You must love. But you have written abusive words in your love letter and that is stupid. Does anyone have to write foul words in a love letter? If it was up to me, I would teach you how to write a love letter. This love letter is wrong, but it is not wrong to write a love letter. It is absolutely natural."

But when unnatural things are imposed – and when you are told you should consider all girls as your mother and your sister – it will bring the reverse effect. The boy will superficially say that he thinks of all girls as his mother or his sister, but his whole nature will force him to love a girl. Then he is compelled to do perverted things such as throwing acid, throwing stones, writing abuse, or writing abusive verses in the bathroom – he is bound to do all that. All that will happen. And the society will be vulgar; it will not be cultured.

Love has its own divinity. What can be more sacred than love? But we have destroyed its purity by separating man and woman from each other. We have polluted it. Slowly, slowly we have obstructed every natural thing and made it unnatural. And there will be inevitable results.

India cannot move in the direction of celibacy until a healthy and scientific approach to sex is born. The madness that is going on must stop. It should be prevented – these wrong teachings should be banned. The amount of damage caused by them is hard to imagine. You cannot imagine how much harm we are doing to our children!

All the doctors of the world say that it is natural for boys and girls to be curious about each other after sexual maturity, when they are fourteen or fifteen years of age. If it does not happen, there is a danger. It is absolutely natural; now, how we guide this curiosity on a sophisticated cultured path is in our hands. The more we guide this curiosity toward a more refined path, the more we can support our children in maintaining their life force and preserving their vigor and that will help them to move toward celibacy.

But what are we doing? We build a stone wall between them and leave open all the back doors. An interesting thing is that on the one hand we go on preaching celibacy and on the other hand the whole society advertises sexuality. Children are tortured round the clock by the advertisement of sexuality from one side and teachings of celibacy from the other side. These contradictory teachings come together and make their lives a living hell.

Indian children have as much vigor as children of any other country. But the main reason for a lack of vigor is poverty and starvation. And the even greater reason behind it is our unscientific approach to sex. If our approach becomes scientific, our children can become more dynamic and forceful than children of any other country.

But stupid saints go on saying anything: they neither know anything about biology nor about physiology, nor anything about the functioning of the body, nor about the production of semen. They have nothing to do with all these scientific matters and they go on preaching so many stupid things. The Indian saints preach that the semen is stored in our body as a fixed quantity and if it is spent, you will die.

Semen is not a fixed quantity like a deposit in a bank. The more it is spent, the more it is produced. Hence, there is no need to worry about releasing semen. There is no need; this is what science says. But it does not mean that someone should just waste it. Semen is produced daily and people preach that if you lose a drop of semen, your whole life will be destroyed. These people should be charged with crimes because when a child reads this kind of thing and then loses a drop of semen, he gets very worried that he is going to die soon.

No one dies and no life gets destroyed. It is an interesting point that semen is part of the body – all these saints give so much importance to body parts, so we can see how body-oriented they are! Semen does not have so much value. And remember, there is no harm in releasing semen; the harm is caused by the idea that if the semen is spent, it is harmful. This mental conditioning brings perversion and damage.

This does not mean that I am saying you should be spending semen to the extreme. Those with a deep understanding say that nature has arranged it in such a way that you cannot release too much semen. Nature has a totally automatic arrangement for the body; you cannot release too much. But if you want, you can stop spending semen completely; that is possible.

Try to comprehend these two things. You cannot release too much. Your release is limited; no one can expend more than that because the body will deny it. It is automatic, the body will immediately prevent it. The body will refuse to expend more than it can. But if you want, you can stop expending completely.

Not to release at all can happen in two ways. It can happen forcefully, then you will go mad: as if steam is held in a kettle and you have closed all openings, then the kettle will burst – that is what will happen. A man who forcefully stops his semen from being released will go mad. Out of a hundred psychiatric cases, eighty have gone crazy because of sexual repression.

There is another way also: the whole attention of a man moves upward instead of moving downward. The attention moves upward. The attention gets involved in the search for the ultimate, in the search for the truth. The attention is shifted to a space where one attains a millionfold more bliss than sexual pleasure. If attention is focused on that dimension, all the energy starts moving upward. That man does not even feel that there is anything like a sexual pull. He does not even notice. Sex does not even stand in his way. If your attention...

For instance, a child is playing, collecting pebbles, and someone tells him that there is a diamond mine nearby. He will run there and if he finds diamonds and gems, will his attention go back to the pebbles? It is finished; now his whole energy will be absorbed in collecting diamonds.

Until someone moves in the dimension of godliness, he is bound to be pulled in the direction of sexuality. The moment he starts moving in the dimension of the ultimate, at the same moment all his energy moves on a different journey.

Do you understand the meaning of the word *brahmacharya*? *Brahmacharya* implies: a life, *charya*, of godliness, *brahman*. The meaning of the word *brahmacharya* has no connection to sex. It means living like the divine, living like the ultimate. It has no relation to semen and so on.

And how can our living become like the divine? When consciousness is flowing toward the divine, our way of life slowly, slowly becomes like the divine. And when our consciousness moves upward, it stops moving downward. The downward flow stops. If someone starts playing on a *veena* while I am speaking, all your attention will move toward the *veena*. You will not have to force it to; rather, it will move naturally. Within a moment, you will find that you have forgotten to listen to me and you are listening to the *veena*.

When the *veena* of the innermost being starts playing its melody, then our consciousness moves away from the body and it moves toward the self-nature. And that which flowers is called *brahmacharya*, celibacy. That celibacy has incredible bliss, that celibacy has extraordinary peace, that celibacy has miraculous mysteries.

But it is not available to those people who suppress and repress. So you say that the faces of our young people look weak, there is no shine in their eyes, but have you observed a procession of holy men? Then there should be shining in their eyes, but they look sicker than us, more feverish. Their condition is worse than ours. But we say that they are practicing austerity and that is why they look like that.

The reasons behind low life energy are deficiency, poverty, and starvation. And the reasons for all this vulgarity and sexuality are due to moving in a wrong direction and the preaching of celibacy – the training of suppression.

There are a few more questions; I will discuss them during

the evening talk. I am grateful that you listened to my talk with so much peace and love. And I salute the godliness within you. Please accept my respect.

CHAPTER 9

grasp the knack of meditation

SOMEONE HAS ASKED:

> *Osho,*
> *You have said that inner revolution is a sudden explosion. And then you suggest we practice meditation. Isn't this contradictory?*

No, there is no contradiction between these two statements. If I say that when water evaporates it is an explosion, and that it evaporates at one hundred degrees – and also I say to someone that he should heat up the water so that it can evaporate... He can say, "You were saying that water evaporates suddenly, so why do we need to warm it up slowly, slowly? Isn't there a contradiction between these two?" And I will say to him that there is no contradiction.

When we heat water, water warmed to one degree or ninety-nine degrees does not become vapor. Water warmed to one degree is still water and water heated to ninety-nine degrees is still water. At one hundred degrees, the water suddenly turns into steam.

But while heating it up to one hundred degrees, the temperature increases gradually. That level of heat does not happen suddenly.

So when I say that water turns into vapor suddenly, I am saying that it is not that water first turns a little into vapor, and then a little more, and then a little more. The water turns into steam at one hundred degrees with a sudden explosion. The vapor replaces the water. But when I say you should heat it up, it means that the hundred-degree temperature comes slowly, slowly. I say that inner revolution is an explosion, but before the revolution, the warming up of the consciousness takes place slowly, slowly. It does not happen suddenly. Otherwise there would be no need to practice meditation. Hence, I said that when the explosion happens, it happens.

But your consciousness is not at that point where the explosion can take place; the explosion has a boiling point and after reaching that point, the explosion happens. But you are not there. If you are at that point, the explosion can happen this very moment. The explosion does not take time, but it takes time to reach the point of explosion.

We plant a seed; it suddenly bursts into a sprout. But before sprouting, it remains underground: it disintegrates, it breaks, it cracks – and then it sprouts. Sprouting happens like an eruption.

A baby is born out of the mother's womb. The birth is an explosion. It is not that the child is born a little now and then he will be born a little more a while later. Birth is not a gradual happening. The birth takes place in a moment. But before the birth, the baby is gradually growing for nine months. He is getting ready to be born, he is preparing. Then the birth will happen instantaneously. But the preparation will take nine months continuously. When birth happens, there will have been a preparation of nine months behind it. If that preparation is not there, birth cannot happen instantly. There is a gradual growth to reach the point of birth, but birth is an explosion.

Revolution is an explosion and meditation is a gradual growth. And meditation is the primary preparation for that life revolution. I am talking about that preparation; the day the preparation is complete, that very day the explosion will take place. When it happens, you will not say, "I am a little enlightened, I will be more enlightened in a while." It will not happen like that.

The day enlightenment happens, it happens as a sudden explosion and all the doors will be broken down. But until it happens, the primary preparation for it will continue step by step.

There is no contradiction between these two.

Osho,
Will there be any indication of coming closer to enlightenment?

Certainly there will be. For instance, someone is going to walk in a garden. The garden is far away, he cannot even see it yet, but as he comes closer, he can feel the cool breeze and the fragrance of the flowers on the wind. He says, "It seems the garden is close now." He says, "The garden is close." Neither the garden has been seen yet, nor the flowers have been seen yet, but the breeze has become cooler and it carries a little fragrance. And as he continues, the fragrance increases, the freshness grows, and the air becomes cooler. He says, "Certainly I am reaching closer to the garden."

As you reach closer to enlightenment, when you reach closer to the inner revolution, you will start having a few glimpses. For instance, the disturbances you felt inside until yesterday will become less. The anger that was there until yesterday will become less intense. Your hatred will start disappearing. The ego was heavy on you until yesterday and it will be lighter. The anxiety of yesterday will be less today. Desires will evaporate. All this will show that you are reaching closer to the point of revolution, where you disappear and the ultimate is revealed. Before you reach the point of godliness, all these changes will start happening.

But if all these things are *increasing*, you should know that you are moving farther away from *samadhi*. If anger is increasing day by day, anxiety is increasing, hatred is increasing, wickedness is increasing, you will know that you are going in the opposite direction. If these things are decreasing, you know that you are moving toward meditation. These changes are just indications. And each person has to think over it for himself because each person has one basic weakness which will be the criterion for whether his meditation is growing or not. Everyone's fundamental weakness is different.

Someone's basic weakness is anger. His whole personality is built around anger. It is as if, after going around and about, he always comes back to the same point – anger. Then he will have to observe closely whether his anger is becoming less or not. If his anger is decreasing, it means that a fundamental transformation in his personality has begun. Someone else may have another weakness and others will have other kinds of weaknesses. So, each person has to find out the basic center of his personality and watch the minute changes that start to happen. The transformation will start happening and you will see the difference. At first only you will notice the changes. Slowly, slowly others will see it too; those who are close to you will notice. But initially only you will perceive it.

Just remember this much: if the things that are called sins start decreasing, then understand that there is a growth in meditation. And if the qualities that are called virtues start increasing, then understand that you are moving deeper into meditation.

What I am saying is that sin is that which takes you in the opposite direction of yourself. And virtue is that which takes you closer to yourself. Remember that sin and virtue have no other meaning. The second thing to remember is that your awareness should gradually be increasing. Whatever work you are doing, you will do it more consciously. You did the same thing yesterday and the day before yesterday, but you did not do it with so much awareness. You will even eat your food with awareness. If you are talking, you will talk consciously. When you are walking on the road, you will walk with awareness. Awareness will increase. And that will bring about the first difference: the more awareness grows, committing mistakes becomes more difficult. How can a man of awareness get angry? How can a conscious man fight? How can a man full of awareness steal? The personality of a man of awareness starts to change.

So remember two things: all the things that increase the disturbance of the mind start disappearing, and awareness starts growing. Know then that meditation is growing. But this is the fragrance of the garden, not the garden.

This is the difference between a seeker and an enlightened being. A seeker is one who is coming closer to the garden. He has not yet arrived. He is becoming a good man, a virtuous man, but still standing outside the garden. Now he can feel the fragrant breeze, but he has not yet stepped into the garden. And an enlightened being is one who has stepped into the garden. He is neither good nor bad. Now he has reached a space where there is neither good nor bad. Good and bad were the measures of the outside. Now, in the garden, they do not apply.

If virtue is increasing, then understand that meditation is growing. And try to understand the meaning of virtue. It does not mean that you start wearing the ochre clothes of a sannyasin or anointing sandalwood on your forehead or covering yourself with a sheet on which the mantra "Rama, Rama" is written. All these have nothing to do with virtue.

If you look at it carefully, you will see that someone does things such as wearing ochre clothes, covering his mouth to avoid killing insects, wearing something saying "Rama, Rama" and so on, in order to express his fundamental weakness of exhibitionism. His basic weakness, exhibitionism, is compelling him to do all these things. The word *exhibitionism* implies: others must see me, others should know me, others should recognize and acknowledge that I exist. This is his basic weakness. He could have become a movie actor, then it would have been all right. He could have worked in a theater, then it would have been all right. That would have been the right soil for him to grow. That world would have been according to his weakness. But he became a saint – what has a saint got to do with exhibition?

But he will go on expressing his basic weakness. So, if someone has the weakness that he enjoys exhibiting himself, it will decrease with the deepening of his meditation. We need to inquire within and find out what our weakness is. And we all know our weakness; there is no need to ask someone else. You know at what point your personality is obsessed.

Someone goes on clinging to money – that is his weakness. When meditation deepens, the clinging to money will decrease. Whatever is your weakness, these are the two results that you will see. And if you keep watching like this, within six months to a year you will be able to decide whether there is any difference or not, what difference you feel, and in which area of your life the change has occurred. Transformation is certain. With the deepening of meditation, there will be changes in your life. It cannot be prevented.

The whole personality and behavior go through a transformation. But remember, all this belongs to the outside of the garden. Inside the garden, there is no way to keep any account of what is happening. There is no longer even any need to keep an account. It is only needed before entering the garden. Once in the garden, no one ever asks, "How can I know that the explosion has happened?" If a man's house has caught fire, does he go outside and ask someone, "How can I know that my house is on fire?" When the explosion happens, such a great revolution takes place that all the past is burned, a completely new beginning happens. Then there is no need to ask someone. You know it.

But until the explosion has happened, you want to ask about the kind of changes that will take place. That is why there are a few indications that will help you to know your growth outside the garden; inside the garden, no sign will work. There you perceive directly, you just know.

Osho,
How long should we meditate each day?

It is not a matter of time. The question is not how long you should do it for; rather the question is how to approach it. It can be ten minutes or fifteen minutes or half an hour. The question of quality is more important. The quantity and length of time is not important. But anyway we can give it a thought: you can meditate at least half an hour in the morning and half an hour in the evening. At least this much!

But it is not a fixed rule. One should not think that if he cannot meditate for half an hour he should give it up. Whatever you can manage will be significant. But if you can manage thirty minutes in the morning and thirty minutes in the evening, the results will come faster.

But even then, the focus is not on the length of time, but on the depth of meditation. Even if it is for five minutes, your whole being is totally involved. Otherwise, you can just sit for half an hour with closed eyes. Many people are sitting in the temples for their whole lives and nothing happens to them because they are just wasting their time. They look at their watches and when thirty minutes are over, they get up and leave.

There is no need to pay too much attention to quantity. Time has some utility, because what will happen without it? Thirty minutes plus thirty minutes – take one hour out for meditation in twenty-four hours; let the worldly things continue for twenty-three hours. And in the final day of your life, you will find out that what you earned in those twenty-three hours is lost and what you earned in spending one hour in meditation each day is going to be with you forever.

Today, you will feel that it is an hour! You are not aware of the treasures that will be revealed through meditation, so a minimum of one hour! And you should also select the time for yourself. Generally, on waking up in the morning, it is valuable if you can finish your shower as soon as possible and then sit for meditation. Why? Because your mind rests the whole night; in the morning it is fresh, joyful, and can become serene quickly.

If you can meditate before the daily routine of work begins, it will also affect your daily work because someone who has gone through half an hour of meditation on waking up cannot work in the same way as someone who has gone to work without meditation. There will be a difference between these two individuals. There will be a difference between their interiority. There will be a difference in their behavior. So, before the daytime world begins, sit for half an hour. Just as we bring freshness with us after a shower, in the same way, if you come from an inner shower, you will bring an inner freshness with you. It will influence your whole day's work.

So, early in the morning – as soon as possible, right after waking up. And right before sleeping at night; just the last moments before you fall asleep, meditate and then immediately sleep. These two moments in time are called the turning point: when we wake up in the morning, at that moment, and when we move into sleep again at night. At those two points, the state of our consciousness changes. When the consciousness moves from waking into sleep, at that moment the whole environment of the mind changes, and in the morning when we wake up from sleep, the whole environment changes. If you can sow the seed of meditation at those moments of transition, it is the most significant moment for meditation because at that moment, consciousness goes through a shift and reaches the spaces it does not generally reach.

As you go to sleep at night… When you start falling asleep, slowly, slowly wakefulness disappears and sleep descends. And a moment comes which, if you have observed, you must have noticed: there is a moment before which you were awake and after which you are asleep. There is a very subtle moment in the middle, which is the door through which waking enters sleep. Consciousness turns into unconsciousness. If the wave of meditation sustains at that very door, the wave descends deeper with sleep. And all night during sleep, the inner current of meditation goes on flowing. That door opens only at that moment. Generally the door is closed, but when someone is entering it opens, and if you enter at that moment, you can go within. Then the door closes again.

So the door of consciousness opens for sleep. The conscious mind goes into sleep and the unconscious mind wakes up – at that moment, a new state, a new door opens in the consciousness. Whatever state or feeling you bring to that door will be locked in as a treasure of your consciousness for the whole night.

That is why, before a student is to appear for an examination, he goes on taking the exam during his sleep. He goes to sleep thinking continuously about the exam. His exam enters his sleep. The whole night he is taking the exam, the whole night the work of the exam is going on.

A shopkeeper goes to sleep counting money, and even in his dreams, he goes on counting money. You must have heard about a cloth merchant who tore his bedsheet during his sleep. He was selling it to someone in his dream.

We continue doing the same thing in sleep that we do at the last moment before sleep. If you have not noticed this, then try to observe it tonight. The last thought before sleep will be the first thought on waking up. Whatever thought is the last before sleep will be the first thought at the moment of waking up. The last thought remains present in the consciousness for the whole night and appears as the first thought in the morning. You can see this by experimenting. If you experiment, you will know.

Hence, at the last moment before sleep, the more peaceful,

silent, and blissful your state of mind is, the better it is. It will continue like an inner current during the night. That is why someone who goes into sleep meditating transforms his whole sleep into meditation slowly, slowly.

Nowadays no one has so much time that he can devote six hours to meditation. But we sleep for six hours. And if the whole period of sleep can become meditation, we will get the benefit of six hours meditation.

So, meditate at the last moment before sleep at night, and at the first moment after waking up in the morning. If you can take these two periods for meditation, it will be very good. If someone has more time, or if he can take some time out for meditation, ten or fifteen minutes anytime during the day, he can do that. Remember one thing: there cannot be an extreme of meditation. No matter how much you meditate, it can never become too much. You can meditate as much as you wish; it can never be too much.

Can there be an extreme of silence? Can we say that this man is extreme in peace? We cannot say such things. There is no amount that is extreme in peace. And there is no limit to meditation. So don't worry about an extreme at all – whenever and whatever time you get!

When you have grasped the knack of meditation, while you are sitting in a bus you can close your eyes... What is the use of listening to the stupid, useless talk of people and looking at the road outside the window? What will you gain from it? Close your eyes. If you are sitting in the bus for two hours, try to dissolve those two hours in meditation.

When you are sitting in your office with nothing to do, or you are sitting in a waiting room, you've got nothing to do, instead of doing something useless, it is better to close your eyes. That way you will avoid uselessly looking here and there with no purpose, thinking futile things, listening to pointless things. You can invest that much time in something that is ultimately significant. And if a man can just give his spare moments – which he wastes uselessly – to meditation, that is enough. That is absolutely enough.

A man is sitting in a train: if he has to sit in the train for the whole day, he reads the same newspaper again and again. I see it every day in the train. He has read the newspaper many times, but what else to do now, so he starts reading it again! He has listened to the same songs so many times, but once again he turns on the radio and starts listening to them. You have talked about the same things so many times, and again you start the same conversation.

If a man watches what he is talking about throughout the day, how many times will he see that he has spoken about the same thing? And if he observes how much of what he is talking about is useless and he can do without…? Then he will find himself in difficulty. He will be shocked to see that out of a hundred, ninety-eight things he is saying are futile!

When you send a telegram, how do you reduce the number of words? You find that fewer and fewer words can convey the message. Altogether, eight or ten words are enough. In a telegram you are able to convey a message which you would write in two pages if you were to write a letter. All that can be said in ten words. And the message works faster than a letter because all the power is condensed into ten words. Hence, a telegram is so effective. In a letter, the same message becomes long and expanded and when it is expanded over two pages, its effect becomes less.

One should be telegraphic in talking, listening, walking, strolling, and all other activities, so that the time saved can be invested in meditation.

Should we do the night meditation sitting or lying down?

As far as possible, the night meditation should be done lying down. If you fall asleep immediately when lying down, then meditate in a sitting posture. The night meditation should be done lying down so that you enter sleep while meditating. That is, you should not notice when meditation ends and when you go to sleep. You should go to sleep while meditating. So, it should be practiced lying down. If you meditate in a sitting posture, then you will have to lie down to go to sleep. That will create a hindrance. It will become an obstruction in the flow and will create a distance; first you will finish your sitting meditation and then you will lie down to go to sleep. So it should be practiced lying down, unless someone feels that he falls asleep immediately after lying down, that he is absolutely unable to meditate lying down. Then he can practice the night meditation in a sitting posture for two or three months and then slowly, slowly try doing it while lying down.

What if people are chattering?

That is not a problem. Your mind should not be chattering. If everyone is chattering, that is not your concern. You are meditating; they are not meditating.

But just now, when the children were talking, your attention was drawn to that, wasn't it?

No, no. My attention was drawn there – I am not trying to meditate here. I am speaking here and if during my talk ten more people start speaking, I have no objection, I can speak, but my speaking will have no purpose at all. I am not practicing meditation here. If I was meditating, you could bring all your children, but it would not make any difference. Do you understand? I am talking here and if during my talk a couple of children are crying and shouting, the very purpose of my talking will not be fulfilled. My talks will not reach you.

Talking can be hindered by other people talking. Now if you put a couple more microphones right here and start speaking, it would not make any difference to me, but I would stop talking because there would be no point. The very meaning of meditation is... You are going to meditate; now you have no right to control any child. You cannot ask all the children of the world to become silent so that you can meditate! It is none of your business. You are moving into meditation, enjoy it. The children are not supposed to meditate, so why should they keep silent?

Will that not become a distraction?

The distraction happens because you are not able to move into meditation. Do you understand the meaning of meditation? It means witnessing, as I mentioned earlier. If the child is crying, just witness it: the child is crying and I am witnessing. But you don't remain a witness, you become a doer. You say, "I will strangle this child, he is making a lot of fuss!" Then the disturbance starts. You are no longer a witness, you have become a doer. You say, "Take this child away. I don't want to hear him."

Just remain a witness. If the child is crying, let him cry. If he is laughing, let him laugh. If he is not crying, he is not crying. If you remain a witness, whether the child is crying or someone is chattering, or someone is blowing a horn, or something else is happening, does not make any difference because the process I am talking about is that of witnessing.

Yes, it can make a difference in concentration. If a man is chanting a mantra, "Rama, Rama" and someone else starts saying something else very loudly, it will become a hindrance because he is saying something and the other is also saying something. One person talking can disturb another person talking.

But I am not speaking about talking at all. I am not saying that you should chant "Om" or do anything else. I am just asking you to be a witness. Whatever is happening, be a witness to that. If there is any disturbance inside you, be a witness to that too. Just go on witnessing. Whatever is taking place, be a witness to it. The final result of that will be meditation. So, you can do it while you are sitting in a shop, or in a bus. There is no need to go to the Himalayas. You can do it sitting by the side of a road. Rather, you will enjoy it greatly if you are doing it sitting at the side of a road. Then you will see how strange your mind is; it does not remain a witness at all! It says immediately, "Strangle this one, stop that one! Stop that man speaking!" Our minds say all that.

Can it happen anywhere?

Absolutely! It can happen right now. It is just a matter of a little effort.

I was staying in a guesthouse and a politician was staying at the same place. In the evening, we both returned to the hotel to sleep. I went to sleep immediately. He came into my room fifteen minutes later, shook me, and said, "Are you sleeping? I can't sleep – it's impossible for me to sleep!"

All the dogs of the town were gathered near the hotel, making such a noise. They must have been used to gathering there every day. He went out a couple of times to chase the dogs away, but each time he chased them away, they brought back more dogs with them. Dogs cannot be chased away so easily; it's not possible even to chase human beings away so easily, so how could he chase the dogs away? They all came back. He became restless and said, "I won't be able to sleep. These dogs are barking so much, making so much noise."

I said to him, "The dogs are not aware that you are sleeping here. And they are not concerned either. What have they got to do with you? You should sleep easily. What connection do you have with the dogs?"

He replied, "It's not a matter of connection. They make a noise, so I can't sleep."

I said, "The disturbance doesn't come from the noise the dogs are making. Rather, it comes from the idea that they shouldn't bark. This idea of yours is disturbing you. Dogs are dogs, they are going to bark. You have to sleep, so just sleep."

Then he asked, "What shall I do?"

I told him, "The dogs are barking, just listen to that, with witnessing. Just listen: the dogs are barking and I am listening. Then we will talk in the morning."

Within fifteen minutes, he must have fallen asleep. On waking up in the morning he said to me, "Miraculous! When I started witnessing that the dogs were barking and I was just listening, even their barking sounded to me as if it was a lullaby. It was bound to send me to sleep. I slept deeply the whole night. I have no idea when they stopped barking."

I said, "Why would they have stopped? They have no relation to you. They are not concerned with whether you slept or not. They must have continued barking, but your mind had dropped its resistance. As long as it was resisting and thinking about preventing them from barking, there was a problem. Then you accepted that if they wanted to bark, they could bark."

To witness that which is happening around us is what I call meditation. Hence, nothing can hinder that.

Is it necessary to close our eyes?

No, it is not necessary at all. But in the beginning, generally you'll find it easier to experiment with closed eyes because then you will need to be a witness only at the windows of your ears. If you keep your eyes open, you will have to be a witness at two places – at the windows of your ears and also at the windows of your eyes. And to be a witness at the windows of the eyes is a little more difficult than at the windows of the ears because the impressions we receive on the eyes affect us more deeply.

But if you can manage it, then it is very good. What I am saying is to move slowly, that when you have mastered witnessing at the ears, then you can also keep your eyes open. But if you feel it is difficult to keep your eyes closed, keep them open from the beginning. If someone finds it difficult, if he finds it difficult to close his eyes, he can keep his eyes open. But then he will have to be a witness at two points. Then you must witness what you see. You witness who is passing by: you don't need to keep an account of the man who is passing by, whether he is your friend or your enemy, or the woman who is going by is your wife, and so on. You should not keep a report like that because the moment you start reporting, your witnessing is gone. When you are just a witness, you are just observing that someone is passing by. You don't make any judgment about it. You are just perceiving and observing.

In order to avoid the double work, I tell you to keep your eyes closed. It is in fact better to keep both of them open, but if that is difficult, first try to master witnessing just at the ears. And then you can practice it at the eyes also. When both are mastered, a great joy comes; then you can remain a witness while walking on the road with open eyes. Then there is no need to sit down for meditation: you can remain a witness while doing all kinds of work because then there is no need to close the eyes. But in order to avoid difficulty in the beginning, try to focus all your energy at just one window first. If you can manage that, then try it at both. There is no problem in that.

Osho,
When I meditate one day and I don't do it the next day, it becomes a suffering and guilt.

If you make it so, then it will become so. If one day you

meditated and the next day you did not, if you turn it into a suffering, it will become a suffering. Otherwise there is no need to be sad about it. Feel gratitude for whatever you could manage. There is no need to feel guilt for what you couldn't manage. Why? – because guilt will create a hindrance in your next meditation and gratitude will support your next meditation.

If I can sit in meditation, if I can meditate, I should feel gratitude toward existence that I was able to meditate today. It is a great blessing from existence. If you have this attitude, tomorrow this feeling will be helpful in your meditation because the feeling of gratitude makes the mind serene. But if you are unable to meditate one day and you start regretting it – that it was so bad and is a great disturbance, it is a great harm and a big loss, and you make your mind suffer... This miserable state of mind about missing meditation today will not allow you to enter deeply into meditation tomorrow either.

You must understand that guilt becomes an obstacle in meditation, so feeling guilty is meaningless. Also, you should be a witness to everything. You are witnessing the fact that you meditated today, then be a witness also to the fact that you could not meditate another day. Why create unnecessary conflict? There were two facts: you observed both that yesterday you could meditate and that today you could not.

Ramateertha used to talk about himself in the third person. He was not using "I." He wouldn't say, "I feel thirsty," he used to say, "Ramateertha is feeling thirsty." He would say, "Today Ramateertha met a few people along the way and they started abusing Ramateertha. I was standing there and laughing that Ramateertha was facing abuse."

When he went to America for the first time, people asked him, "We don't understand what you are saying. What do you mean? You are Ramateertha, aren't you?"

He replied, "I am not Ramateertha. People call this body Ramateertha. I am beyond this and far away."

Ramateertha went to visit somewhere and he got caught up with a few people who started fighting. He just stood there laughing: "Good, now Ramateertha has been caught. Now you are in trouble, son! Now there is no way to escape."

This is the meaning of witnessing. Slowly, slowly it settles so deeply that you are observing, "I am sitting for meditation today" or you are watching, "I could not sit for meditation today." You are witnessing even the process of meditation. And then with the benefits you get from meditation there will be even deeper insights because the witnessing has started penetrating even deeper within. Now you don't have the feeling of being a "doer" of the practice of meditation, whether you meditated or did not meditate. Otherwise the doer comes in. The "I' comes in and catches hold of the act.

No, today, watch that you meditated and another day in the same way, observe that you could not meditate. You are just the watcher, you are not a doer. Then the momentum will become much stronger. And on that level there is no regret, no suffering, there is no question of such things. Whatever happened, you observed.

What do you mean by gratitude?

Gratitude means thankfulness toward the whole, because nothing is possible without this whole existence. We cannot even breathe. I am breathing, then I feel gratitude toward the wind; gratitude toward the trees, for producing oxygen. Gratitude toward the sky, toward the stars, toward the sun, and toward all of you. I do not mean toward Rama, Krishna, Buddha or any other person like that.

We cannot be alive even for a second without this whole existence, this whole expansion of life. Whatever we are, that is through existence. So whatever is happening through us is happening with the support of existence. Otherwise it would not happen. The gratitude is toward all of that.

And in the feeling of gratitude, the emphasis is not on who you are grateful to, that is irrelevant. You felt gratitude; that is helpful. Whether there is someone to receive it or not is not important. It is not valuable.

Should I repeat in my mind, "I am a witness, I am a witness..."?

Witnessing is not a matter of repeating, it is a matter of being.

Because I'm explaining it to you, I have to say it in words: "Feel in yourself, 'I am just a witness.'" There are two things in it... This is a very significant question. If you go on repeating in your mind "I am a witness, I am a witness," it will work as a mantra. Then slowly, slowly it will become something like chanting, "Rama, Rama. Rama, Rama, Rama, Rama."

Don't repeat in words, "I am a witness." You have to experience, "I am a witness." There is a difference between these two. You have to experience, "Who am I?" in relation to whatever is taking place. "What is my relationship to it?" Then you will discover the relationship of the witness. Witnessing does not mean you go on repeating the words, "I am a witness." Otherwise it will have no more significance than a mantra. "I am a witness. My experience of this must go on deepening."

For instance, with the sounds going on all around, what am I toward this sound? I am a witness. Even these words I am creating just in order to convey it to you. You don't need to create any words within yourself. Just this much knowing is needed: "This is my situation." To be a witness is "...my situation."

When you are eating, for a moment bow down your head and look within: "What am I doing?" Then you will know: "The body is eating, I am just a witness." This witnessing must be an experiencing. It is not a repeating of words. Repetition in words is pointless.

Because I am explaining it to you, the difficulty arises; I have to explain it through words. If I am talking to you, I have to use words. And then I am aware of the danger that somebody may sit down and start repeating every day, "I am a witness, I am a witness." If he continues doing it, after just a couple of times it will become a dead routine. He won't even be aware of what he is saying. He will go on repeating, "I am a witness, I am a witness." He will look at the clock, get up after half an hour and nothing will be gained. He will remain exactly the same. On top of that, he wasted half an hour. And the stupid work he did during that half an hour – "I am a witness, I am a witness" – also disturbed his mind.

It is not a question of repeating in words – it is an experiencing. Everything which is happening around me, toward that, my attitude is of a witness.

Osho,
How can a revolution happen in spite of the intolerable, dirty, and corrupt politics of India?

The first thing is that whether it is a society, or a government, or an economic system, when we say that it is "intolerable" we make a mistake because the moment it becomes intolerable, that very moment, change will start happening. So the first thing to remember is that it has not become intolerable yet.

You say that politics is corrupt, but it is not intolerable, otherwise it could not continue. Anything intolerable cannot continue.

So, my first effort is that, if you want to end something, you have to make it intolerable. And making it intolerable means to awaken people's consciousness and sensitivity so that the situation becomes unbearable. It is not unbearable because whatever is happening we are tolerating it; that is why it is happening. As long as we tolerate it, it will continue to happen.

The truth is that our governments cannot be worthier than our own level of intelligence. It is not possible. We feel that there is corruption in the government; it is very bad, but not intolerable. Otherwise it would not continue even for a second. In fact, how does a revolution happen? When a system becomes intolerable, a revolution takes place.

There has not been a revolution in India for the last five thousand years because nothing ever becomes intolerable here. And there is a psychological reason for that in this country. The whole purpose of my talking is to break those psychological reasons, so that the situation becomes intolerable. Otherwise it will never become unbearable.

There are psychological mechanisms in India. It is just as we install a suspension in a car, so that we don't feel the bumps on the roads. There are bumps on the road, but the car is equipped with shock absorbers. When the car crosses the bumps, the springs absorb the shock and the person sitting in the car doesn't feel it. And unless the springs are removed, the passenger will never feel the bumps on the road.

Trains are equipped with buffers; there is a buffer installed between two compartments in a train. If there is a collision, the shock absorber is so powerful that it can absorb a collision up to two feet. The passenger in the compartment won't feel that there was an impact. Unless the buffers are removed, the outside impacts won't be felt inside the compartment.

The most dangerous thing in the Indian mind is that there are buffers and shock absorbers installed inside it for the last three or four thousand years. And because of that, anything intolerable in life is absorbed by the buffers. We don't notice that it has become unbearable. Those buffers are of great cunningness: they are installed very skillfully and they are very pleasant too, so we never become aware of any trouble, we never feel any problem.

Take the example of poverty in India. There has never been so much poverty in any other country. If there was so much poverty anywhere else in the world, everything would be on fire; it could not continue for even a second! No other nation in this world could agree to remain so poor even for a second.

But India has buffers. And the buffer is that the saints and the holy people of this country are convincing people that poverty is the result of your past-lives karma. That is the buffer. And because of that buffer, the poor man says, "What can I do? The rich man in front of me has nothing to do with my poverty. My poverty is due to my past lives." And now nothing can be done about those past lives. What can you do about them? The past life is gone. Now you cannot do anything. Now you can do something only with the next life, and if you did something very wrong, then even that chance will be gone. Hence, tolerate everything peacefully. Tolerate so that you are not poor in the next life, so that wealth is given to you. This is the reason you must not do anything wrong. Now, this is a buffer.

There will be no revolution in India until all the buffers are broken. Nothing becomes unbearable here!

So, the first thing is that the law and order system of the state *is* very corrupt; it is beyond tolerance. But the mind of the country is able to tolerate so much, it endures everything. So the biggest question in front of me is how to destroy this buffer. I continuously talk to you from every dimension and from every angle in order to shatter the buffer, so that it starts breaking from here and there. At the places where it breaks, the system will become intolerable. And even if it becomes intolerable for just a small group of people here, it will bring about a revolution in this nation. There is not much difficulty in bringing about a revolution, but the situation needs to be unbearable.

And how can we remove the corruption? When we ask a question such as this, we have an idea in our minds, thinking, "What can we do so that this filth can be eradicated?" I don't think that the dirt can be removed this way. There are two kinds of dirt: one is outer dirt, such as the dust which gathers on your body. That is called dirt. A man is covered with dust, dripping with sweat, and becomes dirty. He takes a shower and the dirt is removed. The dirt was only outside. But suppose a man gets cancer? That too is a toxin, but it will not wash off in a shower. It has to be operated on, it needs surgery. It will be removed only by surgical treatment.

The dirt that has gathered on Indian politics is not the kind of dust that gathers superficially, where you can give the politicians a good shower and everything will be all right. It is not like that. Its tumors are deep within; there are cancers in the whole political system of India. And there is no treatment other than surgery. There is no other way than amputating its arms and legs.

Nothing is going to happen through superficial reforms here and there. The roots are very deep, and they are so fundamental that we don't even think it possible that roots can spread so deeply and fundamentally.

I will give you one example for this. And then, if there are still more questions, we can talk about them in the evening.

The roots have spread so deeply that they are not visible to us. And the measures we take are so superficial that the roots don't even get the news that something has been done. Suppose that someone goes on trimming the leaves of a tree – the roots will not even notice that the leaves were pruned. The roots will produce new leaves immediately because the function of the roots is to produce leaves. So, when you prune one leaf, the root sends two leaves. The roots take it as pruning the tree. The function of the roots is not to let the leaves die off. If the leaves have died, then send new leaves. When someone cuts leaves off a tree, he is not harming the tree. The plant becomes double the thickness in a few days.

All reformists multiply the sickness of the society: all reformists, without exception! For they prune the leaves. A revolutionary man talks about cutting the roots. Try to understand this.

After my last visit to Ahmedabad, I received letters regularly for a couple of days. The secretary of the untouchables wrote to me. They have a magazine, and its editor wrote to me, "Why don't you stay in the home of a harijan as Gandhi did?"?

I told him that if they all came together, I would talk to them and around ten or twenty people came to visit me in the evening. They asked me, "Why don't you stay with us as Gandhi did? You too should stay with us in our homes."

I said to them, "I don't consider anyone a harijan, so what criterion would I use to find out who is a harijan, which house belongs to a harijan? In order to stay in a harijan's house, I have to take it for granted that a group of people are untouchables.

"I usually stay in someone's house. If you say, 'Come and stay in our home,' I am ready to go. But if you say, 'Stay in an untouchables' home,' I am not ready to go because I do not consider anyone an untouchable.

"You are so stupid that you announce that you are harijans, so I should stay at your home! You can talk about inviting me to your homes, why do you talk about being a harijan? On the one hand you wish that being a harijan should end and on the other hand you want recognition as a harijan, you want respectability for it."

The man who insists that he will stay only in a harijan house considers them as untouchable as the man who says that he will not allow a harijan to enter his house. There is no difference between these two. Both accept that harijans exist. They both water the deep roots; they water the roots of social difference. Superficially it seems that the untouchables are being called harijan – the children of God – and the harijans thought that it was a great thing that happened to them!

Actually it was the worst thing to happen to them. The shock they were experiencing in being called untouchables was gone. No one wants to be called an untouchable, but a man feels pride in being called a harijan. It is a very dangerous thing.

It is as if we give a good name to a disease. Instead of calling a cancer a cancer, we start calling it the name of a goddess. Then a man can say, "I am suffering from something that is a goddess." But it is still a cancer. What difference does it make? Untouchables are untouchables. To give them a name like *harijan* is very dangerous because the disease will hide behind the good word *harijan*. And even the harijan will start saying arrogantly, "I am not an ordinary person, I am a harijan!"

The roots are not removed. Only the leaves are pruned superficially and they come back again and again. And many times it can also happen that the tree can become upside-down, but the sickness will continue: that is, it is possible that the brahmins could end up being in the same condition as the sudras, and the sudras could move up to the condition of a brahmin, but the same disease will continue. It will be no different.

My whole concern is how to catch hold of the very roots of this society, this nation and this system, from where all the lies originate, to find the seeds in those minds that create the roots, and to see how to destroy them.

If a few conscious people in India do not listen to the superficial, bureaucratic notions – such as where to make a road, where to open a hospital and so on... Even though all this is good, nothing is going to happen by it. If they ignore all these bureaucratic details and just focus on breaking the conditioning of the eternal Indian mind, then within twenty years such fresh minds will be born in India that you will not have to do anything for revolution. There will be an instantaneous revolution. Otherwise it can never happen.

If the mind is not prepared, then violence is needed for a revolution. But if the mind of the nation is prepared, then revolution happens through nonviolence. There is no other way for a revolution to happen nonviolently. If we all agree that this building should be demolished, there is no need for violence. But if we have only one person among us who says that the building should be demolished and the others do not agree, then there will be violence, there will be fighting and killing. Those who do not agree will have to be destroyed. Then there will be chaos.

Until now, violence has been needed for all the revolutions in this world, because only a few people understood something and the rest of the population did not agree. Then violence was needed.

If there is the right psychological environment, a revolution can be absolutely nonviolent. And a revolution that is not nonviolent is an incomplete revolution. It means that it has been forced: a few people have forced their ideology onto the masses. My view is that when a few people forcefully impose something on the masses, then even though it can be for their own good, it is wrong.

So, first we have to make it intolerable for everybody. We have to make it clear in everybody's minds where all these things are coming from, and that because of these ideas we tolerate everything.

Then the revolution will take place. There is no great difficulty for a revolution to happen.

CHAPTER 10

the only goal is life itself

MY BELOVED ONES.

People have asked many questions about the talks of these last three days. I will try to answer as many as possible.

One friend has asked:

Osho,
You talk about "the revolution of new thoughts." Can something that has never happened before happen now? Everything under the sky is old, so what is the new?

The first thing I want to say about this is that everything under the sky is *new*; what is there which can be called old? The old does not survive for even a moment. The new is born every moment. The illusion of "old" is created because we are unable to perceive the difference between the old and the new.

The sun rose yesterday morning, clouds gathered yesterday and the winds blew yesterday too. And we say, "It is the same!" But nothing is exactly the same. The way the clouds were shaping and reshaping yesterday will never happen "under the sky" again in the same way. Or the winds which were blowing yesterday evening – the same winds are not blowing today. You came here yesterday; if you think that the same "you" has come here today, you are mistaken. Neither I am the same, nor you are the same. In twenty-four hours, a lot of water has flown down the Ganges.

Everything is new from moment to moment. Existence does not tolerate the old at all. It cannot tolerate the old even for a moment. This is the very meaning of life. Life implies: that which is ever new. But man has dared to try to save the old.

Existence does not tolerate the old at all, but man makes such an effort to try to save the old. That is why human society is not a living thing; it is a dead society. And a nation that tries to save the old is a dead nation in the same proportion. Our country, India, is one of those dead nations.

We arrogantly say that the ancient nations like Babylon, Syria, Egypt, and Rome could not survive, but our ancient India still goes on. But if you look carefully, you will find that they don't exist anymore because they changed, they became new. And we exist in our ancient form because we could *not* change; we made a tremendous effort to remain old. If we have changed at all, it has been forced on us by existence. Our continuous effort has been to resist change: the same old rut which was there should continue.

If the bullock cart has become out of date, it is not because of us. We made a tremendous effort – all our saints, all our respected men of the society, and all our leaders made a joint effort to save the bullock cart. But existence does not agree with them, and manufactures jet planes instead. We are dragged toward the new as if forced to move toward it.

The situation is the reverse in the rest of the world. In the rest of the world, people stay with the old only when they have to. In our country, we move toward the new only under compulsion. In the rest of the world, the new is welcomed and invited, but in our country the new is accepted as if it is a defeat. That is why a five-thousand-year-old culture stretches out its begging hands toward a culture which is only three hundred, or one that is fifty years old. And we don't even feel ashamed of it.

Our culture must be five thousand years old or even older – the known history is of at least five thousand years. And in five thousand years we have not been able to produce enough wheat or houses or clothes for the population.

The United States is only three hundred years old. Within three hundred years, America has become capable of feeding the whole world. The Soviet Union is only fifty years old. And within fifty years, Russia has come off the list of poor nations and is counted as a rich country. Those who were starving children fifty years ago are today planning to reach the moon and stars. What happened within fifty years? What magic did they learn?

They have not learned any magic; they have learned only one secret: a society which clings to the old slowly, slowly dies, rots, and degenerates. They have learned the secret of inviting the new, calling upon the new, welcoming the new, invoking the challenges of the new – and as soon as possible bringing forth the new, saying good-bye to the old. The result is that they have become more alive. And us? We have almost died.

This friend is also asking if anything new can come into existence.

I remember a story. You must also have heard it...

One day, the mice held a meeting about how to avoid the cat. One clever mouse suggested... All clever mice give this kind of suggestion. The advice is good, but never executed. This is the difficulty with the clever mice. The clever mouse said, "Let's hang a bell around the cat's neck."

All the other mice clapped and said, "A perfect solution."

But the question arose, "Who will hang the bell?"

The clever mouse said, "I just propose the theory. You will have to find out how to apply it. My function is to create a theory, now you have to find out how to do it. The theory is simple: hang a bell around the cat's neck and there will be no danger anymore. Whenever a cat will come, the bell will ring and all the mice will become alert."

This incident was recorded in the mice scriptures. It happened thousands of years ago. And every time the question arose, "How to avoid cats?" the mice would say, "Look in the scriptures." They opened their ancient book and there it was written: "Hang a bell."

The mice all say, "This solution is absolutely perfect; we have been told by our ancestors that a bell should be hung around the cat's neck. But who is going to hang it?"

Once again the question was getting stuck at the same point.

A few days ago it happened… All the mice once again called a meeting. And they said, "Now it is very difficult, the cat is torturing us. Once again the same old book…!"

Then two new mice got up and said – they must have been young mice studying at college. They said, "Drop this nonsense of an ancient book. Enough is enough; the same old talk, the same old book, again the same question will come."

But still the others said, "We cannot act without looking into the scriptures. Has anything new ever happened in this world? Whatever has happened is recorded by our ancestors. Can anything happen more than that? Were our ancestors ignorant? They were so knowledgeable that they knew everything, they were omniscient. They have written that we should tie a bell."

The scriptures were opened again, and the matter was stuck at the same point again. Those who depend on scriptures always get stuck at the same point where they have been getting stuck forever; they never move forward. Again the same question, "Who will tie the bell?"

The young mice said, "Stop this nonsense! Tomorrow we will tie the bell." They were just young mice.

The old mice objected: "Have you gone mad! You are spoiled and don't understand. Has a bell ever been tied? It has never happened before. Have you ever heard that a mouse could manage to tie a bell around a cat's neck? It has never happened before nor can it ever happen."

The young mice said, "No more talk! Tomorrow a bell will be hung on the cat."

And in morning, to their great surprise, the bell was hanging around the cat's neck. The older mice were very puzzled. They asked, "It is very strange. How did you manage to tie it?"

The young mice said, "It is no big deal." They had gone to a medical store, brought some sleeping pills, and dropped them into the cat's milk. The problem was solved. The cat fell asleep and the mice tied the bell around its neck.

The old mice had always been saying that nothing new had

ever happened: "Has any mouse ever tied a bell?" But now the mice have managed to tie a bell.

Whether they have tied it in your village or not, I don't know. There are many different types of villages. And these villages of Rajasthan are very backward. Perhaps the mice of this area have not yet managed to tie a bell. And they go on thinking: "Has anything new ever happened? Can there be any revolution of thought?"

All over the world, there has always been revolution of thought, except in this country. We are the only unfortunate country where we don't bother to think that something new can happen. And if someone raises the topic of the new, we immediately start doubting him.

In the future there will be living spaces on the moon, so the Russian young people think about building a colony on the moon. American children dream of traveling in space. And our children? They go to watch Ramleela, a drama about an ancient Hindu epic!

There is nothing wrong in watching Ramleela. Rama is very lovable. And if you sometimes watch a play about him it is pleasant. But to always go on watching Ramleela is dangerous. It is a wrong attitude. Our youth don't just watch the drama, rather they dream about creating the state of Rama.

This shows our illusion that whatever has happened in the past was golden. This is wrong thinking: everything that happened in the past was not good. The future is always going to be better than the past because we always come out of the past with more experience, we become more experienced. Time passes by, history passes by, and we learn something from it, don't we? Or have we no ability to learn at all?

We don't have to recreate the state of Rama. Now we will bring about a new state, so that even if Rama descends to earth again, he will get such a shock about what has happened here! But we have this idea that whatever has happened before was all good. It is a totally wrong idea; and because of this wrong idea, we are tied to the past and tied to the old and unable to think about the new.

We all have this notion in this country that the "Golden Age" has already happened. Other countries think their Golden Age will come in the future. This makes a difference. Those who think it will come in the future try to make it happen. Those who think it has already happened sit down with closed eyes. They say, "It has already happened. It is not going to come now. Now everything will become worse day by day. The darkest age will come: darkness, more darkness, and then the absolute annihilation of everything."

In this country, if a man starts preaching that the great annihilation is coming, he immediately becomes a guru. A crowd gathers around him and they say, "You are right! You are speaking the truth. Everything is going downhill. Everything is being destroyed. Total destruction is coming! All the bad days are coming." All those bad days are not coming because they *have* to come. Rather, they are coming because we have lost the capacity to make our lives better. And they are coming because the mind of our country is lethargic, weak, and fearful, so much so that it says, "Just hold on to the old, otherwise it will be gone. Whatever is happening is happening. Nothing new can happen. So live in the old house and when you feel afraid that it will fall, just chant 'Rama, Rama.' Just build a fence around the old house so that it feels protected, but don't leave it. If the old is gone and nothing new is created, then what will happen?" There is so much fear.

There are reasons for this fear. Try to understand a couple of things. First, this false idea has been spread that everything in ancient times was good. It is totally false. But there is a reason for this idea to spread. After one thousand or two thousand years, no one will remember people like me or you. But they will remember a great name like Gandhi. People will remember Gandhi after two thousand years. And then what will they think? They will think, "What an incredible man Gandhi was! How great people of his age must have been."

And we are the people of his age! We will be forgotten, there will not be an account of us in history. Nobody will write about us in the history books, about the kind of people we were. We are the real people of this age. Gandhi is just an exception, he is not the rule. Only the exception will be kept in the history books and the real people like us will disappear from the record. We will be remembered by his name, the Gandhi-era! People will say that in the Gandhi-era, people must have been great; such nonviolence must have been practiced. There must have been such love.

What love and what nonviolence? Exactly the same mistake has always happened. We remember great people like Rama, but we forget the crowd of real people around him. There is no account of them. What was that crowd like?

We think on the basis of Rama that in Rama's era, people must have been good. On the basis of Buddha, we think that in that age there must have been great people. This is a wrong idea. Don't think on the basis of Buddha because, according to me, if people were so great in the age of Buddha or Mahavira, we would not even have a memory of Buddha or Mahavira. Only people who are the exception are remembered, not all are remembered.

Just imagine: if there were ten thousand people like Gandhi – not a big number – even then it would not have been easy to keep a record of Mohandas Karamchand Gandhi. He would have been lost in the crowd. When there are ten thousand good people like Gandhi, who will remember one Mohandas Karamchand Gandhi? In the same way, Buddha or Mahavira are standing alone in a crowd of millions and millions, so they are remembered. Otherwise they would have been forgotten.

The very fact that they are remembered shows that they were either alone or very few in number. And remembering them also shows that other people must have been their opposite, and that is why they could shine in their eyes. Otherwise they would not have been reported to be so luminous or bright.

If you visit any small primary school, you will realize what a primary school teacher knows – we are not even aware of it. He doesn't write on a white board with white chalk. He could write like that, the words could be written, but it would not be readable. He writes on a blackboard with a white chalk. White chalk shows on a blackboard. Similarly Rama, Buddha, Krishna, and Mahavira, and similar people show on the blackboard of the society; they would never have been noticeable otherwise.

If society was not so inferior, all these saints would not have been so visible; in spite of being great, they would not be noticeable. For the birth of a great saint, an inferior society is needed; otherwise such "great saints" would not happen. A blackboard of an inferior society is needed for a saint to be visible on it; otherwise he wouldn't be visible. Even if he was born, he would not be recognized.

So I say that the day a great society is born, that day, great men will stop being born. They will not stop being born, but they will not get any recognition. The day a great humanity is born, that day the era of saints will end. Then they will not be needed. They will certainly be born, but they will not even be known about.

If we look carefully at the teachings of Buddha, Confucius, Lao Tzu, Mohammed, or Zarathustra, what is there in their teachings? You will find something very interesting: Mahavira is trying to convince people from morning till evening, "Don't steal, don't kill, don't commit adultery, and don't be dishonest." What kind of people are they saying this to? Good people? Was he crazy that he would teach such things to good people? And they go on singing the same song around the clock – both Buddha and Mahavira – singing the same song: "Don't steal, don't be dishonest, don't be violent, don't kill, and don't lie." Who are they talking to?

There are only two possibilities. Either they had the sort of people it was necessary to preach these things to, not only one day but regularly day and night, or they were so crazy that they did not care who they were talking to!

I have heard…

A mystic was invited to a church to speak on truth. The mystic said, "You want me to speak on truth in a church? Why should I speak on truth here? The truth is a topic for the inmates of a prison! This is a church, a temple – the good people of the village are gathered here. If I speak on truth, people will think me crazy. No, I can't do it."

But the people in the church did not accept it. They said, "Please teach us something about truth."

The mystic said, "This is very strange. If you insist, I will speak on it, but let me ask you a question first. Have you all read the Bible?"

They all said, "Yes, we have read the Bible." They all raised their hands.

He asked, "Have you read the sixty-ninth chapter of Luke's gospel?"

They all raised their hands, except one person.

He said, "Then it is right, I should speak on truth. And I should tell you that there is no sixty-ninth chapter in Luke's gospel. And all of you have read it! Now I understand the kind of people that are here in this church."

This mystic must be naïve. In churches, only people like that congregate. No one else goes to the religious places except the irreligious. At pilgrimage and holy places, no one congregates except the sinners. No one prays and worships except the dishonest people. Our minds are upside-down. The mind of someone who is a sinner says, "Now pray, because you have to wash away your sins with prayers." Someone who digs a ditch in one place carries the soil to another place, because he needs to compensate.

The mystic said, "Now I understand. But I was surprised that one man did not raise his hand. Where did a truthful man come from?" He said to the man, "Thank you sir, for coming here. But why didn't you raise your hand?"

The man was sitting in the front row. He replied, "Please excuse me! I have a hearing problem. Did you ask about the sixty-ninth chapter of Luke? I read it every day. But I couldn't understand your question earlier, so I thought that it wasn't right to raise my hand without understanding the question."

We think of a time with great people as a great era, but if you look at their teachings and what people were getting out of them, it will be clear that their very teachings show the people around them were not so good. But the illusion remains that the people of that time were really great. And until this illusion is gone, we cannot generate a new society and a new man.

I say to you that the new is constantly being born. If we don't create obstacles, then the new is bound to be born. We create obstacles; we try to save the old. This very effort to save the old slowly, slowly creates such a sick and rotten system that it is difficult to live in it. And it is difficult to die in it as well. This is the condition of India.

New knowledge is needed. New rules of life are needed. Every day we need new rules, because every old rule becomes dangerous after a while.

It is as if we give a child a pair of pants to wear and even when he grows up, we go on insisting that he has to wear the same pants. Once we make a commitment, we do not change. Now the child is dying in those pants because he keeps on growing, but the pants are not growing. No rule grows because rules are lifeless things and man is alive. A man grows, and because rules are dead, they just go on tightening. Now those pants are too short and the boy goes on growing; he says, "You are causing me great difficulty, these pants are taking my life away!"

Now there are only two ways for him: either he stands naked or he changes his pants. You don't allow him to change his pants, so he tries to stand naked.

In the Indian society there is such nakedness, shamelessness, such rudeness, such meanness, such unkindness, because all the rules are too small. We don't make new rules, nor do we want to change the old rules. Then man tries to stand without any rules. He says, "At least let me breathe. I want to live; just keep your laws to yourself." Or he becomes a hypocrite. On the surface he shows, "The rules are absolutely right. I always follow them" and from the back door he does not follow them.

Everybody in this country has become a hypocrite. Each and every person has a split personality. There is one personality to show to others, you just put it on when needed. When you come home back, you take it off and the real man starts functioning. The real man functions in privacy. We are all like that: the false man is used as a cover. This country's society has created such great difficulties for us because the rules have become so dead that they don't allow any movement.

But movement is bound to happen. And in order to think in all these directions, with new thinking, of a new society, a new revolution, you must keep the doors of the mind open. Please don't think things such as "Old is gold" or "Nothing is new under the sky, so there is no need for the new." Nothing is old under the sky, every day demands the new.

A friend has asked something else related to the same topic; so we will discuss it next. He has asked:

Osho,
Does each person have to discover truth by themselves?
Does truth that was discovered in the past have no significance for us?

This subject is a little delicate. It is delicate because truth is not something that can be given to you by someone else. Even so, there are shops where truth is being sold: the Hindus' shops, the Mohammedans' shops, the Christians' shops, and so on. But still, truth is not something that can be purchased from a shop. And now even a few new shops have opened and claim: Truth is sold here.

But truth can neither be sold nor can it be received from someone else. No one can experience truth without going through the discipline to attain it. It is attained only by passing through meditation, the discipline of truth.

A man went to visit a mystic and said to him, "I want to meet the most blissful man of this world. I am very miserable; I feel like no one is as miserable as me. Then the idea came to my mind that perhaps everyone is unhappy. So I want to find the happiest man."

The mystic told him to go on a journey and instructed him to visit a certain mountain peak. He laid out the whole route he should take. And he told the man that he would be able to find the person he was looking for.

The mountain peak was very far away and the path the mystic had told him to take was very long. But the man really wanted to find out; he went on his search. He met so many people along the way and asked them, and they all said, "We are happy, but there is a man who is more blissful than us, you should go there." Each time, when he reached the place they told him about, he got the same answer: "We are happy, but there is someone who is happier than us."

He searched for twelve years and faced all kinds of troubles. He completely forgot that there was any happiness or sadness inside him; he was totally occupied with the one search: Who is the most blissful man? Finally after twelve years, he reached the mountain peak mentioned by the mystic. He saw an old man sitting there, who immediately said, "Yes, I am the most blissful man. What do you want?"

The man said, "My search is over now. I went in the search of happiness, but being concerned with other people's happiness and sadness, I totally forgot my own suffering. And now I am experiencing that when there is no suffering, how can there be happiness?"

Then he looked at the old man carefully and saw that his face looked familiar. He said to the old man, "Can you remove your turban please, it is covering your eyes and I want to see you properly." The old man started laughing. He removed his turban. It was the same mystic the man had met twelve year before.

The man who had been searching for so long said to him, "Why did you put me through this arduous search? You could have told me the same day that you are the most blissful man."

The mystic replied, "That day you would not have understood. This twelve-year journey was necessary. Only then could you understand what I am saying to you now. I ask you, 'Would you have been able to understand that day?'"

The man replied, "You are right. I wasn't able to understand that day."

Those who have known truth have told it, but you cannot understand unless you go through a long journey of searching. Once you go through that journey, you will understand. That search is an essential preparation to understand what has been written down. But that writing has no significance! Unless you go through this search, so that your consciousness reaches the space where things are crystal clear, until then, you will not be able to perceive anything from anywhere. And the interesting thing is that you will be able to perceive directly, that day – on your own. So whether you look into the scriptures or not has no meaning, rather you must become the holy book yourself.

The truth is not something that someone can give to you. You have to go through a long journey, a search. That search simply transforms you, it does nothing else. Truth is already right here; it is standing right by your side, but you don't have the ability to perceive it. The day you have that ability, you will find out that what you were searching for in every nook and corner is actually present everywhere. What you are searching for is right here. You have been unnecessarily troubled. But no one is pointlessly troubled: that trouble is an essential part of the preparation.

So, don't think that you can learn what is truth by reading about it in a book. By reading about it in a book, you will only collect answers. You will prepare an answer for the question, but that answer will be stale and borrowed; it will not be yours. It won't have any roots in you. It is a flower which you have purchased from the market; it has not come from your life source.

I have heard...

An emperor was going to visit a village, and all the important people of the village were going to be introduced to him. There was an old mystic in the village and the villagers said, "We will introduce our mystic first. He is the most honored man of the village."

But the state officials said, "This mystic is a little eccentric. No one knows what he will say to the emperor; perhaps he won't behave well, won't behave with manners, do something strange, and there will be trouble. So if he is going to be introduced, we'll have to train him beforehand. First he needs to be prepared for the conversation, only then can he can be brought to the emperor."

The villagers agreed, saying, "He is a simple man. You can train him."

The officials said to the mystic, "When the king comes, he will ask you a few things about yourself. He will ask, 'How old are you?' Please don't give spiritual answers such as 'What is age? The soul is eternal, there is no age to the soul' and so on. Don't talk like that, otherwise the king will be very puzzled. Just say directly that you are sixty years old."

The mystic said, "As you wish. I will certainly say that I am sixty years old. Am I supposed to do anything else?"

They said, "Just be sure that when he asks your age, you reply 'Sixty years old.' He might even ask you how long you have been meditating for. Don't answer, 'My meditation has been going on for many lives, it is without any beginning or end' and so on. It won't make sense to the king. He is asking you about this life, so just say you have been doing it for thirty years."

After his training the mystic said, "As you wish, I am ready."

The king came and everybody went to see him. The mystic also went, but everything went wrong. The king was supposed to ask first, "How old are you?" But he asked, "For how long you have been practicing meditation?"

The mystic replied, "Now here is the trouble. For sixty years!" ...since his answer was prepared.

The king asked, "Sixty years! How old are you?"

And the mystic replied, "Thirty years old." The answer was ready. The officials became nervous that things were going wrong.

And the king said, "That is crazy! Either you are crazy or me."

The mystic said, "Both."

The king asked, "What do you mean?"

He replied, "What I mean is that you asked the wrong question and I gave the wrong answer. I have been trained what to answer. If it was my own answer, I could have corrected it before giving it. Now I am in difficulty. First you are crazy, then I am also crazy to come here with readymade answers. And you are asking the wrong questions!"

We learn from the Gita, the Koran, the Bible and so on. When life brings you challenges and your answers are conditioned by books, they are not going to match the question. There will be no synchronicity. Life will ask something and you will answer something else, because the answer will not come from your interiority. It will never be in agreement. It will always be absurd.

And in a nation where so many people become knowledgeable by reading books, there are many fashionable answers, but there are no responses. Everyone will answer: everyone has memorized the Gita, Ramayana, and all their verses. Great stupidity! Everybody has a readymade answer. You can ask any question, their answer is readymade. Their answer is searching for a way to come out, so the moment someone asks something, they throw out the answer.

This readiness to answer is all any scripture can do. The search has to be done on your own. Yes, the day your search is fulfilled, you will have a direct experience and then all the scriptures will become relevant. No one can know truth by reading the scriptures; rather, once you know truth, then you can read the scriptures.

You have to experiment with what I am saying to you and go through it individually, only then can you experience something. And only experience reveals truth.

Another friend has asked:

Osho,
Is what you are saying your experience or the truth?

Perhaps he has the idea that experience and truth are two different things. Experience means truth. But what kind of experience is truth? There are false experiences too. For example, a man is walking down the street at dusk and, seeing a piece of rope lying on the ground, he mistakes it for a snake and runs for his life. Arriving home, he says that he has experienced a snake. But there was no snake there at all, it was just a rope.

False experiences do happen. Perhaps that is why the questioner has asked, "Is what you are saying your experience or the truth?" There are false experiences also, but if it is false, for how long will the experience be there? And when do experience and truth become the same thing? As long as the "I" is working, experiences cannot be trusted as the truth. In fact as long as there is "I" within, there cannot be any experience of the truth. "I" makes every experience false. But as the "I" disappears, when there is no more "I," then there is only experiencing. You don't say, "I have experienced," you say, "When there was no 'I,' the experience happened." Then there is no untruth; the factor that was creating false experiences has dissolved.

For instance, if we put a stick of wood into water, it appears to be crooked. The stick is not crooked, but it appears bent. The medium of water makes the stick appear bent. The stick does not become crooked – when you pull it out, it is straight. If you put it back in the water, it becomes bent again. The medium of water makes the stick appear crooked. Similarly, the medium of ego distorts truth into untruth.

So, as long as someone perceives the world through the medium of the ego, he is bound to experience non-truth. That is, the experience of non-truth implies that you are perceiving things through the medium of the ego. And the experience of truth means: perceiving in the state of non-ego, where there is no "I."

Hence, never think even by mistake that the "I" will know truth. "I" can never know truth; when truth is perceived, there is no "I." As long as the "I" persists, there is no experience of truth. And we all are filled with "I." Our whole life we just strengthen the "I." We gather all the experiences that have happened through the medium of the ego. As long as the foundation of the "I" continues, all our experiences are bound to be un-true, no experience can be true.

So, if you understand it rightly, existence seen through the "I" is what we call maya, an illusion. The ultimate seen through the "I" is called the world. Through the medium of "I," what is perceived is only that which is not. And the day the "I" dissolves, whatever experiencing takes place is the ultimate, and truth. You can give it any other name; it does not make any difference.

Another friend has asked:

Osho,
What is the purpose of life? Is ultimate liberation the goal of life? Is enlightenment the aim of life?

No, neither ultimate liberation nor enlightenment is the goal of life. The purpose of life is the total experiencing of life itself. When you experience life totally, that very moment, ultimate liberation happens; that very moment, enlightenment takes place. That is the byproduct. It is not the goal of life.

It is just as when a man cultivates wheat his purpose is not to produce straw. He cultivates wheat, the wheat grows and ripens. The straw comes with it, it is a byproduct. It is produced along with the grain.

The purpose of life is the total fulfillment of life. But on its total fulfillment, all bondages disappear and ultimate liberation takes place. So the ultimate liberation is a byproduct, it is like the straw.

But there are thousands of people who treat the straw as the main product and they treat the wheat as a byproduct, so they get into difficulties. They sow the straw in the fields and then neither straw is produced nor wheat is cultivated; instead, even the straw they had ends up rotting. And then in utter frustration they start saying there is nothing like enlightenment: "It is useless trouble! Nothing like that happens."

For hundreds and thousands of years, people have made ultimate liberation into a goal and that has created the trouble. It is not the goal. The fulfillment of life is the goal. To know life in its absolute bliss and in its total significance is the purpose. And when life dances in its total bliss, then all chains are dropped. When life is revealed in all its glory, then all obstacles disappear. When life unites itself totally with the whole, it becomes liberated.

A partial life is bondage, a total life is freedom. Ultimate liberation is not the goal. The goal is always life itself! If you make ultimate liberation your goal, there is great danger because you go in a different direction.

The man who says that ultimate liberation is the goal starts escaping from life. He says, "Drop life, our goal is liberation." He will withdraw from life, will run away and escape because he doesn't accept life. He will torture and destroy himself: "We believe in dying." The man who believes in ultimate liberation becomes suicidal. He says that he will commit suicide. There are a few courageous people who commit suicide at once and there are weak people who do it slowly, slowly. There are people who say that they will die by dropping things one by one. That they will live as a dead man lives. They are called renunciates.

These holy people have caused great harm; they have poisoned all the roots of life. Their condemnation of life has taken away all the joy of living. Their opposition of life has declared and condemned all those who are living life as sinners. Even they are facing life as if they are criminals! To live life has become a crime, to laugh has become a crime, to be joyful has become a crime, to dance has become a crime – everything has become a crime. Depressed long faces have become the only evidence of virtue. Escape, drop life! And the more a man escapes from life, the more he shrinks into a corner, into a cave, the greater saint he becomes, because "This man is going toward ultimate liberation!" He is not moving toward liberation; he is just moving toward death. He is suicidal and he is just searching for his grave.

Only someone who moves toward more life is actually moving toward freedom. He embraces the whole of life. He drinks life from the rays of the moon and the stars, dances with the aliveness; he drinks the juice of the life force from other people's eyes; he celebrates the life that is present all around in every flower and leaf. His each and every cell throbs with life and he unites his each and every breath with the whole of life. He stands up, sits, wakes up, dances, and sings – with life. He becomes life itself. That kind of man attains liberation, because who will put him in bondage then? He has merged with the whole of life, so who will create bondage for him? This kind of man is called an enlightened one. This kind of man creates liberation while being alive.

The liberation of an escapist always happens after death. A living man can never become liberated according to them, because for their liberation, total death is essential. A living man is going to be alive no matter how much he pretends to be dead – at least he is going to breathe or open his eyes. Even that much life remaining is a hindrance. He can attain liberation only after death. And liberation that happens after death has no value. Only the liberation that takes place in the total bliss of living, while being totally alive, is eternal and only that is significant.

As I see it, if existence was favoring that kind of death-based enlightenment, there was no need for life to be. Then life is happening in opposition to existence. If existence is against life and wants all of us to be liberated, it should finish it all at once and release us from all the trouble. But existence seems to be favorable to life. Existence constantly creates new leaves, no matter how hard you try to destroy life. No matter how many atom bombs you blast, existence goes on creating new lives. No matter how many obstacles you create, existence goes on creating life. Existence is a great lover of life.

But the saints are great enemies of life; the holy people are often the enemies of existence. And this world is under the influence of holy people. This has no relation to existence. That is why religions have slowly, slowly become suicidal and life negative. Religion should be life affirmative, it should be accepting life; it should acknowledge life in all its expressions. Such a religion and such a religious vision will not be focused on liberation after death. It will say, "Now and here! Why can't the ultimate liberation happen right now?"

I am emphasizing that the goal of life is life itself. Remember that the purpose of any ultimate experience in life is the experience itself.

If you are in love with someone and you are asked, "What is the purpose of love?" and you are able to give an answer, your love is of no value. Then love becomes a means and something else will become the end. But the lover knows it, he will say, "There is no goal or purpose to love! No, there is no goal to love at all. Love itself is the purpose of love. I love, that is enough, nothing more is needed."

Ask someone what the purpose is behind speaking the truth. And if the man answers that the purpose is to increase his respectability in the town, then that poor man has nothing to do with being truthful. He is concerned with earning respectability in the town. And if it is a town of thieves, he may even become a liar or a dishonest person, because that will gain him respectability among the thieves. His concern is totally different. He has nothing to do with truth. His concern is with respectability.

Someone says that he is truthful because he wants to go to heaven. If he comes to know that all the politicians go to heaven, he will say, "There is no need to work so hard to get to heaven. Even the politicians live there. Certainly, there must be corruption even in heaven; then I will also get into heaven by bribing. Why take so much trouble?"

Politicians cannot enter heaven without bribery, although they are all supposed to be living in heaven after death. It is as if after death no one ever goes anywhere but heaven. Whoever dies, we say that now he is in heaven. So-and-so has gone to heaven. People make a statue and erect a gravestone for them – and most of those whose statues are built in the streets must be residents of hell! But if you write below their statue "Resident in hell" then a fight will break out.

If a man realizes that even the politicians are going to heaven, then what is the problem: "Then I will also go there. I will make some arrangements to be able to go there." He will not be truthful after that.

Someone who says that speaking truth is the goal in itself – it is my bliss that I speak truth, there is no other motive behind it – that man is a lover of truth.

Whatever is magnificent and beautiful in life is an end in itself. It is not a means to something else; it is an end in itself. And life is the ultimate end. It cannot become a means for something else. If someone says that life is the means to attain ultimate freedom, he is saying something wrong. Life is an end to itself. Yes, when life is fulfilled, the experience is called ultimate liberation. Then there is no bondage, no obstacle, no limit, no end, and no death. In that moment of absolute fulfillment of life, the feeling of ultimate liberation is also included. But ultimate liberation is not the goal. And one who considers life as an end attains ultimate liberation.

I say: the end of life is life itself.

One last thing. A friend has asked:

Osho,
If you were asked to become president of the country, would you accept?

You have asked a very interesting question.

The first thing to be understood is that only people who suffer from an inferiority complex are desperate for a high position in life. People who have an inferiority complex become frantic about achieving a high status.

If someone seems desperate to get a high post, you can know that he feels very inferior: "If I can climb up onto this chair, my inferiority will disappear." They will climb up onto something just to get rid of their inferiority complex. Hence, a great man rarely agrees to have a high position. Very rarely!

An inferiority complex is behind all greed for position, so the most inferior people have gathered on the highest posts all over the world. The most inferior people have gathered on the highest positions. That is why the whole world is in chaos. The people with the worst inferiority complex have reached the top political positions; there is no possibility of a flowering of prosperity in the world, only misfortune will be the result.

The second thing to be understood is that improvements to society do not come by a good man reaching a good position. Improvements to society don't depend on one good man reaching somewhere. It does not depend on one man; it depends on the whole life vision of a society.

India has made that mistake often enough. It has put many good people in high positions over the last twenty-five years. When they reached the high post, they were good, but afterward they turned out to be a totally different type of person. It was not that all of them were bad – some of them were very good, but even the good people could not succeed in this web of a wrong system.

The whole life vision of society needs to be transformed. Nothing happens through the changeover of individuals. A change of individual just gives a little relief for a while. It is as if, when people carry a dead man on a stretcher to the funeral pyre and one shoulder starts hurting, they change to the other shoulder. It gives relief for a while; one shoulder feels light. But the weight of the stretcher is exactly the same. After a while the second shoulder starts aching.

We go on changing the person, but nothing happens by changing the person in power. It gives a little relief for a while, and it seems that because a new man has come to power something will happen. Then again, everything is exactly the way it was before. The system is the same old one. An individual is such a small thing that even if he has changed, still the system is so huge that it grinds the individual down; it grinds the individual in its mill. The man gets crushed in the mill and starts following the system.

The whole social and political system, the whole machinery and grinding mill of the Indian socio-political system, need to be transformed and demolished. Nothing will happen by changing the individuals. Right now, the main economic and social systems of India are such that if God himself becomes the president of the country, even then nothing is going to happen – other than giving him a poor reputation. Nothing is going to happen. It is not a question of any individual; we should stop thinking about individuals. And we should drop the hope that by putting a good man in a powerful position everything will happen.

No, we have to replace the old vision with a new vision of life. The day a new vision of life is established, that day even an ordinary man can take on the work of a high position. But you have to change the whole system.

For example, someone is driving a bullock cart and you start shouting at him that he is driving it too slowly. And you bring a good man and put him on the driver's seat. Then what will happen? The bullock cart is still a bullock cart. He may drive it faster and may even end up in a ditch. Or he can even create more trouble if he drives it too fast: the bullocks could get loose or die, or something could happen so that the whole cart will just collapse.

No, it is not a question of the bullock cart. If you want more speed, then you'll have to replace the bullock cart with a jet plane. Then it is possible that the same man who was driving the bullock cart, given the chance to drive a more advanced machine, can generate speed.

All the countries that are developing so much, the reason behind their development is not that they have better people than you. That is not the question. It is that their whole system has changed. Our country's system is very old and has deteriorated. Whoever is part of it will be trapped. And nothing is going to happen through it.

Hence, my interest is not in bringing someone new to a political position or removing someone. All these things are worth nothing. My interest is in how to change the mind of the country. When the mind has changed, any *ABC* can do the job. That is not very significant.

But one of the reasons for the wrong mind-set of India is that we always look up to individuals, we don't look at the system. This mistake has been going on for thousands of years. We think that if a Krishna could come back, everything would be all right. Krishna has already come and nothing was right then. What will be made right if he comes back again now?

We read in the Gita that whenever religion will be in danger, God will appear. So many times religion has been in danger, God has reincarnated, and still everything is the same as it ever was. So please drop such ideologies now; nothing is going to happen by God's arrival. Perhaps that is why he has stopped coming here, because he understood that there is no point in coming to this country again and again.

A society dependent on individuals is not progressive, because what is the capacity of a single individual? He is totally crushed when facing an established system. The issue is to change the system. Then even a small individual becomes significant.

We sent our best people to govern this country: after the independence of India, we had the best people and they all joined the government. They all rotted in the system. None of them could do anything. Now we don't even have such great people anymore. Now the people we will put in power, we can expect nothing from them. But still our attention is focused on the wrong thing. We always ask, "Who shall we elect to the highest position in the government? Who shall join the government?" And then we hope that this person will do something.

It is not a question of the individual. The social structure of this country, our way of thinking, our philosophy, and our vision of life, everything is wrong. All our troubles are because of that wrong vision of life. Hence, my interest is in changing the whole vision of life. I am not interested in individuals, in *ABC* – whoever works can do the job, it does not make a difference.

If you understand this rightly, you will see that when Lenin or his comrades came to power, it was not because of them that something happened. Please do not think that way. Perhaps Kerensky, who was in power before Lenin, was a man of no less wisdom or goodness. He was a very good man. But he did not have the idea to change the structure of the whole system. Lenin came with the notion that the structure of the whole society had to change. And the very notion of changing the structure worked. Then any individual could do the work, once the idea of changing the social structure was clear.

According to my vision, India should take its focus away from the individual and should focus on the society and its fundamental ideologies. Otherwise it is a great deception: we will go on changing the individual and keep on thinking that now this person is in power or that person is in power and so on. Nothing happens by that and we become more and more depressed. Then we abuse the individuals. Then we think, "He was bad, he disturbed things. He must be the wrong person." But nobody sees that our whole system and our whole structure are immensely dangerous. The intention to change the system must spread.

And remember, one cannot change the country's mind-set by sitting at the highest position. The country's mind-set needs to be fundamentally changed. Minds are not changed superficially. It is not that you elect someone to a high position and then he convinces people through his talks on national radio, and the mind-set changes. The mind-set has to change fundamentally. One has to enter the places where the mass mentality has spread and cut the roots there, focus the attention there. When the mind-set starts transforming, then insight comes into being on its own. That insight becomes what can transform this country. Try to think in this way.

The same friend has asked another question. He has asked:

Osho,
You said that poverty is pleasant. Then why don't you stay in poor people's houses? You also said that the cottage of a poor man is bigger than the home of someone who is rich. Then why do you stay in rich people's homes?

You have asked a good question. There are two things to be understood. The first thing, when I said that the hut of a poor man is bigger than the house of a rich man, it does not mean that if you measure it, the hut of the poor man will be bigger and the house of the rich man will be smaller. Don't take it that way. What I said was that the mind of the rich man is always small; there is very little space in it. The mind is so stuffed with wealth that there is no more space. Where more money is stuffed, there is less space for love. He *does* have a bigger house; don't think that the house of the poor man is bigger.

I am reminded of a Sufi mystic. He had a small hut. It was night and it was raining, and the mystic and his wife were asleep. Someone knocked on the door. The mystic said to his wife, "Please open the door. It is a dark rainy night and a guest has come."

The wife asked, "But where is there space in the house for another?"

The mystic said, "There is a lot of space. We were both lying down asleep, now the three of us will sit. Three of us cannot lie down." The wife opened the door. The guest came in, sat down, and started gossiping.

Again someone knocked on the door. The mystic said to the man who was sitting closer to the door, "Please open the door, it seems we have more guests."

The man said, "But where is the space?"

The mystic said, "There is enough space. We have been sitting with space between us, now we can sit a little closer to each other. Please open the door."

Unwillingly the man opened the door. Two more people came into the hut. Now they were all sitting very close to each other. They started chatting near the fireplace.

Meanwhile, a donkey hit on the door with his head. The mystic said, "Friend, please open the door! It seems we have another guest."

One of the men said, "It is not a guest, it is a donkey."

The mystic replied, "I don't differentiate. A guest is a guest. I didn't open the door for you just because you are a human being. You are a guest, so I opened the door. So, please open the door."

They said, "But it is a donkey!"

The mystic replied, "This discrimination between a donkey and a human being… If you knock on the door of a rich man, even a man at the door turns into a donkey. This is the hut of a poor man; it is not the palace of a rich man. The donkey has come, so we have to invite him in. Open the door!" They had to open the door and the donkey came in.

They all said, "What do we do now?"

The mystic said, "We have been sitting, now we can stand up." They all stood up.

The hut of the poor man was small – and his heart? But his heart was not big just because he was poor. Keep this in mind. The heart of the poor man is big because he has love in it and no money. But it does not mean that if you have money, you will not have love. And it does not mean either that I support poverty or that people should remain poor.

Also, remember that what I said does not mean that people should remain poor. I said this so that some space will be created even in the heart of the rich. You can take my statement in a wrong way: I did not say that the poor should remain poor. If the poor man remains poor, it is not good. The poor should become rich and the rich should create as big a space in their heart as the poor do. The poor should not be prevented from becoming rich. The rich have to be prevented from becoming poor inwardly. The poor should become rich outwardly and the rich should not become poor inwardly. Both kinds of richness should be present – outer and inner.

The friend is asking, "Why don't you stay at the house of a poor man?" I have no problem with it. But the problem is that the poor man does not even have a house; in this country, the poor man does not even have a house. The poverty of this country is so great that they don't even have houses to live in. And what you call his house, is it really a house? You should drown in shame if you call that a house! What is the poor man's house – he ties a few leaves together and puts some tiles on top and you call it a house. Only if a society has remained absolutely impotent for the last ten thousand years can you call it a house. It is not a house! Is that a house? That is not a house at all! If you count that as a house, you will never be able to build a house, remember. It is not a house, it is just helplessness. It is evidence of the lack of intelligence and skill in this country. Even houses have not been built in such a long time!

Try to understand what I am saying. I have no respect for poverty at all. And I consider anyone dangerous who respects poverty because if people follow him, the world will remain poor. I do not respect poverty.

I do say that the love a poor man has in his heart, a rich man should also have. But the discomfort a poor man faces should be removed; he too should have all the luxuries available to him. But there are people who respect poverty and call the poor: "God in the form of the poor." Madness without end! If you call the poor God, how will you remove poverty? How will you remove God? You have to worship God, not remove him. Poverty is a plague, it is not God. We have to erase it.

I have also said that poverty is a kind of joy. That statement also has to be understood. The happiness of poverty can be felt only by those who have experienced wealth. It is not available to the poor. Try to understand this last thing, and then I will finish.

It can be a pleasure to be poor. But that pleasure is not available to the poor. Mahavira may have had that pleasure, Buddha may have had it. Mahavira was the son of a king. He had known everything – palaces, all the luxuries, all the wealth. And through that experience, all those things became futile. Hence Mahavira stood naked in the street.

If there is a beggar standing naked on the road, do you think that the nakedness of Mahavira and the nakedness of that beggar are of the same quality? Mahavira's nakedness was his own choice. That poverty was taken on willingly. That poverty was pleasure.

Mahavira's poverty was a joy and it had a fragrance. Mahavira's poverty was liberation, it was a culmination. But we tell the naked beggar standing by the side of the road, "You are great and God has showered great blessings on you. See, Mahavira had everything and he had to renounce it all and become naked like you. You have God's grace on you; he has made you naked from the beginning. Enjoy it! You have avoided all the effort that Mahavira had to go through"... But can a naked beggar ever attain the nakedness of Mahavira? These two kinds of nakedness are basically different.

For example, many people are starving. If you go to the districts where there is famine – here in Rajasthan there is famine. People are dying of starvation. If you say to someone, "You have God's grace on you. So many people fast through effort, but God is helping you to fast, so be happy and feel grateful," he will reply, "What fasting? I just need some bread. I don't want to fast at all."

Only someone who has overeaten can enjoy fasting. Fasting is enjoyed only by overfed people. Hence, the more overfed a society is, such as the Jaina society in India, the more the cult of fasting becomes fashionable. The concept of fasting is prevalent among overfed people.

Now a fashion has started in America. Many naturopathy centers have opened in America where they make people fast. And people are happy to do it. In India, people are dying of hunger, and these people are enjoying fasting. What is happening there? Something is certainly happening: their bodies have gathered too much nourishment. Their bodies have collected surplus fat which needs to be released, and that release gives them joy. For instance, a hungry man does not have enough fat on his body and if he starts getting proper nourishment and so gains some fat on his body, he will become very happy. In the same way, an overfed person gets pleasure when he loses fat.

A poor man can never have the pleasure of poverty. Only a

rich man can enjoy the pleasure of poverty; poverty is the last luxury of the rich, the final luxury.

Take the example of the hippies and dropouts in America; they are all the children of rich people. They are sons of millionaires and billionaires. When I was in Varanasi, a few hippies came to visit me. I asked them, "You are the sons and daughters of millionaires and you are begging in Varanasi for a few coins?" They said, "It is such a joy, it is beyond imagination."

But can we feel that much joy in begging? We cannot feel that. They said, "Such freedom! We can sleep under a tree, wherever we want. We have never known such joy." Joy in being a beggar can be felt only by the children of a millionaire.

Someone else can say, "If you anyway have to drop wealth at the end and become poor, and we are poor already, why first become rich and then drop everything?" I remember a story about this.

I have heard...

Some people were going to visit Hardwar by train. Most of them were already on the train and were shouting, "Hurry up, get your luggage on the train! Come in, don't delay, the train is about to leave." A man was standing on the platform and about eight people were trying to drag him onto the train.

The man was saying, "Tell me first, do I have to get off the train in Hardwar? If I have to leave the train there, why should I get on the train now? When I have to get off it later, getting on the train now is pointless. I won't get on! Those who have got onto the train are stupid. They will anyway have to get off in a while."

His friends were saying, "The train is leaving, we will explain to you on the way. Please don't talk high philosophy right now. First come in, and then we will talk afterward."

He was saying, "Tell me!" But when his friends saw that the train was about to leave, they pulled him forcefully onto the train.

When they arrived at Hardwar, the man went on sitting with closed eyes. They all started to leave the train and again they had to shout, "Come out! Hurry up and get your luggage out." The man was surrounded by his friends again. They were saying, "The train is about to leave the station. Get off the train!"

He was saying, "I am not getting off! Once I've boarded the

train, why get off again? I am not someone who changes commitments so easily – I am firm in my principles. I have boarded the train, now I'm not going to get off again. I am surprised to see that you have changed your mind within just two hours! Just two hours ago you forced me to board the train, now you are forcing me to get off. You are very dishonest people."

His friends were saying, "Have you gone mad? Get off the train, it's about to leave!"

But he continued, "That is why I was not getting on, I told you earlier." They dragged him forcefully off the train.

Was he saying the right thing or was he wrong? His logic was right. He was saying, "If one is going to get off, why bother getting on?" But he was forgetting that you have to board the train at one station and get off it at a different station. If he hadn't boarded the train, he wouldn't have arrived at Hardwar.

One day, even a rich person has to adopt poverty, but that is like getting off the train at Hardwar station. If a poor person never experiences wealth, he can never accept poverty willingly. And until poverty is voluntary, it does not become a joy.

I was telling you the story of Diogenes earlier. In that context, even poverty is a joy. He was not an ordinary poor man. He was not really a poor, poor man. His poverty was chosen; it was bliss. He was not helplessly poor. What pleasure can someone who is forced to be helplessly poor derive from his poverty? But someone who becomes poor willingly has a different kind of joy.

That is why I am in favor of society becoming richer and richer, so that everybody has the opportunity to become poor if he wants. The society should grow richer. The society should be so rich that everybody can have the pleasure of voluntary poverty. Everybody has the possibility of becoming a poor wandering mystic. But in a place where all are just poor, how can poverty be a joy?

Try to understand rightly what I am saying. I don't support poverty – the poverty you see all around. I am its enemy: it should be erased. Even to allow it to exist for a moment is dangerous. It should be burned down. It should not be spared.

I do support another kind of poverty, but that is available only to those who adopt it voluntarily. And when does someone accept poverty willingly? It happens when everything becomes futile through experiencing it; then it happens. When someone has experienced wealth, wealth becomes useless. When someone has experienced fame, fame becomes useless. Whatever is experienced becomes futile. You go beyond it. From poverty to wealth and from wealth to a different kind of poverty, but that poverty is a totally different thing altogether.

Jesus said, "Blessed are the poor, those who are truly poor." A very strange statement. Blessed are those who are *really* poor. It means Jesus does not count these poor people as truly poor. Hence, those who are trying to become rich inwardly cannot be called poor. The poor person is trying to become rich, he desires being rich, he is money-minded, he wants to build a bigger house, and he wants to have everything that others are having. He is not capable of having all that, so he is tortured, depressed. He is not truly poor.

Very few people have become truly poor, because there is not much wealth in the world. If the wealth in the world increases and the whole of this country becomes wealthy, the way it was for Buddha and Mahavira... There should not be only a few dynasties of kings, rather every family in this country should become like a dynasty of kings. Then thousands, millions of Buddhas and Mahaviras will be born. They cannot be born in this poverty.

When someone has the opportunity to become truly poor, the joy is different. But who gets that opportunity? It is available to those who go through the extreme experience of luxury and comfort. Only they get that opportunity.

I do not support poverty – and I am in favor another kind of poverty! But there are two types of poverty. One station is for departure and the other station is for arrival. One day you have to get off, but in order to do that, you have first to board.

Hence, if you understand what I am saying, I do not support that there should be any poor people's huts nor do I support poverty. But I *am* in favor of the rich man not being rich only outwardly, rather he should become rich inwardly too. And inner richness is a different matter.

Inner richness means having a great heart. Not only a big house, but a great heart. Inner richness implies having an expanded vision. Inner richness means having not only outer wealth, but inner wealth too. Until someone attains inner wealth and the inner kingdom, his outer affluence, outer wealth, and outer kingdom have no value. But it does not mean that I want people to remain poor, helpless, inferior, and downtrodden.

No one should remain poor and helpless because if even one person remains poor, we all are responsible for his poverty. If even one person is suffering, we are responsible for his suffering. And so we all are criminals. But if this awareness develops, a new society and a new nation can be born.

You listened to my talks during these four days with so much peace and so much love that I am very, very grateful to you. And finally I salute the godliness within you. Please accept my greetings.

about osho

Osho's unique contribution to the understanding of who we are defies categorization. Mystic and scientist, a rebellious spirit whose sole interest is to alert humanity to the urgent need to discover a new way of living. To continue as before is to invite threats to our very survival on this unique and beautiful planet.

His essential point is that only by changing ourselves, one individual at a time, can the outcome of all our "selves" – our societies, our cultures, our beliefs, our world – also change. The doorway to that change is meditation.

Osho the scientist has experimented and scrutinized all the approaches of the past and examined their effects on the modern human being and responded to their shortcomings by creating a new starting point for the hyperactive 21st Century mind: OSHO Active Meditations.

Once the agitation of a modern lifetime has started to settle, "activity" can melt into "passivity," a key starting point of real meditation. To support this next step, Osho has transformed the ancient "art of listening" into a subtle contemporary methodology: the OSHO Talks. Here words become music, the listener discovers who is listening, and the awareness moves from what is being heard to the individual doing the listening. Magically, as silence arises, what needs to be heard is understood directly, free from the distraction of a mind that can only interrupt and interfere with this delicate process.

These thousands of talks cover everything from the individual quest for meaning to the most urgent social and political issues facing society today. Osho's books are not written but are transcribed from audio and video recordings of these extemporaneous talks to international audiences. As he puts it, "So remember: whatever I am saying is not just for you...I am talking also for the future generations."

Osho has been described by *The Sunday Times* in London as one of the "1000 Makers of the 20th Century" and by American author Tom Robbins as "the most dangerous man since Jesus

Christ." *Sunday Mid-Day* (India) has selected Osho as one of ten people – along with Gandhi, Nehru and Buddha – who have changed the destiny of India.

About his own work Osho has said that he is helping to create the conditions for the birth of a new kind of human being. He often characterizes this new human being as "Zorba the Buddha" – capable both of enjoying the earthy pleasures of a Zorba the Greek and the silent serenity of a Gautama the Buddha.

Running like a thread through all aspects of Osho's talks and meditations is a vision that encompasses both the timeless wisdom of all ages past and the highest potential of today's (and tomorrow's) science and technology.

Osho is known for his revolutionary contribution to the science of inner transformation, with an approach to meditation that acknowledges the accelerated pace of contemporary life. His unique OSHO Active Meditations™ are designed to first release the accumulated stresses of body and mind, so that it is then easier to take an experience of stillness and thought-free relaxation into daily life.

Two autobiographical works by the author are available:
Autobiography of a Spiritually Incorrect Mystic,
St Martins Press, New York (book and eBook)
Glimpses of a Golden Childhood,
OSHO Media International, Pune, India (book and eBook)

OSHO international meditation resort

Each year the Meditation Resort welcomes thousands of people from more than 100 countries. The unique campus provides an opportunity for a direct personal experience of a new way of living – with more awareness, relaxation, celebration and creativity. A great variety of around-the-clock and around-the-year program options are available. Doing nothing and just relaxing is one of them!

All of the programs are based on Osho's vision of "Zorba the Buddha" – a qualitatively new kind of human being who is able *both* to participate creatively in everyday life *and* to relax into silence and meditation.

Location

Located 100 miles southeast of Mumbai in the thriving modern city of Pune, India, the OSHO International Meditation Resort is a holiday destination with a difference. The Meditation Resort is spread over 28 acres of spectacular gardens in a beautiful tree-lined residential area.

OSHO Meditations

A full daily schedule of meditations for every type of person includes both traditional and revolutionary methods, and particularly the OSHO Active Meditations™. The daily meditation program takes place in what must be the world's largest meditation hall, the OSHO Auditorium.

OSHO Multiversity

Individual sessions, courses and workshops cover everything from creative arts to holistic health, personal transformation, relationship and life transition, transforming meditation into a lifestyle for life and work, esoteric sciences, and the "Zen" approach to sports and recreation. The secret of the OSHO

Multiversity's success lies in the fact that all its programs are combined with meditation, supporting the understanding that as human beings we are far more than the sum of our parts.

OSHO Basho Spa
The luxurious Basho Spa provides for leisurely open-air swimming surrounded by trees and tropical green. The uniquely styled, spacious Jacuzzi, the saunas, gym, tennis courts…all these are enhanced by their stunningly beautiful setting.

Cuisine
A variety of different eating areas serve delicious Western, Asian and Indian vegetarian food – most of it organically grown especially for the Meditation Resort. Breads and cakes are baked in the resort's own bakery.

Night life
There are many evening events to choose from – dancing being at the top of the list! Other activities include full-moon meditations beneath the stars, variety shows, music performances and meditations for daily life.

Facilities
You can buy all of your basic necessities and toiletries in the Galleria. The Multimedia Gallery sells a large range of OSHO media products. There is also a bank, a travel agency and a Cyber Café on-campus. For those who enjoy shopping, Pune provides all the options, ranging from traditional and ethnic Indian products to all of the global brand-name stores.

Accommodation
You can choose to stay in the elegant rooms of the OSHO Guesthouse, or for longer stays on campus you can select one of the OSHO Living-In programs. Additionally there is a plentiful variety of nearby hotels and serviced apartments.

www.osho.com/meditationresort
www.osho.com/guesthouse
www.osho.com/livingin

for more information

www.**OSHO**.com

a comprehensive multi-language website including a magazine, OSHO Books, OSHO Talks in audio and video formats, the OSHO Library text archive in English and Hindi and extensive information about OSHO Meditations. You will also find the program schedule of the OSHO Multiversity and information about the OSHO International Meditation Resort.

http://OSHO.com/AllAboutOSHO
http://OSHO.com/Resort
http://OSHO.com/Shop
http://www.youtube.com/OSHO
http://www.Twitter.com/OSHO
http://www.facebook.com/pages/OSHO.International

To contact OSHO International Foundation:
www.osho.com/oshointernational,
oshointernational@oshointernational.com